The Coffin Texts

Sacred Spells of the Afterlife's Journey

Volume 3

M L Ruscsak

Trient Press
3375 S Rainbow Blvd
#81710, SMB 13135
Las Vegas,NV 89180

Ordering Information:
Quantity sales. Special discounts are available on quantity purchases by corporations, associations, and others. For details, contact the publisher at the address above.
Orders by U.S. trade bookstores and wholesalers. Please contact Trient Press: Tel: (775) 996-3844; or visit www.trientpress.com.

Printed in the United States of America

Publisher's Cataloging-in-Publication data
Ruscsak, M.L.
A title of a book : The Coffin Texts: Sacred Spells of the Afterlife's Journey Volume 3
   ISBN
Hard Cover   979-8-88990-041-2

Paper Back   979-8-88990-042-9

Ebook   979-8-88990-043-6

Disclosure for the book "Coffin Text: Sacred Spells of the Afterlife's Journey Volume 3":

In this book, we present a collection of spells, incantations, and rituals that are inspired by and closely aligned with ancient Egyptian hieroglyphs. While we have made efforts to translate and interpret these texts as accurately as possible, it is important to note that the numbers assigned to each entry are for ease of reference within this book and do not necessarily reflect a definitive chronological or organizational order. Many scholars continue to study and analyze these ancient texts, seeking to confirm their age and the periods in which they were written.

The concept of the afterlife holds a significant place in ancient Egyptian culture and religion. Therefore, numerous books with similar texts have been written throughout history to provide guidance, teachings, and inspiration that resonate with modern-day spirituality and various religions today.

It is crucial to approach these spells, incantations, and rituals with an open mind, understanding that they are rooted in the ancient Egyptian belief system and cultural context. While they may offer insights into the human quest for spiritual understanding and growth, they should be viewed as a part of the rich tapestry of human religious and spiritual exploration.

Readers are encouraged to interpret and adapt the contents of this book in a way that aligns with their personal beliefs and spiritual practices. The aim of this book is to shed light on the wisdom and traditions of ancient Egypt while providing a source of inspiration and guidance for individuals seeking to deepen their spiritual journey.

Please approach the text with respect for the ancient culture and its religious practices, and consider these spells, incantations, and rituals as tools for personal growth, reflection, and connection with the mysteries of the afterlife.

May the exploration of these ancient texts bring you insight, enrichment, and a deeper appreciation for the enduring wisdom of the ancient Egyptian civilization.

1. Incantation to guide the deceased through the perilous realm of the Duat

Journey with me now, O departed soul,
Through the realm of shadows, to reach your ultimate goal.
With this sacred incantation, I shall guide you true,
To navigate the Duat, as ancient Egyptians once knew.

"Djehuty, god of wisdom, I call upon your name,
Guide this soul, through darkness, to transcend mortal frame.
Anubis, guardian of the gates, protect and lead the way,
Through trials and tests, let the deceased safely sway.

I invoke the power of Ra, the sun's eternal light,
To illuminate the path, banishing all fright.
Ma'at, goddess of truth, let justice be your guide,
Balance the heart's feather, with righteousness by your side.

O Osiris, lord of the afterlife, hear my plea,
Open the gates of paradise, for the soul to be set free.
Isis, goddess of magic, weave your spells of grace,
Grant the deceased solace, in your loving embrace.

By the sacred words I speak, let the Duat be revealed,
May the deceased find solace, from fears to be healed.
Through peril and darkness, the soul shall rise above,
To a realm of eternal peace, bathed in divine love.

As above, so below, may this incantation hold true,
Guiding the deceased to their destiny anew.
In harmony with ancient wisdom, this journey shall be blessed,
As the soul embarks on its Duat's quest."

Let the words resonate, through the realm of the Duat,
Guiding the departed, in their sacred pursuit.
May they find enlightenment, as their journey unfolds,
Through the perilous realm, where their destiny beholds.

2. Ritual for the purification of the deceased's spirit through sacred herbs and oils

Prepare, O faithful seeker, the sacred space,
Where the essence of the departed shall find solace.
Gather now the herbs and oils of divine grace,
To purify the spirit, in this sacred embrace.

In the vessel of wisdom, blend the herbs with care,
Sage for cleansing, lavender for peace to share.
Rosemary for remembrance, myrrh for spiritual ascent,
Frankincense for purification, a sacred scent.

Ignite the sacred flame, and let it burn bright,
As the smoke rises, it cleanses with its pure light.
Hold the vessel of herbs and oils in your hand,
And with reverence, let the purification expand.

Speak these words, with intention and belief,
To purify the spirit, to offer relief:

"By the power of sacred herbs and oils,
I cleanse this spirit from earthly toils.
May the smoke and fragrance purify,
Remove all darkness, let the spirit fly.

With sage, I banish negativity's hold,
With lavender, serenity unfolds.
Rosemary, bring forth memories pure,
Myrrh, elevate the spirit to endure.

Frankincense, purify and sanctify,
Release the burdens, let the spirit rise.
As these sacred elements combine,
The deceased's spirit becomes divine.

May this ritual bring purification deep,
In the afterlife's journey, its essence shall keep.
Restored, rejuvenated, and free from strife,
The spirit shines forth in eternal life."

Let the smoke waft and fill the sacred space,
As the herbs and oils purify with grace.
Feel the presence of the deceased spirit cleanse,
In this ritual of purification, their essence transcends.

When the smoke subsides, and the ritual is complete,
A purified spirit soars, in realms bittersweet.
May their journey be guided by love's embrace,
In the afterlife's realm, they find their rightful place.

3. Spell for the restoration of the deceased's physical body in the afterlife

Preparation:

✧ Choose a quiet and sacred space where you can perform the ritual undisturbed.
✧ Gather the necessary ingredients: sacred herbs (such as sage, lavender, rosemary, myrrh, and frankincense), sacred oils, a vessel for burning the herbs, a lighter or matches, and a written copy of the Spell for Restoration.

Creating the Sacred Space:

✧ Cleanse the space by smudging with sacred herbs, such as sage or palo santo.
✧ Arrange the ritual items on a clean altar or sacred surface.
✧ Light a candle or lamp as a symbol of divine presence.

Invocation and Setting Intentions:

✧ Close your eyes, take a deep breath, and center yourself.
✧ Invoke the presence of divine forces, ancestors, or deities associated with the afterlife, such as Anubis or Osiris.
✧ State your intention clearly, focusing on the purification of the deceased's spirit and the restoration of their physical body in the afterlife.

Ritual of Purification:

✧ Take the vessel and place a small amount of each sacred herb inside.
✧ Light the herbs with the flame from the candle or lamp, allowing them to smolder and release fragrant smoke.
✧ Hold the vessel in your hand and walk around the sacred space, allowing the smoke to purify the area and create a spiritual atmosphere.
✧ As you move, visualize the smoke cleansing the space and purifying the energy.

Anointing with Sacred Oils:

✧ Take a small amount of sacred oil in your hand.
✧ Gently rub your hands together to warm the oil and activate its energy.
✧ Begin at the crown of your head and slowly anoint your body, moving in a downward motion.
✧ As you anoint, visualize the oil infusing your being with divine purification and spiritual enlightenment.

Spell for Restoration of the Deceased's Physical Body:

- ✧ Hold the written copy of the Spell for Restoration in your hands.
- ✧ Read the spell aloud, with clarity and conviction, directing your intention toward the deceased's physical body being restored in the afterlife.
- ✧ As you recite the spell, visualize the deceased's physical body being rejuvenated, healed, and restored to its divine perfection.

By the powers of the ancient ones, I call upon the divine forces of the afterlife. Hear my words and heed my plea.

In the realm beyond life's veil, where spirits dwell and journeys are made, I beseech you to restore the physical body of [Name of the deceased].

From the sands of time, let the essence of life flow through their being. Let their limbs regain strength and vitality, their form rebuilt with grace and beauty.

May the wounds and ailments of their mortal existence be washed away, replaced by the divine touch of restoration.

With each breath of the eternal winds, let the vital energy fill their cells, rejuvenating every part of their being.

O divine forces of the afterlife, hear my invocation. Restore [Name of the deceased]'s physical body to its divine perfection, so they may journey through the realms of the afterlife whole and restored.

As it was, as it is, as it shall be. So mote it be.

Closing and Gratitude:

- ✧ Offer gratitude to the divine forces, ancestors, or deities you invoked at the beginning of the ritual.
- ✧ Extinguish the candle or lamp, symbolizing the completion of the ritual.
- ✧ Express gratitude for the opportunity to perform this sacred rite and for the blessings received.

4. Invocation of the god Anubis for guidance and protection in the journey of the soul

"O mighty Anubis, guide and guardian of the souls,
I call upon your divine presence to join me in this sacred space.
With reverence and respect, I seek your guidance and protection,
As I embark upon the journey of the soul beyond earthly realms.

Anubis, the jackal-headed deity of the afterlife,
Bearer of wisdom, conductor of souls,
I beseech you to lend me your guiding hand,
To lead me through the veil that separates the living and the dead.

With your keen insight and unwavering vigilance,
Protect me from the perils that may lie ahead,
Guide me along the paths of the underworld,
And keep my spirit safe from harm's way.

As I navigate the realms of the afterlife,
Grant me clarity of mind and courage of heart,
Illuminate my path with your divine wisdom,
And help me discern the true nature of my journey.

Anubis, ancient god of embalmers and protectors,
I humbly invoke your presence and seek your favor,
As I embrace the mysteries of the soul's passage,
Grant me your guidance and protection throughout.

May your divine presence be my steadfast companion,
As I traverse the realms of the great unknown,
With your guidance, I shall find solace and purpose,
And emerge from this journey transformed and reborn.

Thank you, Anubis, for your benevolent presence,
For your unwavering guidance and protection.
I honor you, mighty guardian of the soul,
In this journey and beyond, eternally grateful."

Invoke this invocation with sincerity and respect, knowing that Anubis hears your call
and will offer his guidance and protection on your soul's journey.

5. Ritual of anointing with sacred waters for spiritual rejuvenation

Prepare a sacred space: Find a quiet and peaceful area where you can perform the ritual undisturbed. Cleanse the space by burning sacred herbs or incense and set up a small altar with a bowl of fresh water.

Purify yourself: Before starting the ritual, cleanse yourself physically and mentally. Take a shower or bath, imagining the water washing away any negativity or stagnant energy. Center yourself through deep breathing and meditation.

Invoke sacred intentions: Stand before the altar and set your intention for the ritual. Visualize the sacred waters as a source of spiritual rejuvenation, healing, and purification. Connect with the energy of the water and its ability to cleanse and renew.

Bless the sacred waters: Hold your hands over the bowl of water and close your eyes. Envision a divine light surrounding the water, infusing it with positive and healing energy. Say a prayer or invocation, expressing your gratitude for the sacredness of the water and its ability to purify and rejuvenate.

Anoint yourself with the sacred waters: Dip your fingers or a small cloth into the bowl of water, and gently touch it to your forehead, heart, and palms. As you do so, visualize the water purifying your mind, heart, and spirit, washing away any negativity or heaviness. Feel the rejuvenating energy of the water flowing through you, restoring your vitality and inner balance.

Offer gratitude: Express your gratitude to the sacred waters for their cleansing and rejuvenating properties. Thank the divine forces and energies that support you on your spiritual journey.

Closing the ritual: Take a moment to bask in the renewed energy and sense of spiritual rejuvenation. You can leave the bowl of water on your altar as a symbol of ongoing purification and connection to the sacred waters.

Remember, the ritual of anointing with sacred waters is a personal and sacred practice. Modify the steps as per your intuition and preferences. May this ritual bring you deep spiritual rejuvenation and a sense of inner harmony.

6. Spell for the transformation of the deceased into a vessel of divine love and compassion

In the presence of sacred space and with sincere intent,
I call upon the forces of love and compassion, heaven-sent.
By the power of divine grace and cosmic light,
May the spirit of the departed shine ever so bright.

From this realm to the next, I beckon the heart,
To open wide and embrace love's sacred art.
Let all barriers and limitations dissolve away,
As the soul awakens to love's eternal sway.

With each breath, let love flow through,
Infusing every cell and being, old and new.
May the deceased embody love's gentle embrace,
Radiating compassion, spreading warmth and grace.

Let kindness be their language, forgiveness their guide,
May their spirit uplift and heal far and wide.
In the realms beyond, let love be their eternal song,
A vessel of divine love, they forever belong.

By the power of love and the cosmic divine,
I seal this spell, knowing it shall align.
As the deceased transforms into love's sacred vessel,
Their journey in the afterlife filled with love's eternal wrestle.

This spell is cast with reverence and pure intent,
May love and compassion be the deceased's eternal ascent.
So mote it be, and may it manifest,
In perfect harmony and divine love's behest.

Remember, the spoken words hold power, but it is your intent and belief that bring them to life. Use this spell with love and respect, knowing that the energy you invoke can have a profound impact on the deceased and their journey.

7. Incantation to invoke the blessings of the celestial rivers and lakes

By the rivers and lakes that flow through the heavens high,
I call upon the spirits that dwell in the celestial sky.
With reverence and awe, I seek your sacred grace,
To bless and guide me on this spiritual embrace.

From the depths of the celestial waters, ancient and deep,
May the blessings of purity and abundance seep.
Flowing with the currents of celestial love,
Bring forth your blessings from the realms above.

Let the rivers of wisdom wash away all strife,
And bring clarity and harmony to my life.
As the lakes of serenity reflect the stars above,
May I find peace and tranquility in your divine love.

O spirits of the rivers and lakes, I humbly implore,
Pour your blessings upon me, now and forevermore.
Grant me strength and guidance, like a gentle stream,
As I navigate life's currents, fulfilling my dreams.

With gratitude and reverence, I honor your sacred might,
For in your waters, I find solace and delight.
Blessed be the rivers and lakes of the celestial plane,
May their blessings forever flow and sustain.

As I speak these words, I align with your divine flow,
In harmony with the currents, my spirit shall grow.
I thank the celestial rivers and lakes, spirits so grand,
For their blessings bestowed upon me, as I stand.

So mote it be, in accordance with divine will,
May the blessings of the celestial waters fulfill.
In the embrace of their currents, I find solace and peace,
And may their sacred blessings never cease.

Remember, when invoking the blessings of the celestial rivers and lakes, do so with reverence and respect. The energies and forces invoked are powerful, and it is important to approach them with a pure heart and genuine intent.

8. Ritual for the transfiguration of the deceased into a divine conduit of divine energy

Materials needed:

✧ A sacred space or altar
✧ Candles (white or gold)
✧ Incense (frankincense or sandalwood)
✧ A small bowl of water
✧ Anointing oil (such as lavender or rose)

Procedure:

✧ Prepare your sacred space or altar by cleansing it with the elements of fire, air, water, and earth. This can be done by lighting a candle, wafting incense, sprinkling water, and placing a small dish of salt or earth on the altar.

✧ Light the candles and the incense, creating an atmosphere of reverence and divine presence.

✧ Take a moment to ground yourself and connect with the energy of the divine. Breathe deeply and visualize yourself surrounded by a golden light.

✧ Hold the bowl of water in your hands and say the following words:

"By the sacred waters, pure and divine,
I call upon the ancient powers to shine.
Let this water be blessed with divine grace,
To transfigure and transform in this sacred space."

✧ Gently dip your fingers into the water and anoint the forehead of the deceased (or an image or representation if performing the ritual for someone else), saying:

"With this sacred water, I cleanse and bless,
May the divine energy within you manifest.
As the water touches your earthly form,
Let the transfiguration of divine energy be born."

✧ Take the anointing oil and apply a small amount to your fingertips. With gentle strokes, anoint the deceased (or the representation) on the forehead, heart, and palms of the hands, saying:

"By this sacred oil, I invoke the divine,
May you become a vessel, pure and aligned.
Let the energy of the heavens flow through,
Transfiguring you into a conduit of divine virtue."

✧ Sit in quiet meditation for a few moments, envisioning the deceased being filled with divine energy, radiating light and love.

✧ Express gratitude to the divine energies and powers that have been invoked, acknowledging their presence and assistance in the transfiguration process.

✧ Close the ritual by extinguishing the candles and offering a final prayer or affirmation of blessings for the deceased's journey into becoming a divine conduit.

Remember, when performing this ritual, do so with utmost respect, love, and intention. It is a sacred act of honoring the deceased's journey and potential for spiritual transformation.

9. Spell for the reunion of the deceased's soul with their ancestral lineage

Recite the following incantation with focused intention and a clear connection to the divine:

"Ancestors of blood and bone,
I call upon you, hear my tone.
Through time and space, we are entwined,
In this sacred union, let our souls bind.

Guide the spirit, now set free,
Back to the roots of ancestry.
Open the gateways, let them pass,
To reunite with kindred souls at last.

Through generations, wisdom flows,
Through lineage, our essence knows.
May the veil be lifted, barriers break,
Let the reunion of souls awake.

Ancestral spirits, I call upon thee,
With love and reverence, hear my plea.
Bring the departed back to the fold,
Where ancestral stories are told.

With gratitude, I honor the past,
May this union forever last.
Bound by love, and in harmony,
Let the reunion of souls be."

Visualize the deceased's soul being surrounded by a loving embrace of ancestral spirits, guiding them towards their ancestral lineage. Feel the presence and connection to the ancestors as the spell is spoken.

After reciting the incantation, sit in quiet meditation, allowing space for the energy to settle and the reunion to take place. Trust in the divine timing and the wisdom of the ancestors.

Note: It is important to approach this spell with sincerity, respect, and a genuine desire for the highest good of the deceased. The reunion with ancestral lineage can bring healing, guidance, and a sense of belonging to the departed soul.

10. Ritual of purification through the sacred breath of the eternal winds

✧ Find a quiet and serene outdoor location, preferably where you can feel the gentle breeze. Alternatively, you can perform this ritual indoors with good ventilation.

✧ Begin by grounding yourself through deep breathing and centering your energy. Close your eyes and take a few moments to connect with your inner self.

✧ Stand with your feet firmly planted on the ground, feeling rooted and connected to the Earth. Allow your body to relax and your mind to become still.

✧ Extend your arms outward, palms facing upward, as if embracing the unseen currents of the wind. Feel the subtle energy of the air flowing around you.

✧ Take a deep breath in, imagining that you are inhaling the pure essence of the eternal winds. Feel the revitalizing energy entering your body, cleansing and purifying every cell and aspect of your being.

✧ As you exhale, release any stagnant or negative energy, allowing it to be carried away by the gentle breeze. Visualize the wind carrying away all impurities, leaving you feeling refreshed and renewed.

✧ Repeat this deep breathing and visualization process several times, focusing on the purification and renewal of your mind, body, and spirit.

✧ As you continue the ritual, you can also recite a personal affirmation or mantra that resonates with the concept of purification and renewal. For example, you can say, "With each breath, I release what no longer serves me. I am cleansed, renewed, and aligned with the eternal winds of transformation."

✧ Take a few moments to simply stand in stillness and gratitude, feeling the energy of the wind embracing you. Acknowledge the purification and revitalization that has taken place within you.

✧ When you feel ready, gently bring your hands to your heart center and express gratitude to the eternal winds for their cleansing and purifying presence.

✧ Slowly open your eyes, maintaining a sense of inner peace and clarity. Carry this purified state of being with you throughout your day.

Remember, the key to this ritual is intention and focus. Allow yourself to fully immerse in the experience, surrendering to the power of the eternal winds and their purifying energy.

11. Spell for the liberation of the deceased's soul from karmic bonds

✧ Find a quiet and peaceful space where you can perform this spell without distractions. Light a white candle and place it in front of you as a symbol of purity and divine guidance.

✧ Take a few deep breaths to center yourself and connect with your intention. Focus your mind on the liberation of the deceased's soul from any karmic bonds that may be holding them back.

✧ Hold a clear quartz crystal in your hand, symbolizing clarity and amplification of energy. Close your eyes and visualize the soul of the deceased surrounded by a golden light, signifying divine protection and assistance.

✧ Recite the following incantation with conviction and intention:

"By the power of the divine,
I call upon the karmic ties to unwind.
Release the soul from burdens past,
Free them from karmic chains that last.

Let the winds of change blow strong,
Dissolving all that has been wrong.
May the soul soar to heights unknown,
Liberation and freedom now be shown.

With this spell, I set them free,
Unbound from karmic destiny.
May their soul journey with joy and grace,
Released from karmic bonds, they embrace."

✧ Visualize the golden light surrounding the deceased's soul growing brighter and expanding, breaking any karmic bonds that are holding them back. See the soul becoming lighter and more liberated, free to move forward on its spiritual journey.

✧ Hold the intention of love and forgiveness towards the deceased and any karmic connections between you. Send out thoughts of compassion and understanding, allowing the healing energy to flow.

✧ Place the clear quartz crystal near the lit candle and let it absorb the energy of the spell. Allow the candle to burn down completely, signifying the completion of the spell.

✧ Express gratitude to the divine forces and energies that have assisted in this spell. Thank them for their guidance and support.

✧ Close the ritual by grounding yourself, feeling your connection to the Earth beneath you. Take a few deep breaths, allowing yourself to fully return to the present moment.

Remember, the power of this spell lies in your intention and belief. Trust in the process and have faith that the liberation of the deceased's soul from karmic bonds is taking place. May this spell bring freedom and spiritual growth to all involved.

12. Incantation to awaken the dormant wisdom within the deceased's spirit

✧ Sit in a quiet and sacred space where you can connect with the spiritual energies around you. Light a candle or some incense to create a peaceful ambiance.

✧ Close your eyes and take a few deep breaths, centering yourself and entering a meditative state. Allow your mind to become still and receptive to the energies of the universe.

✧ Visualize the deceased's spirit surrounded by a gentle golden light, symbolizing divine wisdom and knowledge. See this light permeating their being, awakening and illuminating the dormant wisdom within.

✧ Begin reciting the following incantation with focus and intention:

"Oh spirit awakened, hear my call,
Rise from slumber, stand tall.
Dormant wisdom, now arise,
Unveil the truth that lies.

Ancient knowledge, buried deep,
I summon you from eternal sleep.
Awaken, awaken, with every breath,
Embrace the wisdom that conquers death.

Let the rivers of wisdom flow,
Unveil the secrets we yearn to know.
Ancient teachings, profound and true,
Reveal themselves in shades of blue.

Spirit of wisdom, guide us through,
Illuminate paths both old and new.
Unleash the wisdom that's been concealed,
Let truth and understanding be revealed."

✧ Repeat the incantation several times, allowing its words to resonate with the energy of the space and the deceased's spirit. Feel the vibration of the words as they echo through the realms, awakening the dormant wisdom within.

- ✧ After reciting the incantation, sit in silence and open yourself to receive any messages, insights, or symbols that may come through. Trust your intuition and remain receptive to the wisdom that may be revealed.

- ✧ Express gratitude to the spirit and the divine forces that have assisted in this awakening. Thank them for their guidance and presence.

- ✧ Slowly bring yourself back to the present moment, grounding your energy by connecting with the Earth beneath you. Take a few deep breaths, allowing yourself to fully return.

Remember, the power of this incantation lies in your intention and belief. Trust in the process and have faith that the dormant wisdom within the deceased's spirit will be awakened. May this incantation bring forth profound insights and guidance for the journey ahead.

13. Ritual for the communion with the spirits of the celestial constellations

✧ Choose a clear night and find a peaceful outdoor space where you can connect with the night sky. Ideally, away from city lights for better visibility of the stars.

✧ Set up your sacred space by placing a comfortable mat or blanket on the ground. You may also choose to create a small altar with symbols or objects that represent the celestial realm, such as crystals, star maps, or celestial-themed artwork.

✧ Light candles or small lanterns around the area to create a gentle, ambient glow. Consider using colors that resonate with the cosmos, such as deep blues and purples.

✧ Take a moment to ground yourself by standing barefoot on the earth. Feel the energy of the earth beneath you and imagine roots extending from your feet, grounding you to the core of the earth.

✧ As you gaze up at the night sky, bring your awareness to the vastness and beauty of the stars. Feel a sense of reverence and connection to the celestial realm.

✧ Begin to quiet your mind and enter a meditative state. Close your eyes and take a few deep breaths, allowing yourself to relax and become receptive to the energies around you.

✧ Visualize yourself surrounded by a sphere of gentle, radiant light, representing your personal energy field. See this light expanding to encompass the entire sacred space, creating a harmonious and protected environment.

✧ Raise your arms out to your sides, palms facing upwards, and begin to chant or speak the following invocation:

"Oh, celestial spirits, I call upon thee,
Guardians of the stars, shine your light upon me.
From Orion to Ursa Major, Gemini to Leo,
I seek communion with your celestial glow.

Ancient constellations, keepers of wisdom and lore,
I open my heart to your cosmic core.

Guide me, inspire me, reveal your divine mysteries,
Let your celestial energies flow through me."

✧ Allow yourself to feel the energy of the celestial constellations as you continue to chant or speak the invocation. Visualize their radiant light merging with your own energy, creating a profound connection.

✧ Spend some time in quiet contemplation, allowing yourself to receive any messages, insights, or inspirations that may come through. Be open to the guidance and wisdom of the celestial spirits.

✧ When you feel ready, express gratitude to the celestial spirits for their presence and guidance. Thank them for the wisdom and energy they have shared with you during this communion.

✧ Slowly bring your awareness back to the present moment. Gently close the ritual by offering a final prayer or affirmation, acknowledging the connection you have established and expressing your intention to carry the wisdom of the celestial constellations with you.

Remember, this ritual is a sacred and personal practice. Adapt it to suit your own beliefs and preferences. May your communion with the spirits of the celestial constellations bring you deep insights, cosmic wisdom, and a profound sense of connection to the vastness of the universe.

14. Spell for the transmigration of the deceased's soul into the realm of eternal knowledge

✧ Find a quiet and sacred space where you can perform the spell without distractions. Create a peaceful ambiance by lighting candles and placing crystals or other meaningful objects around you.

✧ Sit in a comfortable position and take a few deep breaths to center yourself. Close your eyes and enter a state of focused awareness.

✧ Begin to visualize a brilliant, golden light surrounding you. Feel this light permeating every cell of your being, illuminating your mind, body, and spirit.

✧ Focus your intention on the deceased soul for whom you are performing this spell. Envision their spirit being enveloped by the same golden light, gently guiding them towards the realm of eternal knowledge.

✧ Chant or recite the following spell, infusing it with intention and heartfelt emotion:

"Oh, spirit of the departed, hear my plea,
Across the veils of time, I set you free.
Transcend the limitations of mortal strife,
Into the realm of eternal knowledge, find new life.

Let the gates of wisdom open wide,
Embrace the teachings that forever abide.
Expand your consciousness, soar beyond,
Into the vast expanse, where truths respond.

I call upon the ancient masters and sages,
Guide this soul through the eternal pages.
May they drink from the fountain of wisdom's well,
In the realm of eternal knowledge, forever dwell."

✧ As you recite the spell, visualize the soul of the deceased transcending into a realm of boundless knowledge and wisdom. Imagine them surrounded by ancient masters, teachers, and guides who welcome and nurture their spirit.

✧ After reciting the spell, sit in silence for a few moments, allowing the energy of the spell to settle and integrate. You may feel a sense of peace and connection during this time.

✧ When you are ready, express your gratitude to the universe, the guides, and the deceased soul for their presence and participation in this spell. Offer thanks for the opportunity to facilitate their journey into the realm of eternal knowledge.

✧ Slowly bring your awareness back to the present moment. Take a few deep breaths and open your eyes, feeling grounded and at peace.

Remember, this spell is a sacred and heartfelt invocation. Adapt it to suit your beliefs and intentions, and always approach it with respect and reverence. May it aid the transmigration of the deceased's soul into the realm of eternal knowledge, granting them profound insights and boundless wisdom.

15. Invocation of the god Ptah for creativity and manifestation in the afterlife

✧ Find a quiet and sacred space where you can perform the spell without distractions. Create a peaceful ambiance by lighting candles and placing crystals or other meaningful objects around you.

✧ Sit in a comfortable position and take a few deep breaths to center yourself. Close your eyes and enter a state of focused awareness.

✧ Begin to visualize a brilliant, golden light surrounding you. Feel this light permeating every cell of your being, illuminating your mind, body, and spirit.

✧ Focus your intention on the deceased soul for whom you are performing this spell. Envision their spirit being enveloped by the same golden light, gently guiding them towards the realm of eternal knowledge.

✧ Chant or recite the following spell, infusing it with intention and heartfelt emotion:

"Oh, spirit of the departed, hear my plea,
Across the veils of time, I set you free.
Transcend the limitations of mortal strife,
Into the realm of eternal knowledge, find new life.

Let the gates of wisdom open wide,
Embrace the teachings that forever abide.
Expand your consciousness, soar beyond,
Into the vast expanse, where truths respond.

I call upon the ancient masters and sages,
Guide this soul through the eternal pages.
May they drink from the fountain of wisdom's well,
In the realm of eternal knowledge, forever dwell."

✧ As you recite the spell, visualize the soul of the deceased transcending into a realm of boundless knowledge and wisdom. Imagine them surrounded by ancient masters, teachers, and guides who welcome and nurture their spirit.

✧ After reciting the spell, sit in silence for a few moments, allowing the energy of the spell to settle and integrate. You may feel a sense of peace and connection during this time.

✧ When you are ready, express your gratitude to the universe, the guides, and the deceased soul for their presence and participation in this spell. Offer thanks for the opportunity to facilitate their journey into the realm of eternal knowledge.

✧ Slowly bring your awareness back to the present moment. Take a few deep breaths and open your eyes, feeling grounded and at peace.

Remember, this spell is a sacred and heartfelt invocation. Adapt it to suit your beliefs and intentions, and always approach it with respect and reverence. May it aid the transmigration of the deceased's soul into the realm of eternal knowledge, granting them profound insights and boundless wisdom.

16. Ritual of anointing with sacred crystals for spiritual clarity and protection

✦ Choose a selection of crystals that resonate with spiritual clarity and protection, such as clear quartz, amethyst, black tourmaline, and selenite. Cleanse and purify the crystals by placing them under running water or in sunlight for a few hours.

✦ Find a quiet and sacred space where you can perform the ritual undisturbed. Create a serene atmosphere by lighting candles, burning incense, or playing gentle music.

✦ Sit comfortably and take a few deep breaths to center yourself. Hold the crystals in your hands and close your eyes, entering a state of peaceful awareness.

✦ Begin by setting your intention for the ritual. Focus on the desire for spiritual clarity and protection, envisioning yourself surrounded by a shield of radiant light.

✦ Take one crystal at a time and hold it to your heart. Feel its energy merging with your own, infusing you with clarity and protection. Visualize the crystal's light expanding and enveloping your entire being.

✦ With each crystal, you may choose to recite a personal affirmation or prayer that resonates with you. For example, you can say, "I am open to divine guidance and clarity. I am protected from all negative energies and influences. I walk my spiritual path with confidence and discernment."

✦ When you feel ready, begin anointing your body with the crystals. Start from the top of your head and gently move the crystals in circular motions, following the natural energy flow of your body. Visualize the crystals leaving a trail of shimmering light and a protective aura around you.

✦ As you anoint yourself, focus on the intention of spiritual clarity and protection. Feel the crystals' energy penetrating your aura and dissolving any stagnant or negative energies, allowing your inner light to shine brightly.

✦ Take your time with each crystal, allowing yourself to fully connect with its energy. You may choose to anoint specific areas of your body, such as your forehead for clarity of thought or your heart for emotional protection.

✧ Once you have anointed your entire body, sit in stillness and gratitude. Feel the combined energy of the crystals working harmoniously within you, providing clarity and protection on your spiritual journey.

✧ When you are ready to conclude the ritual, express gratitude to the crystals for their assistance and to the divine forces for their guidance and protection. Acknowledge the power within you and trust in the clarity and protection that you have invoked.

✧ Place the crystals in a sacred space, such as an altar or a special box, and keep them cleansed and charged for future use.

Remember, this ritual is a sacred practice that honors the power and energy of crystals. Adapt it to suit your personal beliefs and preferences, and always approach it with reverence and respect. May this ritual of anointing with sacred crystals bring you spiritual clarity and protection on your path of growth and transformation.

17. Spell for the transformation of the deceased into a vessel of divine healing

✧ Find a quiet and sacred space where you can perform the spell undisturbed. Create a peaceful atmosphere by lighting candles, burning incense, or playing gentle music.

✧ Sit or stand in a comfortable position and take a few deep breaths to center yourself. Close your eyes and visualize a radiant, healing light surrounding you.

✧ Begin by setting your intention for the spell. Focus on the desire for the deceased to become a vessel of divine healing, envisioning their spirit being filled with healing energy and compassion.

✧ Recite the following incantation or create your own heartfelt words:

"Spirit of the departed, I call upon you now,
Transform into a vessel of healing divine.
Let your essence be filled with love and light,
Becoming a conduit for healing in the realms beyond.

May your presence bring comfort and solace,
Bringing peace and restoration to those in need.
Radiate your healing energy far and wide,
Touching hearts and souls with divine grace.

As you transcend this earthly plane,
Let your spirit embody the power of healing.
Heal the wounded, soothe the broken,
And bring divine blessings to all you encounter.

Through the realms of light and shadow,
Your healing essence shall prevail.
So mote it be."

✧ As you recite the spell, visualize the deceased's spirit being enveloped in a vibrant, healing light. See their energy expanding and radiating outwards, reaching those in need of healing.

✧ Hold the intention in your heart and continue visualizing the divine healing energy flowing through the deceased, touching lives and bringing comfort to the afflicted.

✧ When you feel ready, express gratitude to the deceased for their willingness to be a vessel of divine healing. Thank them for their service and their contribution to the well-being of others.

✧ Take a few moments to sit in stillness and allow the energy of the spell to settle and integrate. Feel the presence of healing energy surrounding you and affirm the transformative power of the spell.

✧ When you are ready to conclude the spell, offer a final expression of gratitude to the divine forces for their support and guidance. Trust that the deceased's spirit will continue to be a beacon of healing in the realms beyond.

Remember, this spell is a sacred practice that honors the power of divine healing. Adapt it to suit your personal beliefs and preferences, and always approach it with reverence and respect. May this spell for the transformation of the deceased into a vessel of divine healing bring comfort, restoration, and blessings to all those touched by its power.

18. Incantation to invoke the blessings of the celestial mountains and valleys

✧ Find a peaceful and serene place where you can connect with the energy of nature. It could be outdoors, near mountains or hills, or in a quiet indoor space where you can visualize the grandeur of the celestial landscape.

✧ Stand tall and take a few deep breaths to center yourself. Close your eyes and imagine yourself surrounded by the majestic presence of celestial mountains and valleys. Feel the grounding energy beneath your feet and the vastness of the sky above.

✧ Raise your arms outstretched, palms facing upward, as if embracing the celestial mountains and valleys. Feel the connection between your physical body and the expansive energy of the natural world.

✧ Recite the following incantation or create your own heartfelt words:

"By the power of the celestial heights,
By the grace of the sacred valleys,
I invoke the blessings of nature's embrace,
As above, so below, our spirits interlace.

From mountaintops, wisdom flows,
Like ancient echoes, ancient stories it knows.
In valleys deep, secrets lie,
Where healing waters and whispers reside.

Celestial mountains, ancient and grand,
Bestow upon me strength and courage, hand in hand.
Celestial valleys, fertile and serene,
Shower upon me abundance, calm and serene.

I am one with the celestial realms,
Connected to the earth, sky, and all that dwells.
In harmony with nature, I find my place,
Guided by its wisdom, with love and grace.

Blessed be the mountains and valleys high,
Their energies fill me, as I reach for the sky.

May their blessings flow through me and beyond,
Aligning my spirit with the universe's bond.

So mote it be."

✧ As you recite the incantation, visualize yourself surrounded by the majestic beauty of celestial mountains and valleys. Feel the strength, wisdom, and serenity emanating from these sacred places, infusing your being with their blessings.

✧ Open your heart and mind to receive the energies of the mountains and valleys. Allow their wisdom and abundance to flow through you, filling you with inspiration, resilience, and harmony.

✧ Express gratitude to the celestial mountains and valleys for their blessings and the connection they provide. Acknowledge the sacredness of nature and your role as a steward of the Earth.

✧ Slowly lower your arms and take a few moments to bask in the energy and peace that the incantation has invoked. Feel the unity between yourself and the natural world, recognizing the profound interconnection that exists.

✧ When you are ready to conclude, express a final word of gratitude to the celestial mountains and valleys for their presence and guidance. Carry their blessings with you as you continue your spiritual journey.

Remember, this incantation serves as a conduit for connecting with the celestial mountains and valleys. Adapt it to your own beliefs and connection with nature. Embrace the sacredness of the natural world and allow its blessings to inspire and guide you. May the celestial mountains and valleys bring you strength, wisdom, and abundance on your spiritual path.

19. Ritual for the transfiguration of the deceased into a divine messenger of the gods

✧ Create a sacred space for the ritual, preferably in a quiet and serene environment. Set up an altar or a designated area where you can focus your intentions and perform the ritual undisturbed.

✧ Gather symbolic items representing the gods or deities you wish to invoke. These can include statues, images, or symbols associated with the specific divine beings you seek to align with.

✧ Light candles and burn incense to purify the space and create a sacred ambiance. Choose fragrances that are traditionally associated with divine communication, such as frankincense or myrrh.

✧ Stand before the altar or sacred space and center yourself. Take a few deep breaths to calm your mind and connect with your inner being. Allow yourself to enter a state of reverence and openness to the divine energies.

✧ Invoke the presence of the gods or deities you wish to connect with. Speak their names aloud and express your sincere desire to serve as a messenger on their behalf.

✧ Offer prayers or invocations to the gods, expressing your dedication and willingness to be a conduit of their messages. Speak from the heart, expressing your commitment to sharing their wisdom, love, and guidance with those who are in need.

✧ Hold one of the symbolic items representing the gods in your hands, and envision yourself being infused with their divine essence. Feel the energy of the gods merging with your own, empowering you to carry their messages with clarity and purity.

✧ Recite the following affirmation or create your own heartfelt words:

"By the gods' divine decree,
I offer myself as their messenger, you see.
Transfigured in their sacred light,

I carry their words, shining bright.

With reverence and humble grace,
I bring their wisdom to this earthly place.
Their messages shall flow through me,
A channel of divine truth, for all to see.

As their messenger, I shall convey,
Their love, their guidance, without delay.
With clarity, I speak their words,
Touching hearts, like sweetest birds.

I am the bridge between realms above,
A conduit of divine, eternal love.
As I speak, their presence shall be known,
Their messages embraced, seeds sown.

So mote it be."

✧ Allow the energy and intention of the ritual to settle within you. Feel the transformation taking place as you embody the role of a divine messenger.

✧ Spend a few moments in silent meditation, connecting with the gods and absorbing their divine energy. Listen for any messages or guidance they may impart to you during this sacred communion.

✧ Express gratitude to the gods for their presence and for the opportunity to serve as their messenger. Acknowledge their wisdom, guidance, and love that flows through you.

✧ When you are ready to conclude the ritual, extinguish the candles and allow the sacred space to return to its natural state. Take a few moments to ground yourself and integrate the energy of the ritual into your being.

Remember, this ritual serves as a sacred act of devotion and dedication to the gods you seek to align with. Adapt it to your own spiritual beliefs and connections. Embrace your role as a divine messenger with humility, love, and integrity, carrying the messages of the gods to those in need. May the divine presence guide and empower you as you fulfill this sacred role.

20. Spell for the reunion of the deceased's soul with their spiritual guides and mentors

✧ Find a quiet and peaceful space where you can focus your energy and intention without distractions. This can be indoors or outdoors, whichever feels most comfortable and sacred to you.

✧ Light a white candle to represent purity and divine guidance. Place it on an altar or a designated area where you will perform the spell.

✧ Sit or stand in front of the candle, close your eyes, and take a few deep breaths to center yourself. Allow your mind to relax and your heart to open.

✧ Visualize a gentle and loving light surrounding you, creating a protective and sacred space. Feel the presence of your spiritual guides and mentors, their energy enveloping you with warmth and guidance.

✧ Speak the following incantation from your heart or use it as a guide to create your own words:

"By the light that guides and protects,
I call upon my spiritual guides and mentors,
Across the realms, I seek your connection,
With reverence and love, I make this intention.

Hear my call, beloved guides and mentors,
In this realm and beyond, I seek your presence,
Guide me with your wisdom and truth,
Illuminate my path, provide me with proof.

In this sacred space, we reunite,
Souls entwined, like stars in the night,
Your guidance and support I seek,
Together we journey, wise and meek.

Open the channels, let the messages flow,
From realms unseen, where knowledge does grow,
Reveal to me the insights and signs,
As we walk this path, intertwining our minds.

I honor your presence, oh guides so dear,
In gratitude, I hold you near,
Reunite my soul with your divine embrace,
In harmony and love, we share this space.

So mote it be."

✧ Imagine the presence of your spiritual guides and mentors becoming more tangible and clear. Feel their energy blending with yours, offering guidance, support, and love.

✧ Take a few moments to silently communicate with your spiritual guides and mentors. Listen for any messages, insights, or guidance they may have for you. Trust your intuition and allow the connection to deepen.

✧ Express gratitude to your spiritual guides and mentors for their presence and assistance. Thank them for their continued guidance and support on your spiritual journey.

✧ When you feel ready, slowly extinguish the candle, symbolizing the completion of the spell. Take a moment to ground yourself and integrate the energy of the spell into your being.

Remember, this spell is a sacred invitation to connect and reunite with your spiritual guides and mentors. Adapt it as needed to resonate with your personal beliefs and spiritual practices. Embrace the reunion with gratitude, openness, and a willingness to receive the guidance and wisdom they offer. May your connection with your spiritual guides and mentors be strengthened, bringing clarity, support, and growth on your spiritual path.

21. Invocation of the goddess Hathor for joy and abundance in the afterlife

✧ Find a quiet and sacred space where you can focus your energy and connect with the divine. This can be indoors or outdoors, wherever you feel most connected to the energy of Hathor.

✧ Light a yellow or golden candle to represent the radiance and abundance of Hathor. Place it on an altar or a dedicated space for your ritual.

✧ Stand or sit in front of the candle and take a few deep breaths to center yourself. Allow yourself to become fully present in the moment.

✧ Close your eyes and visualize a warm and vibrant golden light surrounding you. Feel the presence of Hathor, the goddess of joy and abundance, drawing near.

✧ Recite the following invocation from your heart or use it as a guide to create your own words:

"Goddess Hathor, radiant and wise,
I call upon your presence, beyond the skies.
With joyous heart, I invite you near,
To bless my journey, to banish fear.

Oh Hathor, bringer of joy and delight,
Shower me with your blessings, day and night.
In the afterlife's realm, guide my way,
Fill my soul with abundance, I pray.

With your divine grace, let joy unfold,
May my spirit dance and my heart behold
The treasures of life, both seen and unseen,
In the afterlife's realm, a joyous dream.

Abundance flows, as your love abounds,
I embrace the blessings that know no bounds.
Fill my being with your joyful light,
In the afterlife's realm, forever bright.

Goddess Hathor, hear my plea,

In the afterlife, may I be free.
Joy and abundance, I ask you to share,
With gratitude and love, I show my care.

So mote it be."

✧ Open your heart and allow the presence of Hathor to envelop you. Feel her joyous energy infusing your being, bringing a sense of abundance and celebration.

✧ Take a few moments to silently connect with Hathor. Feel her presence, listen for any messages or insights she may have for you. Trust your intuition and allow the connection to deepen.

✧ Express gratitude to Hathor for her presence and blessings. Thank her for the joy and abundance she brings into your life, both in the afterlife and in the present moment.

✧ When you feel ready, extinguish the candle, symbolizing the completion of the invocation. Take a moment to ground yourself and integrate the energy of the ritual.

Remember, this invocation is a sacred invitation to connect with the goddess Hathor, the embodiment of joy and abundance. Adapt it as needed to align with your personal beliefs and spiritual practices. Embrace the presence of Hathor with an open heart, inviting joy and abundance to flow into your life, even in the afterlife. May you experience the blessings of Hathor's joy and abundance throughout your spiritual journey.

22. Ritual of purification through the sacred movements of the eternal dance

✧ Find a quiet and sacred space where you can move freely and connect with the divine energy within you. This can be indoors or outdoors, as long as you have enough space to perform your dance.

✧ Create an atmosphere conducive to the ritual by dimming the lights or lighting candles, playing soft and rhythmic music that resonates with your intention, and setting up an altar with meaningful objects or symbols that inspire you.

✧ Begin by standing in the center of your space, feet firmly planted on the ground, and take a few deep breaths to center yourself. Allow any tensions or distractions to melt away as you focus on the present moment.

✧ Close your eyes and visualize a soft, pure, and radiant light enveloping your entire being. Feel this light cleansing and purifying every cell of your body, releasing any stagnant or negative energies.

✧ As you open your eyes, let the music guide your movements. Start with gentle swaying and gradually allow your body to express itself freely. Let go of any inhibitions or self-judgment and allow the dance to be a reflection of your inner state.

✧ As you move, imagine that with each graceful step, spin, or sway, you are shedding old energies and purifying your spirit. Visualize the dance as a sacred ritual that connects you with the divine and washes away any impurities or blockages.

✧ Explore different rhythms and tempos in your dance. Allow your body to respond intuitively to the music, expressing emotions, releasing tensions, and surrendering to the flow of energy.

✧ As you continue dancing, you may choose to incorporate specific gestures or movements that hold personal significance to you. This could include reaching towards the sky, embracing the earth, or weaving your arms like a serpentine river. Let your body and intuition be your guide.

✧ Throughout the dance, repeat a mantra or affirmation that resonates with your intention for purification. It could be as simple as "I release what no longer serves me" or "I am cleansed and renewed."

✧ After a period of time, when you feel complete in your dance, gradually slow down your movements and come to a gentle halt. Stand still, feeling the energy flowing within you and around you, honoring the purification you have experienced.

✧ Take a moment to reflect on your experience and express gratitude for the purification and renewal you have invoked through your dance. Offer thanks to the divine and any guides or energies you feel have supported you during this ritual.

✧ Finally, close the ritual by taking a few deep breaths, grounding yourself by placing your hands on the earth, and setting an intention to carry the energy of purification and renewal into your daily life.

Remember, this ritual is a personal expression of purification through movement. Feel free to adapt it to your own preferences and incorporate any additional elements that resonate with you. Embrace the transformative power of dance and allow it to cleanse and rejuvenate your spirit, bringing you closer to a state of inner purity and harmony.

23. Spell for the liberation of the deceased's soul from earthly attachments

Gather the following materials:

✦ A white candle
✦ A small piece of paper or parchment
✦ A pen or quill
✦ A fireproof bowl or cauldron

Perform this spell during a quiet and undisturbed time:

✦ Begin by lighting the white candle, representing purity and spiritual illumination. Place it on a sturdy surface in front of you.

✦ Take the piece of paper or parchment and write down any earthly attachments or burdens that you believe may be holding the deceased's soul back from complete liberation. These could be specific emotions, relationships, material possessions, or desires.

✦ As you write, focus your intention on releasing and freeing the deceased's soul from these attachments. Visualize them dissipating and transforming into lightness and freedom.

✦ Once you have finished writing, fold the paper or parchment and hold it between your hands. Close your eyes and take a few deep breaths to center yourself.

✦ Envision the divine energy surrounding you and ask for assistance from higher powers or spiritual guides to aid in the liberation of the deceased's soul. You may address a specific deity or simply call upon the universal forces of love and transformation.

✦ Holding the folded paper over the flame of the white candle, carefully ignite it and place it into the fireproof bowl or cauldron. As it burns, imagine the attachments being consumed by the flames, releasing their hold on the deceased's soul.

✦ While the paper burns, recite the following incantation or create your own heartfelt words:

"From earthly bonds, you now are free,
Released from attachments, let your soul be.
With this fire, I ignite the way,
Liberation and freedom come today."

✧ Sit quietly and observe the burning paper, allowing the energy of transformation and liberation to permeate the space. Feel a sense of lightness and release as the spell works its magic.

✧ Once the paper has completely burned, extinguish the flame of the white candle. Take a moment to express gratitude for the assistance received and for the liberation of the deceased's soul.

✧ Dispose of the ashes from the burned paper in a respectful and environmentally-friendly manner. You may choose to scatter them outside or bury them in the earth, symbolizing the final release of the attachments.

✧ Close the spell by taking a few deep breaths and grounding yourself. Express your intention that the liberated soul find its true path and continue its journey in the afterlife with newfound freedom and clarity.

Remember, intention and belief are key components of any spell. Trust in the power of this ritual and the forces of liberation to bring about the desired results. May this spell serve as a catalyst for the deceased's soul to transcend earthly attachments and find ultimate liberation in the realms beyond.

24. Incantation to awaken the dormant inner strength within the deceased's spirit

✧ Stand in a quiet and sacred space, where you can connect with the energies of the divine. Take a few moments to ground yourself and center your focus on the intention of awakening the inner strength within the deceased's spirit.

✧ Close your eyes and take a deep breath, allowing your body and mind to relax. Visualize a bright and radiant light surrounding you, filling the space with its warmth and power. Feel this light flowing through you, infusing every cell of your being with its energy.

✧ As you recite the incantation, speak with confidence and conviction, allowing your words to resonate with the depths of your being:

"Spirits of ancient might and grace,
Awaken the strength within this sacred space.
From realms unseen, I call forth the power,
To empower the deceased in their eternal hour.

Rise, dormant strength, from the depths below,
Unleash your fire, let it burn and glow.
Break the chains of weakness and despair,
With inner fortitude, let the spirit repair.

Through the trials of life and shadows cast,
Unleash the courage of the distant past.
From the wellspring of resilience and might,
Awaken the spirit, shine with inner light.

Strength of the ancients, flow through their veins,
Unveil their power, release their chains.
Embrace their essence, unyielding and bold,
With unwavering strength, their spirit unfold.

By the power of my will, this spell is cast,
Awakening strength that will forever last.
So mote it be, and let it be done,
As the deceased's spirit rises, strong as the sun."

✧ As you finish reciting the incantation, visualize the dormant strength within the deceased's spirit awakening and shining brightly. Feel the energy permeating their being, empowering them with resilience, courage, and unwavering strength.

✧ Take a moment to offer gratitude to the divine forces and the spirits that have assisted in this awakening. Trust that the dormant inner strength within the deceased's spirit has been ignited, ready to guide and support them on their journey in the afterlife.

✧ When you are ready, slowly open your eyes, knowing that your words and intentions have set a powerful transformation in motion. May the deceased's spirit embrace and embody their inner strength, finding solace, empowerment, and resilience in the realms beyond.

25. Ritual for the communion with the spirits of the celestial rain and thunder

✧ Find a secluded and peaceful outdoor space where you can connect with the energies of the natural elements. Choose a day when rain is anticipated or a time when you can hear the distant rumble of thunder. This will enhance the potency of the ritual.

✧ Stand barefoot on the earth, feeling its grounding energy beneath your feet. Close your eyes and take a few deep breaths, allowing yourself to become fully present in the moment. Visualize a gentle rain shower or the powerful display of thunder and lightning in your mind's eye.

✧ Raise your arms towards the sky, palms open, and speak these words with reverence:

"Spirits of rain and thunder, I call upon thee,
Grant me communion, that I may truly see.
Open the gates to your celestial domain,
Let your essence cleanse and nourish my soul's terrain.

Rain, oh blessed rain, with your gentle touch,
Cleanse away the stagnant, the old, and the much.
Purify my spirit, wash away the pain,
Renew and refresh, like the fertile earth's gain.

Thunder, mighty thunder, with your roaring voice,
Awaken within me strength and courage, my choice.
Resound through my being, shake me to the core,
Ignite the fire of transformation forevermore.

In this sacred communion, I seek your wisdom and grace,
To understand the cycles, the divine's embrace.
Guide me in harmony with nature's sacred dance,
Grant me insight, inspiration, and a newfound chance.

As I stand here, connected to the heavens above,
I honor your presence, spirits of rain and thunder, with love.
May your essence merge with mine, in perfect harmony,
As I commune with you, in sacred unity."

✧ Stay in this open and receptive state, feeling the energy of rain and thunder surrounding you. Listen to the raindrops falling or the distant rumble of thunder, allowing the sound to penetrate your being.

✧ Take a few moments to express gratitude for the spirits of rain and thunder, for their presence and guidance. Trust that through this communion, you have opened a channel of connection and received their blessings.

✧ When you feel ready, slowly lower your arms and gently open your eyes. Carry the energy of this ritual with you, allowing the spirits of rain and thunder to continue to inspire and guide you on your spiritual journey.

Note: It is important to exercise caution and prioritize your safety when performing this ritual. Be mindful of weather conditions and seek shelter if necessary.

26. Spell for the transmigration of the deceased's soul into the realm of eternal harmony

✧ Create a sacred space where you can focus your energy and intention. Light candles or incense, and sit or stand in a comfortable position. Take a few moments to center yourself, breathing deeply and releasing any tension or distractions.

✧ Once you feel grounded, speak the following words with clarity and conviction:

"By the power of the divine and the cosmic flow,
I call upon the forces that guide souls to go.
From this earthly realm to the realm of eternal light,
I seek the transmigration, harmonious and bright.

May the soul of [Name of the deceased] find its way,
To the realm of peace and harmony, I pray.
Release the burdens of the past and the strife,
Embrace the serenity of eternal life.

Guide them, O benevolent spirits, on this sacred quest,
To a realm where harmony and love manifest.
In the embrace of divine grace, may they find,
An eternal home where peace and bliss entwine.

May the transition be gentle, smooth, and serene,
As the soul traverses realms yet unseen.
Into the arms of celestial harmony, they shall reside,
Where all discord and pain shall subside.

As I speak these words with love and reverence,
I ask for the soul's journey, blessed and immense.
Grant them eternal harmony, O cosmic divine,
And let their spirit in eternal bliss forever shine.

So mote it be."

- ✧   Allow the energy of the spell to fill the space around you. Visualize the soul of the deceased being surrounded by a radiant light, gently transitioning into the realm of eternal harmony. Hold this image in your mind, sending your love and well-wishes to the departed soul.

- ✧   When you feel ready, slowly extinguish the candles or incense, and take a few moments to offer gratitude to the divine forces and the spirits that guide souls on their journey.

Remember, this spell is intended to be performed with love, respect, and pure intentions. It is a way to honor the deceased and assist them in their transition to a realm of eternal harmony.

27. Invocation of the god Thoth for wisdom and knowledge in the afterlife

✧ Find a quiet and sacred space where you can connect with the divine. Light a candle or incense to create an atmosphere of reverence. Take a moment to center yourself, closing your eyes and taking deep, calming breaths.

✧ When you feel ready, recite the following invocation with sincerity and intention:

"Oh Thoth, the wise and mighty god,
Bearer of knowledge, keeper of the divine rod.
In this sacred space, I call upon thee,
To guide the departed, grant them wisdom's key.

With your ibis head and scribe's hand,
You hold the wisdom of the ancient land.
Inscribe upon their soul the sacred truth,
Illuminate their path with eternal youth.

Oh Thoth, the master of magic and words,
Unveil the mysteries, as their journey unfurls.
Grant them insight and understanding profound,
In the realm of the afterlife, may wisdom resound.

May their spirit be blessed with your divine grace,
As they embark on their eternal embrace.
Grant them access to the halls of knowledge,
And the realms where wisdom freely flows.

Oh Thoth, I beseech you, hear my plea,
Guide them with your wisdom for eternity.
In the afterlife's realm, may they find,
A sanctuary of wisdom, forever enshrined.

I offer my reverence and gratitude to thee,
Oh Thoth, the god of wisdom, I decree.
With love and respect, I honor your name,
And invite your presence in this sacred flame.

So mote it be."

✧ Allow the energy of your words and intentions to fill the space around you. Visualize the presence of Thoth, the god of wisdom, standing before you, emanating an aura of profound knowledge and guidance. Feel his wisdom and blessings descending upon the departed soul, enveloping them with divine wisdom and understanding.

✧ Take a few moments to offer your gratitude to Thoth for his presence and blessings. Reflect on the power of wisdom and knowledge in the journey of the soul.

✧ When you are ready, slowly extinguish the candle or incense, knowing that your invocation has been heard and the departed soul has been blessed by the wisdom of Thoth.

Remember, this invocation is a sacred act that seeks the wisdom and knowledge of the god Thoth for the departed soul. Perform it with reverence and pure intentions, honoring the divine wisdom that Thoth embodies.

28. Ritual of anointing with sacred symbols for spiritual empowerment and protection

Gather the following items:

✧ A small vial of pure, sacred oil (such as frankincense, myrrh, or sandalwood)
✧ A clean, white cloth or piece of fabric
✧ A sacred symbol or talisman that resonates with you (such as an ankh, a pentacle, a sacred geometry symbol, or a symbol from your spiritual tradition)
✧ Find a quiet and sacred space where you can perform the ritual undisturbed. Light a candle or incense to create a sacred atmosphere. Take a moment to center yourself and set your intentions for the ritual.

✧ Hold the vial of sacred oil in your hands and infuse it with your intentions for spiritual empowerment and protection. Visualize the oil being charged with divine energy and the power of the sacred symbol you have chosen.

✧ Dip your finger into the vial of oil and draw the sacred symbol onto the white cloth. As you do so, focus on the energy and meaning of the symbol, invoking its power to empower and protect you spiritually.

✧ Once the symbol is drawn on the cloth, take a deep breath and hold the cloth close to your heart. Close your eyes and silently recite the following affirmation or prayer:

"With this sacred symbol and anointing oil,
I invoke divine power to strengthen and protect my soul.
Empower me with wisdom, love, and spiritual light,
Shielding me from all negativity, day and night.

May this symbol be a beacon of divine grace,
Guiding me on my spiritual journey's embrace.
Empowered and protected, I stand tall and strong,
Aligned with the divine, where I belong.

As I anoint myself with this sacred symbol and oil,
I am infused with divine power and spiritual toil.
May it be so, and so it is."

✧ Hold the anointed cloth against your heart for a few moments, allowing the energy of the symbol and oil to merge with your being. Feel the empowerment and protection spreading throughout your body and aura.

✧ Afterward, you can choose to keep the anointed cloth in a sacred space, carry it with you, or place it under your pillow during sleep to enhance your connection with the symbol's energy.

Remember, this ritual is a sacred act of empowerment and protection. Perform it with reverence, focusing on your intentions, and connecting with the energy of the sacred symbol. Feel the divine power infusing your being as you anoint yourself and affirm your spiritual empowerment and protection.

29. Spell for the transformation of the deceased into a vessel of divine guidance and wisdom

In a quiet and sacred space, gather the following items:

✧ A white candle
✧ A small piece of parchment or paper
✧ A pen or ink
✧ Sit comfortably and light the white candle. Take a few deep breaths to center yourself and focus your intention on connecting with the divine guidance and wisdom.

Take the piece of parchment or paper and write the following words:

"By the power of the divine, I call forth transformation.
From the realms of spirit, I seek guidance and wisdom.
May the soul of (name of the deceased) be transformed,
A vessel of divine guidance and wisdom, adorned.

Let their spirit be open to receive divine insight,
Guided by wisdom, intuition, and divine light.
May they become a beacon of knowledge and truth,
Guiding the living with wisdom from their eternal youth.

By the power of the divine, this spell is cast,
Transforming (name of the deceased), their past.
Into a vessel of divine guidance and wisdom,
Forever connected to the realms of the kingdom.

As I speak these words, let it be so,
In alignment with divine will, it shall grow.
The deceased shall embody wisdom's flame,
Guiding and inspiring, with a celestial name.

With gratitude and trust, I release this spell,
Knowing divine guidance and wisdom shall dwell.
In the vessel of (name of the deceased) as they transition,
Guiding and enlightening, with divine permission."

◇ Once you have written the words, hold the parchment or paper in your hands and visualize the transformation of the deceased into a vessel of divine guidance and wisdom. See their spirit illuminated with a radiant light, filled with knowledge and the ability to provide guidance to those in need.

◇ Place the parchment or paper near the lit candle and allow it to burn safely until it is completely consumed. As the flame consumes the paper, visualize the transformation taking place and the deceased embodying divine guidance and wisdom.

◇ Sit in quiet contemplation for a few moments, expressing gratitude for the transformation and the blessings it will bring. When you feel ready, extinguish the candle and close the ritual with a final affirmation or prayer.

Remember, this spell is a sacred act of transformation and connection with divine guidance and wisdom. Perform it with reverence, focusing on the intention and visualizing the desired outcome. Trust in the power of the divine to bring forth the transformation and guidance for the deceased's spirit.

30. Incantation to invoke the blessings of the celestial sunrises and sunsets

✧　Stand or sit in a place where you can witness the rising or setting sun. Close your eyes and take a few deep breaths, grounding yourself in the present moment.

✧　Feel the warmth of the sun's rays on your skin, and envision the vibrant colors of a sunrise or sunset spreading across the sky.

✧　With a calm and focused mind, recite the following incantation:

"From the realm of celestial wonders,
I call upon the blessings of the sun.
As it rises or sets with radiant hues,
I invoke its power, ancient and one.

Blessed be the sun's golden light,
A symbol of hope, renewal, and grace.
With each sunrise and sunset's embrace,
I welcome blessings to fill this space.

I draw in the energy of the dawn,
A new beginning, a fresh start.
As the sun rises, so does my spirit,
Filled with strength, love, and heart.

I embrace the colors of the twilight,
A gentle transition, a peaceful sight.
As the sun sets, so does my worries,
Guided by the stars, shining bright.

Celestial sunrises and sunsets divine,
I invite your blessings to shine upon me.
Illuminate my path, bring joy and peace,
As I embrace the beauty of life's tapestry.

By the power of the rising and setting sun,
I am filled with its blessings, one by one.
With gratitude and reverence, I receive,
The celestial gifts that I believe.

As I speak these words, so mote it be,
The blessings of sunrises and sunsets, I see.
May their beauty and power forever remain,
Guiding me on my journey, free from strain."

✧ Open your eyes and bask in the glow of the rising or setting sun. Feel the energy
   and blessings flowing through you, filling you with renewed strength, joy, and
   peace.

✧ Take a moment to express gratitude for the sun and its majestic displays of light
   and color. Carry the energy and blessings of the sunrises and sunsets with you
   throughout your day, allowing them to inspire and uplift you.

Remember, this incantation is a way to connect with the celestial energy of sunrises
and sunsets. Perform it with reverence and a genuine appreciation for the beauty and
power of these celestial phenomena.

31. Ritual for the transfiguration of the deceased into a divine weaver of cosmic destinies

✦ You will need a quiet and sacred space where you can perform the ritual undisturbed. Gather the following items: a white candle, a piece of black fabric, a skein of colorful thread, and a small loom or weaving tool if available.

✦ Begin by creating a calm and focused atmosphere. Light the white candle and place it before you as a symbol of divine light and guidance.

✦ Take the black fabric and hold it in your hands. Close your eyes and visualize the deceased, envisioning their spirit as a vibrant and radiant presence.

✦ With heartfelt intention, speak the following words:

"By the threads of fate and destiny's call,
I invoke the powers that weave over all.
In this sacred space, I stand with reverence,
To honor the departed and their transcendence.

Through this ritual, I seek to transform,
The departed's essence into a cosmic form.
A weaver of destinies, of dreams untold,
Bound to the cosmos, forever enfolded.

✦ Lay the black fabric on a flat surface in front of you. Take the skein of colorful thread and hold it in your hands. Visualize the vibrant threads representing the infinite possibilities and paths that can be woven.

✦ Gently begin to weave the threads onto the black fabric, using your fingers or the weaving tool. As you do so, visualize the deceased's spirit intertwining with the threads, becoming a master weaver of cosmic destinies.

✦ As you weave, recite the following incantation:

"With each thread I place and bind,
A cosmic tapestry of fate, I find.
In each intricate pattern and design,

The deceased's essence forever aligns.

Weaving the destinies of stars and space,
Their spirit embraces universal grace.
From the celestial realms, their presence shines,
A divine weaver of cosmic designs."

✧ Continue weaving until you feel a sense of completion or until you intuitively know that the ritual has served its purpose.

✧ Take a moment to reflect on the transformation that has taken place. Express gratitude to the deceased and the cosmic forces for their presence and participation.

✧ Extinguish the white candle, symbolizing the completion of the ritual. Carefully gather the woven fabric and hold it close to your heart, acknowledging the divine connection established through the ritual.

✧ Place the woven fabric in a sacred space or keep it with you as a symbolic reminder of the deceased's transformation into a divine weaver of cosmic destinies.

Remember, this ritual is a symbolic representation of the transfiguration and cosmic weaving. It is a way to honor the deceased and their connection to the greater cosmic forces. Perform it with reverence, intention, and an open heart, allowing the energy and symbolism to guide the transformational process.

32. Spell for the reunion of the deceased's soul with their soul family and spiritual community

✧ In a quiet and sacred space, gather the following items: a white candle, a small mirror, a piece of paper, and a pen or pencil.

✧ Light the white candle and place it before you as a symbol of divine light and guidance. Sit comfortably and take a few deep breaths to center yourself.

✧ Hold the small mirror in your hands, reflecting the light of the candle onto it. Visualize the deceased's soul surrounded by a loving and supportive energy, encompassed by their soul family and spiritual community.

✧ With sincere intention, write the following words on the piece of paper:

"Across realms and dimensions, I call upon the sacred bond,
To reunite the departed with their soul family beyond.
Through the veil of existence, let connections be revealed,
Guided by love and light, may reunion be sealed."

✧ Place the paper on the mirror, facing up, and hold the mirror up towards the candle. Visualize the light from the candle infusing the words on the paper and radiating outwards, creating a beacon of connection.

✧ Focus your attention on the mirror and recite the following incantation:

"By the light that shines, both seen and unseen,
I invoke the power to bridge the realms between.
Through this mirror's reflection, let souls unite,
Guided by love and grace, beyond time's finite."

✧ Close your eyes and visualize the deceased's soul surrounded by a loving and welcoming energy. See them connecting with their soul family and spiritual community, embracing one another with joy and recognition.

✧ Take a moment to express your heartfelt wishes for the reunion, sending love and blessings to the deceased and their soul family.

✧ Slowly open your eyes and gently blow out the candle, symbolizing the completion of the spell.

✧ Fold the paper with the written words and keep it in a safe and sacred place. You may choose to burn it as an offering in the future, releasing the intention into the universe.

✧ Give thanks to the divine forces and the deceased for their presence and participation in the spell. Trust in the process and allow the universe to work in its own time and ways to facilitate the reunion.

Remember, this spell is a means of setting intentions and opening the energetic pathways for the reunion of the deceased's soul with their soul family and spiritual community. It is a way to send love, support, and invitation across realms. Perform it with sincerity, love, and respect, trusting in the power of connection and the divine plan that unfolds.

33. Invocation of the goddess Isis for nurturing and protection in the afterlife

✧ In a quiet and sacred space, create an altar or sacred space dedicated to the goddess Isis. Gather items that symbolize her energy, such as an image or statue of Isis, a white candle, a bowl of water, and any other offerings or symbols that resonate with you.

✧ Begin by lighting the white candle, representing the divine light of Isis. Take a moment to center yourself and connect with the energy of the goddess.

✧ Stand before the altar and place your hands over your heart. Take a few deep breaths and feel your connection with the goddess Isis growing stronger with each inhale and exhale.

✧ Speak the following invocation from your heart, or recite it aloud:

"Divine Isis, great and compassionate goddess,
I call upon your nurturing presence in this sacred space.
In the realm of the afterlife, guide and protect me,
Embrace me with your loving and motherly embrace.

Goddess of life and magic, holder of wisdom and healing,
I seek your strength and grace in this eternal journey.
Wrap me in your wings of protection and guidance,
Envelop me in the warmth of your unconditional love.

Isis, mighty goddess of the heavens and the earth,
I honor you and invite your presence in my life.
Grant me the strength to navigate the afterlife's path,
Sustain me with your nourishing and nurturing light.

As I walk the realms of the afterlife's mysteries,
May your wisdom guide me and your love surround me.
In your divine care, I find solace and security,
Thank you, Isis, for your eternal guardianship."

✧ After reciting the invocation, spend a few moments in silent meditation, opening yourself to receive the energy and blessings of the goddess Isis. Visualize her presence surrounding you, providing nurturing and protection in the afterlife.

✧ If you have any offerings, such as flowers, incense, or food, place them before the image or statue of Isis as a gesture of gratitude and honor. You may also pour a small amount of water into the bowl, symbolizing the life-giving and purifying qualities of the goddess.

✧ Take a few more moments to express your gratitude and reverence to Isis. Reflect on any messages or insights you may have received during the invocation and meditation.

✧ When you feel ready, extinguish the candle as a symbol of completing the invocation. Express your thanks once again to the goddess Isis for her presence and guidance.

Remember, this invocation is a way to connect with the nurturing and protective energy of the goddess Isis in the afterlife. It is an invitation for her to be with you, guide you, and provide you with the love and support you need. Perform it with sincerity and an open heart, trusting in the power and presence of Isis to watch over and care for you in your spiritual journey.

34. Ritual of purification through the sacred fire of the eternal flame

Note: Fire rituals should be performed with caution and in a safe environment. Ensure you have proper fire safety measures in place before proceeding.

✧ Find a quiet and secluded outdoor space where you can safely perform the ritual. Set up a sacred circle or altar, if desired, with elements that symbolize purification, such as white candles, crystals, and cleansing herbs.

✧ Light a sacred fire in a fire pit or cauldron. As you light the fire, focus on the transformative power of the flames and their ability to cleanse and purify.

✧ Stand before the fire and take a few deep breaths to center yourself. Allow yourself to become fully present in the moment and connect with the energy of the fire.

✧ Hold your hands over the flames, feeling their warmth and energy. Visualize any negative or stagnant energies within you being drawn out and released by the purifying power of the fire.

✧ As you stand before the flames, recite the following affirmation or create your own words:

"Sacred fire, flame divine,
Cleanse my spirit, make me shine.
Burn away all that no longer serves,
Purify my being, as my soul observes.

With your power, I release,
All that holds me back, I now release.
Transform me with your sacred flame,
Purify my spirit, in your name.

As this fire burns and glows,
May my essence pure and free-flow.
Release the past, embrace the new,
Purify my spirit, in love and truth."

✧ Allow yourself to meditate and focus on the flames for a few moments. Feel the purification process taking place within you, as the fire consumes and transmutes any impurities or negative energies.

✧ When you feel ready, take a step back from the fire and express your gratitude for its purifying energy. Thank the fire for its cleansing power and for the transformation it has brought to your spirit.

✧ To conclude the ritual, you may choose to perform a closing ceremony, such as grounding yourself by placing your hands on the earth or offering a final prayer of gratitude.

Remember, fire is a powerful element, and it should be treated with respect and care. Always ensure you are in a safe environment and have the necessary precautions in place when working with fire. This ritual is meant to purify and cleanse your spirit, allowing you to release any negativity or stagnant energy. Embrace the transformative power of the sacred fire and allow its energy to uplift and purify your being.

35. Spell for the liberation of the deceased's soul from the chains of illusion and ignorance

✧ Find a quiet and sacred space where you can focus without distractions. Set up an altar or a special place with items that represent clarity and wisdom, such as a clear quartz crystal, a white candle, and a symbol of enlightenment.

✧ Light the white candle, symbolizing the illumination of truth and wisdom. Take a few deep breaths and allow yourself to become centered and present in the moment.

✧ Hold the clear quartz crystal in your hands and close your eyes. Visualize the soul of the deceased surrounded by a bright, purifying light. See this light dispelling all illusions and ignorance that may be hindering the soul's journey.

✧ Recite the following spell or create your own words:

"Spirit released from earthly bind,
Chains of illusion left behind.
Ignorance fades, truth takes flight,
Guided by wisdom's radiant light.

From veils of illusion, I set you free,
Embracing clarity, pure and true to be.
May your soul awaken, ignorance dissolve,
Liberated now, your spirit evolves.

As this spell is spoken and cast,
May truth and wisdom hold steadfast.
Lift the chains of illusion's embrace,
Free the soul with enlightened grace."

✧ Open your eyes and place the clear quartz crystal on the altar or hold it in your hands. Focus your energy and intention on the liberation of the deceased's soul from the chains of illusion and ignorance.

✧ Sit in meditation for a few moments, envisioning the soul becoming free from all limitations and embracing the truth and wisdom that guides its journey.

✧ When you feel ready, express gratitude for the liberation and send blessings to the departed soul. Offer a final prayer or affirmation, expressing your intentions for the soul's continued growth and enlightenment.

✧ Allow the candle to burn out naturally, or extinguish it with gratitude and respect.

Remember, this spell is intended to support the liberation of the deceased's soul from illusion and ignorance. It is important to approach this spell with love, compassion, and respect for the individual soul's journey. May the chains of illusion be broken, and may the soul find clarity, wisdom, and ultimate liberation.

36. Incantation to awaken the dormant divine spark within the deceased's spirit

✧ Find a quiet and sacred space where you can focus your energy and intention without distractions. Set up an altar or a special place with items that symbolize divine energy, such as a lit white candle, a representation of a deity or higher power, and any other objects that hold personal significance.

✧ Stand or sit comfortably in front of the altar and take a few deep breaths, allowing yourself to relax and center your awareness.

✧ Visualize a radiant light surrounding the deceased's spirit, illuminating their being from within. See this light growing brighter and more vibrant, awakening the dormant divine spark within them.

✧ Recite the following incantation or create your own words:

"Divine spark within, awaken and ignite,
In the realm beyond, reclaim your sacred light.
Rise from slumber, spirits so divine,
Rekindle the flame, let your essence shine.

From the depths of spirit, a divine fire burns,
Awaken, oh soul, let your radiance return.
Reconnect with your purpose, your eternal flame,
Embrace your divinity, in your true essence remain.

By the power of the cosmos, this incantation is made,
To awaken the dormant, the divine spark displayed.
May your spirit awaken, shine brightly and true,
In the realms beyond, may your divine purpose renew."

✧ As you recite the incantation, feel the words resonating within your being and vibrating through the space. Envision the divine spark within the deceased's spirit growing brighter and more vibrant with each word spoken.

✧ After reciting the incantation, spend a few moments in silence, holding the intention of awakening the dormant divine spark within the deceased's spirit. Visualize their spirit shining with divine light and connected to the higher realms.

✧   Express gratitude for the awakening and offer a final prayer or affirmation, asking for the continued guidance and nurturing of the divine spark within the deceased's spirit.

✧   Allow the candle to burn out naturally, or extinguish it with gratitude and reverence.

Remember, this incantation is intended to awaken the dormant divine spark within the deceased's spirit. Approach it with reverence, love, and respect for their journey. May the divine spark within them be ignited, and may their spirit shine with its true essence.

37. Ritual for the communion with the spirits of the celestial forests and meadows

✧ Find a peaceful outdoor location, preferably a forest or meadow, where you feel a strong connection to nature and the elements. Choose a time when the energies of the natural world are most vibrant, such as during sunrise or sunset.

✧ Begin by grounding yourself. Stand barefoot on the earth and take a few deep breaths, allowing yourself to feel rooted and connected to the land beneath you.

✧ Create a sacred space by placing natural objects, such as stones, flowers, or leaves, in a circular arrangement around you. This circle represents the boundary between the physical and spiritual realms.

✧ Light a candle or burn some incense, symbolizing the presence of the sacred and inviting the spirits of the forest and meadow to join you.

✧ Close your eyes and visualize the serene beauty of the celestial forests and meadows. Imagine yourself surrounded by the lush greenery, tall trees, and vibrant flowers. Feel the gentle breeze on your skin and the earth beneath your feet.

✧ Call upon the spirits of the celestial forests and meadows by speaking from your heart. Use your own words or recite the following invocation:

"Spirits of the celestial forests and meadows,
I stand before you with reverence and respect.
I seek communion and connection with your divine essence.
Open the doors between our worlds,
And let our energies intertwine and harmonize.

I come with a pure heart and open mind,
To listen, learn, and receive your wisdom.
Guide me through your sacred groves,
Reveal the secrets of the natural world.

With love and gratitude, I invite you to join me,
To dance and sing, to share your essence.
May our spirits unite in harmony and grace,
As we commune within this sacred space."

✧ Sit or lie down within the circle and allow yourself to be fully present in the moment. Listen to the sounds of nature, feel the energy of the environment, and observe any signs or messages that may come to you.

✧ Take your time to meditate, reflect, or simply be in the presence of the spirits. Offer any thoughts, prayers, or intentions you wish to share, and allow yourself to receive their blessings and guidance.

✧ When you feel complete, express your gratitude to the spirits of the celestial forests and meadows for their presence and teachings. Blow out the candle or extinguish the incense, symbolizing the end of the ritual.

✧ Leave the space with a sense of awe and gratitude, carrying the energy and wisdom of the celestial forests and meadows with you in your heart.

Remember, this ritual is a sacred act of communion with the spirits of the celestial forests and meadows. Approach it with reverence, gratitude, and a deep respect for the natural world. May your connection with the spirits and the natural realm bring you harmony, wisdom, and a deeper understanding of the interconnectedness of all things.

38. Spell for the transmigration of the deceased's soul into the realm of eternal peace and serenity

✧ Gather in a quiet and serene space, preferably outdoors or in a place where you feel connected to the elements. Light a white candle and place it before you as a symbol of purity and divine light.

✧ Close your eyes and take a few deep breaths, allowing yourself to enter a state of calm and stillness. Visualize a peaceful and tranquil landscape, where gentle streams flow, and the air is filled with serenity.

✧ Recite the following incantation with sincerity and intention:

"By the power of the sacred flame,
I call upon the realms beyond the earthly plane.
Guide the soul of (name of the deceased) with care,
To the realm of eternal peace and serenity fair.

Let the burdens of earthly existence be released,
As the soul transcends to a place of eternal ease.
May (name of the deceased) find solace and rest,
In the embrace of divine love, eternally blessed.

May peace fill their spirit, like a calm, gentle breeze,
As they traverse the realms with effortless ease.
Grant them serenity, free from sorrow and strife,
In the realm of eternal peace, their eternal life."

✧ Visualize the soul of the deceased being surrounded by a soft, radiant light, gently lifted from the earthly realm and guided towards a peaceful horizon. See them transitioning into a realm of serene beauty and profound tranquility.

✧ Allow the candle to burn for a few more moments, sending your prayers and intentions for the soul's journey. Express your gratitude to the divine forces and the universe for their guidance and support.

✧ When you are ready, extinguish the candle, acknowledging that the spell is complete. Take a moment to reflect on the serenity and peace that you have invoked and offer a final prayer or blessing for the soul's eternal rest.

✧ May this spell serve as a catalyst for the transmigration of the deceased's soul into the realm of eternal peace and serenity, bringing comfort and solace to both the departed and those who mourn.

39. Invocation of the god Sobek for strength and transformation in the afterlife

✧ Stand in a place of stillness and solitude, where you feel connected to the natural world. Visualize the image of Sobek, the ancient Egyptian god of strength and transformation, in your mind's eye. Feel his presence and power surrounding you.

✧ Raise your arms towards the sky, palms facing upward, and speak the following invocation with sincerity and reverence:

"Mighty Sobek, guardian of the Nile,
With scales of strength and a fearsome smile,
I call upon your sacred might,
To guide me through the afterlife's night.

Grant me strength in times of trial,
And courage to face the crocodile,
Transform my spirit, make me anew,
In the afterlife's realm, let me shine through.

Sobek, lord of transformation and change,
Guide me through this sacred exchange,
Grant me the power to transcend and evolve,
In the afterlife's journey, may I revolve.

With your strength, I shall overcome,
In your embrace, I am transformed,
Grant me the fortitude to face each test,
In the afterlife's realm, I manifest my best.

Sobek, mighty god of the Nile,
In your presence, I find solace and guile,
I honor you with love and respect,
In the afterlife's journey, my spirit is perfect."

✧ Take a moment to feel the energy of Sobek flowing through you, empowering you with strength and resilience. Reflect on the transformative power that awaits you in the afterlife, knowing that Sobek will guide and protect you.

✧ Express your gratitude to Sobek for his presence and assistance. Lower your arms and take a deep breath, feeling the connection between yourself and the divine energy of Sobek.

✧ May this invocation of Sobek bring you strength and transformation in your journey through the afterlife, providing you with the courage and resilience to face any challenges that may arise.

40. Ritual of anointing with sacred colors for spiritual transformation and manifestation

✧ Prepare a quiet and sacred space where you can perform this ritual. Gather an assortment of colored oils or paints that hold significance to you and represent the qualities you wish to manifest and embody.

✧ Sit comfortably and take a few deep breaths to center yourself. Hold each bottle of colored oil or paint in your hands, one at a time, and meditate on its energy and symbolism. Reflect on the qualities and intentions associated with each color.

✧ Begin by anointing yourself with the first color. Take a small amount of the colored oil or paint and gently apply it to your forehead, heart, and palms. As you do so, recite a personal affirmation or intention that aligns with the qualities represented by that color. Visualize the color radiating from the anointed areas, enveloping you in its transformative energy.

✧ Continue this process with each color, moving from one to the next. Take your time with each anointing, allowing yourself to fully embrace and embody the energy of the color. You may choose to anoint different parts of your body or focus on specific areas that resonate with your intentions.

✧ As you anoint yourself with each color, imagine the transformative power of the colors infusing your being. Feel yourself aligning with the qualities and vibrations associated with each hue. Visualize your intentions taking shape and manifesting in your life.

✧ Once you have anointed yourself with all the colors, take a few moments to bask in their combined energies. Allow yourself to feel the transformation and manifestation occurring within you.

✧ When you are ready, express gratitude for the ritual and the transformative power of colors. Take a final deep breath, grounding yourself in the present moment.

✧ Carry the energy of the anointing with you throughout your day, knowing that you have invoked the power of sacred colors for spiritual transformation and manifestation. Observe how these qualities manifest in your life, and continue to nurture them through intention and action.

✧ May this ritual of anointing with sacred colors bring you profound spiritual transformation and manifestation as you align with the energies and qualities represented by each hue.

41. Spell for the transformation of the deceased into a vessel of divine protection and healing

Gather in a sacred space where you feel connected to the spiritual realms. Light a white candle and set it before you as a symbol of purity and divine presence. Take a few moments to ground yourself and find inner stillness.

Close your eyes and bring your attention to the energy around you. Envision a radiant sphere of white light forming around you, encompassing your entire being. Feel the purity and protective power of this divine light.

Now, focus on the intention of transformation and healing for the deceased. Imagine their spirit standing before you, enveloped in a gentle glow. Visualize this light growing brighter and more vibrant, filling their entire being.

Recite the following incantation:

"Divine protection, I call upon thee,
Transform this soul, set it free.
Wrap it in light, heal its wounds,
Shield it from harm, in love it blooms.
I call upon the power divine,
Let this vessel radiantly shine."

As you recite the incantation, imagine the white light surrounding the deceased intensifying and permeating their spirit. See it purifying their energy, healing any wounds or imbalances, and infusing them with divine protection.

Hold this visualization and intention for as long as it feels right, allowing the energy to flow and work its magic. Trust in the power of your words and the divine forces that guide you.

When you are ready, express gratitude to the divine for their presence and assistance. Blow out the candle, releasing the intention into the universe.

Know that the transformation and healing process has been set into motion. Trust that the deceased's spirit is now a vessel of divine protection and healing, guided by the forces of light and love.

May this spell bring comfort and support as the deceased undergoes their transformation, becoming a vessel of divine protection and healing in the realms beyond.

42. Incantation to invoke the blessings of the celestial moon phases and lunar cycles

✧ Stand under the open sky, beneath the gentle glow of the moon. Feel the energy of the moon's light bathing you in its ethereal essence. Allow yourself to become attuned to the rhythm of the lunar cycles, feeling the ebb and flow of its mystical power.

✧ Raise your hands to the moon, palms facing upward, as if reaching for its celestial energy. Close your eyes and take a deep breath, grounding yourself in the present moment.

✧ Recite the following incantation:

"By the light of the waxing moon,
I invoke blessings that shall come soon.
With each phase, a new door opens wide,
Revealing secrets that the moon shall guide.

In the fullness of the moon's bright face,
I find wisdom, grace, and divine embrace.
With each waning phase, I release and let go,
Releasing what no longer serves, I grow.

Moon's energy, mystic and sublime,
Align me with the cosmic dance, the divine.
Grant me intuition, insight, and peace,
As I traverse life's cycles with grace and ease.

By the power of the moon, so mote it be,
Blessings and lunar magic flow through me."

✧ As you recite the incantation, envision the moon's light becoming stronger and more vibrant. Feel its energy infusing every cell of your being, awakening your intuition and connecting you to the cycles of life.

✧ Stay in this sacred space for a few moments, basking in the lunar energy and allowing its blessings to fill you. Express gratitude to the moon and the universe for their guidance and support.

✧ Know that by invoking the blessings of the celestial moon phases and lunar cycles, you are aligning yourself with the natural rhythms of the cosmos. May the moon's magic and wisdom guide you on your spiritual journey.

43. Ritual for the transfiguration of the deceased into a divine guardian of cosmic gateways

✧ Gather in a sacred space, where you feel connected to the vastness of the universe. Set up an altar adorned with symbols of the cosmos, such as stars, planets, and celestial patterns. Light candles to create an ambiance of divine energy.

✧ Stand before the altar and take a few deep breaths, centering yourself in the present moment. Visualize the deceased being surrounded by a radiant light, symbolizing their spiritual essence. Invoke their presence and their willingness to embrace their role as a guardian of cosmic gateways.

✧ Begin the ritual by anointing yourself and the sacred space with consecrated oil, symbolizing purification and divine consecration. As you anoint yourself, recite words that resonate with your intention, such as:

"By this sacred anointing oil,
I purify and consecrate my soul.
As I transform and ascend,
I become a guardian, a celestial friend."

✧ Move around the space, anointing each corner and object with the oil, invoking the power of the cosmos to infuse the area with divine energy.

✧ Next, recite the following spell to facilitate the transfiguration of the deceased into a guardian of cosmic gateways:

"From mortal form to cosmic essence,
I call upon divine transference.
May the deceased's spirit rise and soar,
A guardian of gateways forevermore.

Through celestial realms, they shall guide,
Navigating cosmic paths far and wide.
Their presence a beacon of cosmic light,
Guiding souls through the veil of night.

I call upon the cosmic forces above,
To bless and empower this sacred love.
As the deceased transfigures with grace,
They become a guardian, a cosmic embrace.

By the power of cosmic realms, so be it,
The transfiguration is complete and legit.
I honor the deceased's cosmic role,
As a guardian of gateways, blessed and whole."

Visualize the deceased's spirit transforming into a radiant celestial being, their energy expanding and intertwining with the cosmic energies around them. Feel their connection to the cosmic gateways strengthening and their role as a guardian solidifying.

✧ Conclude the ritual with gratitude and reverence for the deceased's new celestial role. Express your appreciation for their guidance and protection as they embrace their cosmic purpose.

✧ Allow the candles to burn out naturally, symbolizing the continued presence of the deceased as a guardian of cosmic gateways. Reflect on the transformative power of this ritual and its connection to the vastness of the universe.

✧ May this ritual empower the deceased to fulfill their divine role as a guardian of cosmic gateways and may their presence bring wisdom, guidance, and protection to all who seek their aid.

44. Spell for the reunion of the deceased's soul with their soulmates and divine counterparts

✧ Gather in a sacred space where you feel connected to the spiritual realm. Create an altar adorned with symbols of love, unity, and divine connection. Light candles to invoke the presence of divine energy and love.

✧ Sit before the altar and take a few deep breaths, centering yourself in the present moment. Visualize the deceased surrounded by a radiant light, their soul shining brightly. Call upon their soulmates and divine counterparts, inviting them to join in the sacred space and time.

✧ Recite the following spell to facilitate the reunion of the deceased's soul with their soulmates and divine counterparts:

"By the threads of destiny, I weave,
A spell of reunion for the souls I believe.
May the deceased find their beloved ones,
The soulmates and divine counterparts, under the sun.

Across time and space, let the bond ignite,
Drawing them close, in love's pure light.
Through the realms of spirit, they shall unite,
Guided by love's compass, shining so bright.

I call upon the forces of love divine,
To align the paths and intertwine.
In the realm beyond, where spirits reside,
Let soulmates and counterparts reunite.

With open hearts and spirits ablaze,
Their souls intertwine in eternal ways.
Love's embrace, a sacred dance,
As they reunite in a cosmic romance.

By the power of love and divine decree,
This spell is cast, so mote it be."

✧ Feel the energy of love and reunion flowing through you and the sacred space. Visualize the deceased's soul connecting with their soulmates and divine counterparts, their spirits intertwining and merging in a harmonious union.

✧ Express gratitude for the reunion and the power of love to transcend boundaries and bring souls together. Allow the candles to burn out naturally, symbolizing the eternal flame of love and connection.

✧ Reflect on the profound nature of soulmate and divine counterpart relationships and the infinite possibilities for love and growth in the afterlife.

May this spell facilitate the reunion of the deceased's soul with their soulmates and divine counterparts, bringing forth deep love, connection, and spiritual growth in the realm beyond.

45. Invocation of the goddess Nut for guidance and expansion in the afterlife

✧ Gather in a sacred space where you feel connected to the celestial realms. Create an altar adorned with symbols of the night sky, stars, and cosmic energy. Light candles to invoke the presence of the goddess Nut, the embodiment of the vast expanse of the heavens.

✧ Stand before the altar, with your arms outstretched to mimic the stretching of the sky. Feel the energy of the cosmos flowing through you, connecting you to the infinite possibilities of the afterlife.

✧ Recite the following invocation to call upon the goddess Nut:

"Oh, mighty Nut, celestial queen,
Whose expanse of stars is wondrously seen,
Guide me in the afterlife's grand flight,
Expand my spirit, show me the light.

With your arms embracing the celestial sphere,
Your wisdom and guidance, I humbly seek here.
Open my eyes to the mysteries untold,
Lead me on a journey of wisdom and gold.

As the night sky reveals its cosmic map,
Unveil to me the secrets that overlap.
Grant me guidance, in your embrace,
In the realm beyond, reveal your grace.

Goddess Nut, with your vast expanse,
I seek your guidance, a divine dance.
Expand my horizons, my spirit unfurl,
In the afterlife's journey, guide this soul."

✧ Feel the presence of the goddess Nut surrounding you, her cosmic energy embracing and guiding you. Open yourself to receiving her wisdom and expansion as you embark on your afterlife journey.

◇ Take a few moments to silently connect with the energy of Nut, allowing any messages or insights to flow through you. Trust in her guidance and know that she is supporting you on your path.

◇ Express gratitude to the goddess Nut for her presence and guidance. Allow the candles to burn out naturally, symbolizing the ongoing connection between you and the celestial realms.

◇ May this invocation of the goddess Nut bring you guidance, expansion, and a deep connection to the cosmic energies in the afterlife, as you navigate the vast expanse of spiritual growth and exploration.

46. Spell for the liberation of the deceased's soul from the illusions of the material world

✧ Gather in a peaceful and sacred space, free from distractions. Light a white candle to represent purity and illumination. Take a moment to ground yourself and connect with the energy of the spell.

✧ Close your eyes and take a few deep breaths, allowing your body and mind to relax. Visualize a radiant light surrounding you, enveloping you in its warm embrace.

✧ Speak the following incantation with conviction and clarity:

"By the power of the divine,
I release the soul from earthly ties.
From illusions of the material plain,
Let the spirit be free, unchained.

No longer bound by worldly desires,
Let the soul ascend higher and higher.
Transcending the illusions that bind,
Into realms of truth and clarity, we find.

May the veil of illusion be lifted,
And the soul's true nature be gifted.
With wisdom and insight, it shall be blessed,
In the eternal realm, it shall find rest.

I call upon the forces of light and love,
To guide the soul to realms above.
Free from illusions that obscure the way,
Let the soul journey to eternal day."

✧ Feel the power of your words as you speak them, infusing them with your intention and love. Visualize the deceased's soul being liberated from the illusions of the material world, ascending to a higher plane of existence.

✧ Sit in quiet contemplation for a few moments, allowing the energy of the spell to settle and integrate. Express gratitude for the liberation of the soul and the divine forces that have assisted in this process.

✧ When you feel ready, extinguish the candle, symbolizing the completion of the spell. Release any attachment to the outcome and trust that the divine wisdom and guidance will lead the soul to its true path.

May this spell bring liberation and freedom to the deceased's soul, freeing it from the illusions of the material world and guiding it towards the realms of truth and enlightenment.

47. Incantation to awaken the dormant spiritual gifts within the deceased's spirit

In a sacred space, where energies converge,
I call upon the spirits to gather and surge.
With reverence and respect, I open the way,
To awaken the gifts hidden in spirit's array.

From the depths of slumber, arise and awake,
The dormant abilities, for the soul's sake.
Ignite the flame of intuition and insight,
Let the gifts shine forth, radiant and bright.

By the ancient forces that guide us all,
I invoke the awakening of gifts, both big and small.
Let the deceased's spirit be touched by grace,
Embracing their gifts, finding their rightful place.

Awaken the clairvoyance, clear as the sky,
The mediumship to communicate with the divine.
Unveil the healing touch, gentle and pure,
And the wisdom to guide, steady and sure.

Unlock the creative flow, like a river unbound,
The psychic senses, attuned and profound.
Open the doors to spiritual perception,
And let the gifts flourish, without exception.

Oh, spirits of ancient wisdom, hear my plea,
Awaken the gifts that were meant to be.
Let the deceased's spirit soar and explore,
Their innate abilities, forevermore.

With gratitude and reverence, this incantation I say,
May the dormant gifts awaken without delay.
For the highest good and the soul's evolution,
Let the spirit's gifts shine with divine resolution.

As the incantation echoes through time and space,
May the dormant gifts awaken, embrace and embrace.

So mote it be, as the spirits decree,
The deceased's spirit shall be set free.

Take a moment of silence to honor the awakening of the dormant spiritual gifts within the deceased's spirit. Trust that the energies have been set in motion and that the gifts will manifest in alignment with the soul's highest purpose.

Remember, this incantation serves as a catalyst for awakening, but the deceased's spirit must continue its own journey of self-discovery and development. May their spiritual gifts bring them closer to their divine purpose and bring light and guidance to their path.

48. Ritual for the communion with the spirits of the celestial oceans and seas

✧ Find a quiet and serene space near a body of water, whether it be an ocean, sea, or even a peaceful lake. Ideally, perform this ritual during the hours of twilight or under the light of the moon.

✧ Begin by centering yourself through deep and mindful breathing. Feel your connection to the Earth beneath you and the vastness of the celestial skies above.

✧ Stand at the water's edge, facing the horizon. Dip your hands into the water and let its cool touch awaken your senses. Visualize the water as a gateway to the celestial realms, connecting you to the spirits of the oceans and seas.

✧ Close your eyes and recite the following invocation:

"Spirits of the celestial waters, I call upon you,
Guardians of the vast and boundless seas,
I seek your presence, your wisdom, and your guidance,
As I commune with your ethereal energies."

✧ Slowly walk along the water's edge, feeling the ebb and flow of the waves beneath your feet. Allow yourself to be in a state of reverence and openness to the messages and energies that may come forth.

✧ As you walk, let your mind and heart open to the voices of the spirits of the celestial waters. Listen for the whispers of ancient wisdom and the echoes of the cosmic tides.

✧ If you feel drawn to do so, you may choose to offer a small and meaningful token to the waters as a sign of respect and gratitude. It could be a seashell, a flower, or any item that holds significance to you.

✧ Spend a few moments in silent contemplation, allowing the energies of the celestial waters to fill you with a sense of peace, harmony, and connection to the greater cosmic flow.

✧ Before concluding the ritual, express your gratitude to the spirits of the celestial waters. Offer words of thanks for their presence, guidance, and the blessings they have bestowed upon you.

✧ Slowly and gently withdraw from the water's edge, carrying with you the energy of the celestial oceans and seas. Reflect upon the insights and experiences you gained during this communion, and integrate them into your spiritual practice and daily life.

Remember, this ritual is a sacred and personal experience. Trust your intuition and let the energies of the celestial waters guide you on your spiritual journey.

49. Invocation of the god Horus for protection and vision in the afterlife

✧ Find a quiet and sacred space where you can focus your energy and connect with the divine. Light a candle to create a sacred ambiance.

✧ Take a few moments to center yourself and enter a state of deep concentration. Close your eyes and take several deep breaths, allowing your body and mind to relax.

✧ Visualize a majestic falcon soaring through the sky, representing the powerful and divine presence of Horus. Imagine its wings outstretched, carrying the essence of protection and vision.

✧ With sincerity and reverence, recite the following invocation:

"Horus, mighty guardian and seer,
I call upon your presence, divine and near.
Wrap your wings of protection around me,
Guide my path in the realm of eternity.

Grant me your vision, eyes sharp and clear,
Illuminate the path as I journey without fear.
Let your wisdom and insight be my guide,
In the afterlife's realm, by your side.

Horus, I honor your sacred name,
Embrace me with your strength, ever the same.
Protect my soul as it finds its way,
In the afterlife's realm, I humbly pray."

✧ As you recite the invocation, visualize a golden light descending upon you, filling your being with the divine essence of Horus. Feel his protective presence surrounding you, and sense his vision infusing your sight.

✧ Take a few moments to meditate and connect with the energy of Horus. Allow any insights, guidance, or visions to come forth, trusting in the wisdom of the divine.

✧ Express gratitude to Horus for his presence and protection. Offer a heartfelt thanks for his guidance in the afterlife.

✧ When you are ready, slowly open your eyes and extinguish the candle, symbolizing the completion of the invocation.

Remember, this invocation is a sacred connection with the god Horus, seeking his protection and vision in the afterlife. Approach this invocation with reverence and sincerity, and trust in the power and guidance of Horus as you embark on your spiritual journey.

50. Ritual of anointing with sacred feathers for spiritual elevation and connection

Prepare a sacred space where you can perform the ritual. This can be a quiet room, a secluded outdoor area, or any place where you feel a strong connection to the divine.

Gather several sacred feathers that hold personal significance to you. These can be feathers from birds that have special spiritual symbolism or feathers that you have collected during meaningful experiences in nature.

Create an altar or a dedicated space where you will perform the ritual. Place a clean cloth or a piece of fabric on the altar, and arrange the feathers on top of it.

Light a candle or several candles to create a sacred ambiance. You may also choose to incorporate other elements, such as crystals, incense, or flowers, to enhance the sacredness of the space.

Take a moment to center yourself and enter a state of deep focus and intention. Close your eyes, take several deep breaths, and visualize a radiant light surrounding you, connecting you with the divine.

Pick up one of the sacred feathers and hold it in your hands. Feel its energy and imagine it carrying the essence of spiritual elevation and connection.

With reverence, gently stroke the feather along your body, starting from the top of your head and moving down to your feet. As you do so, visualize the feather's energy infusing your being, purifying and uplifting your spirit.

As you anoint yourself with each feather, recite a personal affirmation or a prayer that aligns with your intention for spiritual elevation and connection. Speak from the heart, expressing your desires for growth, insight, and divine communion.

After anointing yourself with all the sacred feathers, take a moment to reflect on the experience. Notice any sensations, emotions, or insights that arise within you. Embrace the sacredness of the moment and the connection you have cultivated.

Express gratitude to the sacred feathers for their energy and blessings. Thank them for their role in your spiritual journey and for the elevation and connection they have brought to your life.

Allow the candles to burn out naturally or extinguish them with gratitude, symbolizing the completion of the ritual.

Remember, this ritual is a sacred act of anointing yourself with the energy of sacred feathers for spiritual elevation and connection. Approach it with reverence, intention, and gratitude. As you engage in this ritual, open yourself to the divine energies and allow them to guide you on your path of spiritual growth and connection.

51. Spell for the transformation of the deceased into a vessel of divine strength and courage

✧ Find a quiet and sacred space where you can focus your energy and intention. Light a candle or several candles to create a sacred atmosphere. You may also choose to incorporate other elements that resonate with you, such as crystals or incense.

✧ Take a moment to center yourself and ground your energy. Close your eyes, take several deep breaths, and imagine roots growing from the soles of your feet, anchoring you to the earth.

✧ Once you feel grounded, envision the deceased person's soul standing before you, bathed in a gentle, golden light. Visualize their essence and presence with clarity.

✧ Speak the following incantation, or create your own heartfelt words:

"Divine forces of strength and courage,
I call upon you in this sacred hour.
Transform this soul into a vessel of might,
Let their spirit be filled with courage's light.
Banish fear and doubt, instill bravery within,
Let their strength soar and their courage begin."

✧ As you recite the incantation, imagine a radiant light surrounding the deceased's soul, infusing them with strength and courage. Visualize their spirit growing brighter and more empowered with each word spoken.

✧ Extend your hands towards the image of the deceased and visualize energy flowing from your palms to them, transferring the divine strength and courage you invoke.

✧ Hold the intention of transformation and empowerment firmly in your mind, seeing the deceased person's spirit embodying the qualities of strength and courage.

✧ Express gratitude to the divine forces you invoked, acknowledging their presence and assistance in this sacred work. Thank them for infusing the deceased person's spirit with strength and courage.

✧ Take a few moments to bask in the energy of the spell, feeling the power and transformation that has taken place. Allow the candle(s) to burn out naturally or extinguish them with gratitude, symbolizing the completion of the spell.

Remember, this spell is a channeling of divine energy to transform the deceased person's spirit into a vessel of strength and courage. Approach it with respect, reverence, and the sincere intention to empower and uplift their essence. As you perform this spell, trust in the divine forces you invoke and believe in the transformative power of their energy.

52. Incantation to invoke the blessings of the celestial stars and galaxies

✧ Find a peaceful and open space where you can connect with the vastness of the cosmos. Ideally, go outside under a clear night sky where the stars are visible. If that is not possible, find a quiet indoor space where you can create a serene atmosphere.

✧ Take a few moments to ground yourself and center your energy. Close your eyes and take deep, calming breaths. Allow any tension or distractions to fade away as you focus on the present moment.

✧ With your eyes closed or gazing up at the night sky, raise your hands towards the heavens, palms facing upward. Feel a connection to the vast expanse of the universe and the celestial bodies that reside within it.

✧ Recite the following incantation, or adapt it to your own words:

"Oh, celestial stars and galaxies above,
I call upon your blessings, pure and divine.
Illuminate my path, guide me with your light,
Infuse me with cosmic wisdom and insight.
From the depths of space, I seek your grace,
Shower me with your celestial embrace."

✧ As you recite the incantation, visualize the stars and galaxies responding to your call. See their light shining brightly, enveloping you in a gentle and comforting glow. Feel their energy and wisdom flowing into your being, awakening your intuition and expanding your awareness.

✧ Allow yourself to bask in the presence of the celestial blessings. Feel the vastness of the universe and the interconnectedness of all things. Open yourself to receive the wisdom and guidance that the stars and galaxies offer.

✧ Express your gratitude to the celestial bodies for their blessings and guidance. Thank them for their divine presence and the insights they have shared with you.

✧ Slowly lower your hands, feeling the energy of the stars and galaxies integrate within you. Take a moment to reflect on the experience and the connection you have forged with the celestial realm.

✧　When you are ready, gently open your eyes or shift your focus back to your surroundings. Carry the energy and wisdom of the celestial blessings with you as you continue your spiritual journey.

Remember, this incantation is a channeling of the cosmic energy and wisdom of the stars and galaxies. Approach it with reverence and awe for the vastness of the universe. Allow yourself to be open to the messages and insights that may come from this invocation. Embrace the interconnectedness of all things and trust in the guidance of the celestial bodies above.

53. Ritual for the transfiguration of the deceased into a divine keeper of ancient wisdom

✧ Create a sacred space: Find a quiet and peaceful area where you can perform the ritual without interruption. Cleanse the space by smudging with sacred herbs or lighting incense to purify the energy.

✧ Prepare the altar: Set up an altar with items that symbolize ancient wisdom such as books, scrolls, crystals, and symbols of knowledge. Place a candle at the center of the altar to represent the divine flame of wisdom.

✧ Center yourself: Take a few moments to quiet your mind and center your energy. Close your eyes, take deep breaths, and focus on grounding yourself in the present moment. Allow any distractions or worries to fade away.

✧ Invoke the divine presence: Light the candle on the altar and visualize a divine light shining upon you. Call upon the spirits of the ancient sages and wise beings to join you in this ritual. You can use the following invocation or adapt it to your own words:

"Oh, ancient ones of wisdom and insight,
Hear my call on this sacred night.
I seek your presence, I seek your guidance,
As I perform this ritual of transfiguration.
May the divine flame of wisdom ignite within me,
Transforming me into a keeper of ancient knowledge."

✧ Connect with the deceased: If you are performing this ritual for a specific deceased individual, visualize their presence or hold their photo or an object that reminds you of them. Speak their name aloud and invite their spirit to join you in this ritual.

✧ Channel the ancient wisdom: Begin to recite ancient wisdom teachings, mantras, or prayers that resonate with you. You can also read passages from sacred texts or books of ancient wisdom. As you do so, imagine the words and vibrations infusing you with knowledge and understanding.

✧ Symbolic transformation: Take a moment to reflect on the qualities and attributes of ancient wisdom that you wish to embody. Visualize yourself being surrounded by a radiant light, symbolizing the transformation into a divine keeper of ancient wisdom.

✧ Affirmation and acceptance: Speak aloud an affirmation or statement of intent, declaring your commitment to carrying and preserving the ancient wisdom within you. Embrace your role as a conduit of knowledge and understanding, and accept the responsibility that comes with it.

✧ Gratitude and closing: Express your gratitude to the spirits of the ancient ones, the deceased, and any other divine beings that you invoked during the ritual. Thank them for their presence and guidance. Snuff out the candle on the altar to symbolize the closing of the ritual.

✧ Integration: Take a few moments to sit quietly and integrate the energy and insights you have received. Reflect on the significance of this ritual and how it aligns with your spiritual journey and purpose.

Remember, this ritual is a symbolic representation of the transfiguration of the deceased into a divine keeper of ancient wisdom. It serves as a powerful way to honor their memory and carry their wisdom forward. Embrace the transformation and continue to cultivate your connection to ancient wisdom in your daily life.

54. Spell for the reunion of the deceased's soul with their soul contracts and divine purpose

✧ Set up your sacred space: Find a quiet and peaceful area where you can perform the spell undisturbed. Create an altar or a designated space where you can place meaningful objects, such as candles, crystals, or symbols that represent the divine and spiritual connection.

✧ Center yourself: Take a few deep breaths and close your eyes. Focus your attention on your heart center and imagine a warm, glowing light emanating from it. Allow this light to expand and surround your entire being, creating a sense of peace and serenity.

✧ Invoke the divine presence: Call upon the divine beings, spirit guides, and guardians of the deceased to join you in this spell. You can say the following invocation or adapt it to your own words:

"Divine beings and guardians of the departed,
I call upon your presence and guidance.
Assist me in reuniting the soul of [Name of the deceased]
With their soul contracts and divine purpose.
May their path be illuminated and aligned with the divine plan."

✧ Connect with the energy of the deceased: If you have a specific person in mind, hold an object that belonged to them or a photograph of them. If not, visualize the presence of the departed soul in your mind's eye. Send love and intention towards their spirit, acknowledging their journey and seeking their reunion with their soul contracts.

✧ Recite the spell: Begin reciting the following spell or create your own words, expressing your intentions clearly and sincerely:

"By the power of love and divine connection,
I call upon the soul of [Name of the deceased].
May their spirit be guided to their soul contracts,
Reuniting with their divine purpose and path.
May they find clarity, fulfillment, and joy,
As they align with their highest calling.

With reverence and respect, I speak this spell,
And so it is."

✧ Visualize and feel the reunion: Close your eyes and imagine the soul of the deceased being enveloped in a warm, comforting light. See them surrounded by their soul contracts, their divine purpose, and a sense of clarity and alignment. Feel a deep sense of joy and fulfillment emanating from their essence.

✧ Express gratitude and release: Thank the divine beings, spirit guides, and guardians for their presence and assistance. Express gratitude to the departed soul for their journey and the lessons they shared. Release any attachments or expectations, trusting that the reunion with their soul contracts and purpose is in progress.

✧ Ground yourself: Take a few deep breaths and feel your connection with the Earth beneath you. Visualize roots growing from your feet, anchoring you to the ground. Feel the stability and grounding energy of the Earth supporting you.

✧ Close the ritual: Extinguish any candles or incense you may have used, symbolizing the completion of the spell. Take a moment to reflect on the experience and offer a final word of gratitude. Know that the intentions set in this spell are set in motion and will continue to unfold in divine timing.

Remember, this spell is a way to energetically support the reunion of the deceased's soul with their soul contracts and divine purpose. Trust in the power of the divine and the journey of the departed soul.

55. Invocation of the goddess Sekhmet for healing and empowerment in the afterlife

✧ Find a quiet and sacred space where you can perform the invocation without interruptions. Set up an altar or a dedicated area with representations of Sekhmet, such as a statue or an image.

✧ Light a candle and some incense to create a sacred atmosphere. Take a moment to ground yourself by taking deep breaths and centering your energy.

✧ Stand or sit in front of the altar, facing the image or statue of Sekhmet. Place your hands together in prayer position or extend them outward in a gesture of openness.

✧ Close your eyes and visualize a golden light surrounding you. Imagine this light filling your entire being, radiating warmth and healing energy.

✧ Speak the following invocation, or adapt it to your own words:

"Oh, mighty Sekhmet, lioness of healing and strength,
I invoke your presence in this sacred space.
Hear my call, goddess of the sun's fiery embrace,
Guide me through the realms of the afterlife's grace.

I seek your healing touch, divine mother of compassion,
Bathe me in your fiery light, bring forth transformation.
Release all wounds and burdens that I carry within,
Restore my spirit, and let true empowerment begin.

Grant me the courage to face my fears and strife,
To heal and grow, to reclaim my divine life.
Empower my soul, awaken the dormant power,
In the afterlife's journey, let me truly flower.

Sekhmet, fierce protector and bringer of healing,
I surrender to your wisdom and divine revealing.
Walk beside me in the realms beyond the veil,
Guide me, nurture me, and let your power prevail.

With utmost reverence, I call upon your name,
Sekhmet, goddess of healing, forever the same.
In the afterlife's embrace, I find solace and light,
With gratitude and trust, I honor this sacred rite."

✧ As you recite the invocation, visualize Sekhmet's presence growing stronger. Imagine her fierce but loving energy surrounding you, enveloping you in her healing power.

✧ Take a few moments to meditate and connect with the energy of Sekhmet. Allow her healing energy to flow through you, addressing any areas of imbalance or pain in your spirit.

✧ Express your gratitude to Sekhmet for her presence and assistance. Thank her for the healing and empowerment she brings to your journey in the afterlife.

✧ Close the invocation by extinguishing the candle and offering a final expression of gratitude. Take a deep breath, slowly release it, and open your eyes, feeling the energy of Sekhmet with you.

Remember, this invocation is a way to connect with the healing and empowering energy of the goddess Sekhmet in the afterlife. Trust in her wisdom and guidance as you embark on your journey of healing and empowerment.

56. Ritual of purification through the sacred vibrations of the eternal sound

Find a quiet and sacred space where you can perform the ritual without interruptions. Create a serene atmosphere by dimming the lights and playing soft instrumental music, if desired.

Sit or stand in a comfortable position with your back straight and your feet grounded. Take a few deep breaths to center yourself and bring your awareness to the present moment.

Close your eyes and begin to focus on your breath. Inhale deeply and exhale slowly, allowing any tension or negativity to release with each breath.

Once you feel relaxed and centered, bring your attention to the power of sound. Recognize that sound has the ability to cleanse and purify, both physically and spiritually.

Begin to produce a continuous humming sound, starting at a comfortable pitch and gradually increasing the volume. Feel the vibrations of the sound resonating within your body, purifying and clearing any stagnant energy.

As you continue to hum, imagine the sound waves expanding outward, enveloping your entire being. Visualize the vibrations penetrating every cell and energy center, purifying and harmonizing your physical, mental, and spiritual aspects.

While maintaining the humming sound, you can also introduce sacred syllables or mantras that hold personal significance or are associated with purification and spiritual cleansing. Repeat these syllables or mantras with intention and devotion.

Allow yourself to be fully immersed in the sound and vibrations, surrendering to the purifying energy it creates. Feel the layers of impurities and negativity being dissolved and transformed into pure, radiant energy.

Continue the ritual for as long as it feels right to you, allowing the sound and vibrations to do their work. Trust your intuition and the guidance of your inner self.

When you feel ready, gradually decrease the volume of your humming and slowly bring the sound to a gentle conclusion. Take a moment to observe the stillness and peace within you, appreciating the purification that has taken place.

Open your eyes and take a few more deep breaths, grounding yourself in the present moment. Express gratitude for the cleansing and purification you have experienced through the ritual.

You may choose to journal your experiences and insights or simply take some time to reflect on the effects of the ritual. Be open to any messages or guidance that may arise.

Remember, the ritual of purification through sacred vibrations is a personal practice that can be tailored to your own preferences and beliefs. Trust in the power of sound and vibration to cleanse and purify your being, bringing you into a state of greater harmony and clarity.

57. Spell for the liberation of the deceased's soul from the cycles of birth and death

✧ Find a quiet and sacred space where you can perform the spell without interruptions. Light a candle or incense to create a serene atmosphere.

✧ Sit or stand in a comfortable position with your back straight and your feet grounded. Take a few deep breaths to center yourself and bring your awareness to the present moment.

✧ Close your eyes and visualize a radiant light surrounding you. This light represents the eternal essence and divine nature of the soul.

✧ Focus on the intention of liberating the deceased's soul from the cycles of birth and death. Envision the soul being freed from the constraints of earthly existence and ascending to higher realms of consciousness and spiritual evolution.

✧ Begin to recite the following spell:

"By the power of the divine within,
I call upon the forces of transcendence.
Release the soul from earthly bounds,
Unbind it from cycles that know no end.

With love and light, I set it free,
From birth and death's eternal dance.
Let the soul soar to realms unknown,
Beyond the confines of mortal chance.

By the sacred breath that grants us life,
I release this soul from earthly strife.
May it find eternal peace and grace,
As it transcends to a higher place."

✧ Repeat the spell several times, allowing the words to resonate within you and carry the intention of liberation and freedom.

✧ When you feel ready, take a moment to offer gratitude for the opportunity to perform this spell and for the soul's journey towards liberation.

✧ Gently blow out the candle or extinguish the incense, symbolizing the completion of the spell and the release of the soul.

✧ Take a few more deep breaths, grounding yourself in the present moment and allowing the energy of the spell to integrate within you.

✧ Open your eyes and conclude the ritual with a sense of peace and reverence.

Remember, this spell is intended to support the liberation of the deceased's soul from the cycles of birth and death. It is important to approach it with respect, love, and pure intentions. Trust in the power of your words and intentions to facilitate the soul's journey towards greater spiritual freedom and transcendence.

58. Incantation to awaken the dormant spiritual senses within the deceased's spirit

✧ Find a peaceful and quiet space where you can focus your energy and intention without distractions. Light a candle or incense to create a sacred atmosphere.

✧ Take a few deep breaths to center yourself and connect with your own spiritual energy. Feel the presence of the deceased's spirit and their desire to awaken their dormant spiritual senses.

✧ Close your eyes and visualize the spirit of the deceased standing before you, surrounded by a gentle and radiant light. Feel their presence and their willingness to embark on a journey of spiritual awakening.

✧ With conviction and reverence, begin to recite the following incantation:

"Oh spirit awakened, hear my call,
Rise from slumber, embrace the divine call.
Awaken your senses, both subtle and true,
To perceive the realms beyond what's known and new.

Open your eyes to the ethereal sights,
See the beauty that transcends earthly nights.
Awaken your ears to the celestial sounds,
Hear the whispers of wisdom that know no bounds.

Let your nose inhale the sacred scents,
Fragrances that carry ancient events.
Awaken your touch to the energies unseen,
Feel the vibrations of the realms serene.

Taste the nectar of divine inspiration,
Awaken your senses to revelation.
Spirit awakened, embrace your truth,
As you journey through realms of eternal youth."

✧ Repeat the incantation several times, allowing the words to resonate within you and the spirit of the deceased. Feel the energy building and the awakening of their dormant spiritual senses.

✧ Visualize the spirit of the deceased absorbing the energy of the incantation, as their spiritual senses awaken and become more vibrant and attuned.

✧ Express gratitude for the opportunity to assist the deceased's spirit in their spiritual awakening and growth.

✧ Slowly open your eyes, releasing the energy and intention into the space around you.

✧ Take a moment to reflect on the experience and offer blessings to the spirit of the deceased as they continue on their spiritual journey.

Remember, when performing this incantation, do so with pure intentions and love for the deceased's spirit. Trust in the power of your words and the connection you have with the spirit world to awaken their dormant spiritual senses.

59. Ritual for the communion with the spirits of the celestial birds and winged creatures

✧ Find a serene outdoor space where you can connect with nature and feel the presence of the celestial realm. Choose a time when the energy is calm and conducive to spiritual connection.

✧ Create an altar or sacred space using items that represent the element of air and the energy of flight. Place feathers, bird figurines, and images of birds or winged creatures on the altar.

✧ Light incense or candles with scents that evoke a sense of freedom and lightness, such as lavender, frankincense, or jasmine.

✧ Sit or stand in front of the altar and take a few deep breaths to center yourself. Feel your connection to the earth beneath you and the vast sky above you.

✧ Close your eyes and visualize yourself surrounded by a soft and radiant light. Feel the presence of the celestial birds and winged creatures gathering around you, their energy encompassing the space.

✧ Begin to recite the following invocation with reverence and sincerity:

"Oh, spirits of the sky and air,
Guardians of flight, wise and fair.
I call upon your sacred grace,
To join me in this sacred space.

Feathered beings, spirits bright,
I seek communion, in your flight.
Teach me to soar, beyond the land,
To touch the heavens, hand in hand.

Through your eyes, may I perceive,
The realms where mysteries conceive.
Your songs of wisdom, may I hear,
Guiding me to what is near.

With open hearts and minds set free,
Let us merge in unity.

Divine messengers, I beseech,
Share with me your sacred speech."

✧ As you recite the invocation, visualize the celestial birds and winged creatures surrounding you, their energy merging with yours. Feel their wisdom and guidance flowing into your being.

✧ Sit or stand in stillness, allowing yourself to be open to any messages, sensations, or insights that may come through from the spirits of the celestial birds and winged creatures. Trust your intuition and remain receptive.

✧ Take as much time as you need in this communion, allowing the energies to merge and resonate within you. You may wish to offer prayers or gratitude to the spirits for their presence and guidance.

✧ When you feel ready, slowly come back to your awareness of the physical world. Express your gratitude to the spirits of the celestial birds and winged creatures for their communion and guidance.

✧ Ground yourself by placing your hands on the earth or taking a walk, allowing the energy to integrate and settle.

Remember, this ritual is a sacred act of connection and reverence. Approach it with respect, gratitude, and an open heart, and you may receive insights, messages, or a deeper sense of connection with the spirits of the celestial birds and winged creatures.

60. Spell for the transmigration of the deceased's soul into the realm of eternal light and truth

✧ Find a quiet and sacred space where you can focus and connect with the spiritual realm. Choose a time when you feel most attuned to the energy of light and truth.

✧ Light a white or golden candle to represent the divine light and truth. Place it on a safe and stable surface.

✧ Sit or stand in front of the candle and take a few deep breaths to center yourself. Allow yourself to become fully present in the moment.

✧ Close your eyes and visualize a radiant beam of light descending from the heavens, enveloping you in its warm and comforting embrace. Feel the presence of divine light surrounding you, bringing clarity and illumination.

✧ Recite the following spell with intention and sincerity:

"In this sacred hour, I call upon the light,
To guide the departed on their soul's flight.
From this earthly realm, to realms unseen,
May their spirit be cleansed and serene.

By the power of divine truth and grace,
I invoke the sacred light's embrace.
Transcending time and space, they shall roam,
In the realm of eternal light, their new home.

Oh, radiant light, pure and true,
Illuminate their path, as they journey anew.
Unveil the mysteries and reveal the way,
To the realm of eternal light, they shall stay."

✧ As you recite the spell, imagine the deceased's soul being guided by the divine light, transcending earthly limitations and entering the realm of eternal light and truth. Feel a sense of peace and serenity as you envision their soul finding its rightful place in the cosmic order.

✧ Sit or stand in stillness, allowing the energy of the spell to permeate your surroundings. Visualize the divine light filling the space, bringing healing and transformation.

✧ Express your gratitude to the divine light for its guidance and assistance in the transmigration of the deceased's soul. Offer prayers or words of blessings for their journey.

✧ Allow the candle to burn completely or extinguish it safely if you need to end the ritual. Take a moment to ground yourself by placing your hands on the earth or taking a few deep breaths.

Remember, this spell is a sacred invocation of light and truth. Approach it with reverence, sincerity, and a pure heart, and trust that it will assist in the transmigration of the deceased's soul into the realm of eternal light and truth.

61. Invocation of the god Set for transformation and rebirth in the afterlife

✧ Find a quiet and sacred space where you can focus and connect with the divine energies. Choose a time when you feel most attuned to the transformative forces of the universe.

✧ Light a black or red candle to represent the energy of Set, the god of transformation and rebirth. Place it on a safe and stable surface.

✧ Stand or sit in front of the candle, grounding yourself by placing your feet firmly on the ground. Take a few deep breaths to center yourself and allow your mind to become focused.

✧ Close your eyes and visualize the presence of Set before you. Feel his energy and power surrounding you, invoking a sense of strength and determination.

✧ Recite the following invocation with confidence and intention:

"Mighty Set, god of transformation,
I call upon your presence and inspiration.
Guide me through the realms of the afterlife,
Unleash the power of rebirth and strife.

Grant me the courage to face my fears,
Embrace the changes, shed my old layers.
Transform my spirit, cleanse and renew,
In your divine presence, I find strength anew.

Like the phoenix rising from ashes untold,
I am reborn, empowered, and bold.
Through the trials and challenges I face,
Your guidance and protection I embrace.

Set, I honor your transformative might,
As I journey through the eternal night.
Grant me the gift of rebirth and renewal,
In the afterlife's realm, I find my soul's fuel."

✧ As you recite the invocation, visualize the energy of Set filling your being, igniting a spark of transformation within you. Feel his strength and determination infusing every cell of your being, empowering you to face and overcome any obstacles on your journey.

✧ Take a moment to reflect on the transformative aspects of your life and the changes you seek in the afterlife. Offer your intentions and desires to Set, trusting in his guidance and support.

✧ Express your gratitude to Set for his presence and assistance in your transformation and rebirth. Offer prayers or words of thanks for his continued guidance and blessings.

✧ Allow the candle to burn completely or extinguish it safely if you need to end the invocation. Take a moment to ground yourself by placing your hands on the earth or taking a few deep breaths.

Remember, this invocation is a sacred call to the god Set for transformation and rebirth in the afterlife. Approach it with respect, sincerity, and a genuine desire for growth and change. Trust in the power of Set to guide you on your journey of transformation and renewal.

62. Ritual of anointing with sacred incense for spiritual elevation and purification

Find a quiet and sacred space where you can perform the ritual without any distractions. Choose a time when you feel most connected to the spiritual energies and when you can fully devote yourself to the practice.

Select a high-quality incense that resonates with your intentions. Frankincense, myrrh, sage, or sandalwood are often used for their purifying and elevating properties. Prepare a small charcoal disk or an incense holder to safely burn the incense.

Sit or stand in a comfortable position, taking a few moments to ground yourself and center your energy. Take deep breaths, allowing any tension or stress to dissolve.

Light the charcoal disk or prepare the incense holder and place a small amount of the sacred incense on it. Allow the flame to ignite the incense, and then gently blow it out, allowing the smoke to rise and fill the space.

Hold your hands over the rising smoke and close your eyes. Visualize the smoke carrying away any negative or stagnant energies, purifying your being on all levels— body, mind, and spirit.

Begin to anoint yourself with the sacred smoke by wafting it over different parts of your body. Start with your head, moving down to your shoulders, arms, chest, abdomen, legs, and feet. As you do this, envision the smoke enveloping and purifying each area, lifting you to a higher state of consciousness.

As you anoint yourself, you may choose to recite affirmations or prayers that resonate with your spiritual elevation and purification. Speak words of intention, such as:

"With this sacred smoke, I release all that no longer serves me. I purify my body, mind, and spirit, elevating myself to a higher state of being. May this incense cleanse and uplift me, connecting me with the divine energies of light and love."

Take your time with the anointing process, allowing the sacred smoke to permeate your being and create a sense of spiritual elevation and purification. Pay attention to any sensations, images, or insights that arise during the ritual.

Once you have anointed yourself with the sacred smoke, take a few moments to bask in the purified and elevated energy. Express gratitude for the experience and the transformative power of the sacred incense.

When you are ready to conclude the ritual, gently extinguish the incense or let it burn out completely in a safe and controlled manner. Take a moment to ground yourself by placing your hands on the earth or taking a few deep breaths.

Remember, this ritual of anointing with sacred incense is a personal and sacred practice. Modify it as needed to align with your own spiritual beliefs and intentions. Approach the ritual with reverence and mindfulness, allowing the purifying and elevating properties of the sacred incense to support your spiritual growth and purification.

63. Spell for the transformation of the deceased into a vessel of divine wisdom and understanding

✧ Find a quiet and sacred space where you can perform the spell without any distractions. Choose a time when you feel most connected to the spiritual energies and when you can fully devote yourself to the practice.

✧ Light a white or yellow candle to symbolize divine wisdom and understanding. Place it on a safe and stable surface.

✧ Sit or stand in front of the candle and take a few moments to ground yourself. Close your eyes and take deep breaths, allowing any tension or distractions to melt away.

✧ Once you feel centered, open your eyes and gaze at the flame of the candle. Let the flickering light draw you in, symbolizing the flame of knowledge and enlightenment.

✧ Focus your intention on the deceased, envisioning their spirit being present with you. Feel their presence and their desire for wisdom and understanding.

✧ Repeat the following incantation, or create your own words that resonate with your intention:

"By the light of this flame, I call forth divine wisdom's name. In the realms of spirit, let knowledge flow, May [name of the deceased] be a vessel, wisdom to bestow. Transform their spirit, with understanding deep, Unveil the secrets they are destined to keep."

✧ As you speak the incantation, visualize the deceased being enveloped in a radiant light, symbolizing the transformation of their spirit into a vessel of divine wisdom and understanding. See them embracing this newfound knowledge and experiencing a deep sense of clarity and enlightenment.

✧ Continue to focus on the candle flame and the visualization for as long as it feels appropriate. Allow the energy to flow and the transformation to take place.

✧   When you are ready, express gratitude for the divine wisdom and understanding that will be bestowed upon the deceased. Thank the universe, the divine, or any spiritual entities you feel connected to.

✧   Blow out the candle, symbolizing the completion of the spell. Take a moment to ground yourself, feeling the energy settle and integrate.

Remember, this spell is a personal and sacred practice. Modify it as needed to align with your own spiritual beliefs and intentions. Approach the spell with reverence and respect, allowing the divine wisdom and understanding to flow through the deceased and support their spiritual journey.

64. Incantation to invoke the blessings of the celestial planets and celestial bodies

"Glorious celestial bodies, shining bright,
Planets and stars, sources of cosmic light.
I call upon your ancient wisdom and might,
Grant me your blessings in this sacred rite.

Mercury, messenger of knowledge profound,
Bless me with intellect, let wisdom abound.
Venus, bringer of love, beauty, and grace,
Fill my heart with compassion and embrace.

Mars, warrior spirit, grant me strength and might,
Courage to face challenges, to persevere and fight.
Jupiter, bestower of abundance and growth,
Guide me on a path of expansion and both.

Saturn, keeper of time, teacher of lessons hard,
Grant me discipline and patience, a resilient guard.
Uranus, bringer of change and innovation,
Inspire me to seek new perspectives and transformation.

Neptune, ruler of dreams, intuition, and art,
Unveil hidden truths, ignite my creative spark.
Pluto, guardian of the underworld's embrace,
Help me release what no longer serves, find my true space.

Moon, in all your phases, bring guidance and flow,
Illuminate my path, the mysteries I seek to know.
Sun, radiant and life-giving, source of divine light,
Infuse me with vitality, align me with cosmic sight.

To the celestial planets and bodies, I raise my voice,
May your blessings guide me, empower my choice.
Grant me alignment with the cosmic dance above,
In harmony with the universe, connected with love.

As above, so below, as within, so without,
I embrace the blessings, let the magic sprout.

With gratitude and reverence, I honor this connection,
Celestial blessings, fill me with divine reflection."

Feel free to adapt this incantation to suit your own personal beliefs and practices. Remember to speak the words with intention and focus, allowing the energy of the celestial bodies to flow through you and bless your spiritual journey.

65. Ritual for the transfiguration of the deceased into a divine guardian of sacred knowledge

Items needed:

✧ A quiet and sacred space
✧ Candles (preferably white or blue)
✧ An altar or sacred table
✧ A representation or symbol of knowledge (such as a book, scroll, or an object that represents wisdom)
✧ Incense or herbs associated with wisdom and clarity (such as frankincense, sage, or rosemary)
✧ A small bowl of water
✧ A bell or chime

Procedure:

✧ Prepare your sacred space by cleansing it with incense or smudging with sage, purifying the energy of the area.

✧ Set up your altar or sacred table, placing the representation or symbol of knowledge at the center.

✧ Light the candles and place them on each side of the symbol, creating a balanced and harmonious energy.

✧ Take a few deep breaths to center yourself and connect with the spiritual realm. Invoke the presence of divine energies and beings associated with knowledge and wisdom, such as Thoth, Athena, or Saraswati.

✧ Hold your hands over the symbol of knowledge and visualize it radiating a brilliant light. Imagine this light expanding and enveloping the deceased, transforming their essence into a guardian of sacred knowledge.

✧ Speak the following spell or create your own, focusing on the intention of transfiguration and guardianship:

"By the powers of wisdom and sacred lore,
I call upon the divine, now and evermore.
Transform the spirit of the departed soul,
Into a guardian of knowledge, wise and whole.

May their essence merge with ancient wisdom's stream,
Let them protect and guide as in a sacred dream.
Grant them the power to safeguard sacred texts,
And in realms of knowledge, let them connect.

Through the veil of time and space they shall stride,
A guardian of wisdom, with knowledge as their guide.
Let their spirit shine with wisdom's light,
A beacon of truth in the eternal night.

By the elements of earth, air, fire, and sea,
May this transformation come to be.
In harmony with the universe's flow,
As above, so below."

✧   Sprinkle a few drops of water over the symbol, representing the cleansing and
    purifying of the deceased's spirit, and their rebirth as a guardian of sacred
    knowledge.

✧   Ring the bell or chime three times to seal the ritual, allowing the vibrations to
    carry the intention into the spiritual realms.

✧   Spend a few moments in quiet reflection and gratitude, expressing thanks to the
    divine energies and beings you invoked.

✧   When you feel ready, extinguish the candles, maintaining a sense of reverence
    for the transformed spirit.

Remember, rituals can be customized and adapted to your own beliefs and practices.
Focus on your intention and connection with the spiritual realm as you perform the
ritual, allowing the energy of the divine to flow through you and facilitate the
transfiguration process.

66. Spell for the reunion of the deceased's soul with their spiritual teachers and mentors

"O spirits of wisdom and guidance, I call upon you,
In this sacred space, my intentions I pursue.
With reverence and love, I seek your aid,
To reunite the departed soul with those who've stayed.

By the bonds of learning and shared knowledge,
Bridge the realms between, create a spiritual college.
Guide the soul to its mentors and teachers dear,
In the afterlife's realm, let them draw near.

Through the veils of time and space they'll transcend,
Reunited in realms where souls ascend.
Open the doors to the realms divine,
Let the departed soul's mentors align.

With gratitude and trust, I beseech you now,
Bring the departed soul and mentors together, somehow.
In this sacred union, let knowledge abound,
Support and guidance, let it resound.

By the powers of the divine and the spirits wise,
Grant this reunion, as I visualize.
In harmony and love, let them reconnect,
As student and teacher, their bond resurrect.

So mote it be."

✧ As you recite the spell, focus on the intention of reuniting the deceased's soul with their spiritual teachers and mentors. Visualize a loving and joyful reunion, where wisdom is shared and guidance is given. Feel the presence of the spirits of the teachers and mentors, surrounding and embracing the departed soul.

✧ After reciting the spell, take a few moments of silence to allow the energy of the intention to settle and resonate. Trust that the spirits of the departed's mentors and teachers will hear your call and work towards facilitating the reunion in the spiritual realms.

Remember to perform this spell with respect, love, and reverence for the deceased's journey and the guidance of the spiritual realm.

67. Invocation of the goddess Bastet for protection and grace in the afterlife

"Oh, mighty Bastet, feline goddess of grace,
I call upon your presence, in this sacred space.
With reverence and devotion, I seek your aid,
To protect and guide the departed soul's serenade.

Goddess of joy, protector of the night,
Wrap your divine presence around with all your might.
In the afterlife's realm, where spirits dwell,
Embrace the departed soul, and guard them well.

Grant them your watchful eyes, keen and bright,
Guide them through darkness with your gentle light.
With swift and graceful steps, shield them from harm,
In your loving embrace, keep them warm.

Bastet, goddess of protection and power,
Hear my prayer in this solemn hour.
Defend the soul from all that may dismay,
Lead them on their journey, every step of the way.

May your divine presence be a shield of light,
As the departed soul continues its flight.
Grant them serenity, with your loving grace,
In the afterlife's realm, a sacred resting place.

Oh, Bastet, goddess of protection and grace,
I honor you now, in this sacred space.
With gratitude and reverence, I offer my plea,
Guide and protect the departed soul, forever free.

So mote it be."

✧ As you recite this invocation, envision the divine presence of Bastet surrounding the departed soul with her protective energy. Imagine her graceful and powerful aura providing a shield of light and warmth, ensuring the soul's safe journey in the afterlife.

◇ After the invocation, take a moment to express gratitude to Bastet for her guidance and protection. Trust that her divine presence will continue to watch over the departed soul, offering comfort and grace throughout their afterlife journey.

Remember to perform this invocation with sincerity, respect, and reverence for the goddess Bastet and the departed soul's journey.

68. Ritual of purification through the sacred symbols of the eternal hieroglyphs

Preparation:

✧ Find a quiet and sacred space where you can perform the ritual undisturbed.
✧ Gather materials such as a small bowl of water, a white cloth or piece of parchment, and a writing instrument.
✧ Create a peaceful atmosphere by lighting candles or incense and playing soft, calming music.

Centering and Grounding:

✧ Take a few deep breaths and focus your attention on the present moment.
✧ Close your eyes and imagine roots growing from your feet, grounding you to the earth.
✧ Visualize a pillar of light extending from the top of your head, connecting you to the divine.

Invocation:

✧ Begin by invoking the presence of the ancient Egyptian deities or the higher powers you resonate with.
✧ Call upon their wisdom and guidance as you embark on this journey of purification through hieroglyphs.

Cleansing with Water:

Dip your fingers into the bowl of water and sprinkle a few drops onto the white cloth or parchment.
Gently cleanse your face, hands, and any other parts of your body that feel appropriate, symbolizing the purification of your physical vessel.

Sacred Symbols:

✧ Take the writing instrument and draw or trace the sacred hieroglyphs onto the white cloth or parchment.
✧ Choose symbols that resonate with purification, such as the symbol for water (depicted as waves), the symbol for purity (depicted as a lotus), or the symbol for rebirth (depicted as a phoenix).

- As you draw each symbol, visualize its energy infusing the cloth or parchment, imbuing it with the essence of purification and renewal.

Affirmation:

Speak a personal affirmation or intention that aligns with the purpose of the ritual. For example: "Through these sacred symbols, I release any impurities and invite pure and positive energies into my being. I am cleansed, renewed, and ready for spiritual growth and transformation."

Charging and Blessing:

- Hold the cloth or parchment in your hands and imagine it being filled with divine light and energy.
- Envision the symbols on the cloth or parchment glowing and radiating with the power of purification.
- Offer a heartfelt prayer or blessing, asking for the sacred symbols to bless and protect you on your spiritual journey.

Closing:

- Express gratitude to the ancient Egyptian deities or the higher powers you invoked at the beginning of the ritual.
- Blow out the candles or incense, symbolizing the end of the ritual.
- You may choose to keep the cloth or parchment with the sacred symbols as a reminder of your purification journey, or you can respectfully dispose of it by burying it in the earth or burning it with gratitude.

Remember, the power of the ritual comes from your intention, focus, and connection to the sacred symbols. Allow yourself to fully immerse in the ritual, embracing the purification and transformative energies of the eternal hieroglyphs.

69. Ritual of purification through the sacred symbols of the eternal hieroglyphs

Preparation:

✧ Find a quiet and sacred space where you can perform the spell without interruptions.
✧ Gather materials such as a small candle, a piece of paper, a writing instrument, and a fire-safe container.

Centering and Grounding:

✧ Take a few moments to center yourself and connect with your breath.
✧ Close your eyes and visualize roots extending from your feet, grounding you to the earth.
✧ Feel your body rooted and connected, allowing yourself to enter a state of calm and focus.

Invocation:

✧ Light the candle and invoke the presence of the divine energies or deities you resonate with.
✧ Call upon their guidance and assistance in liberating the deceased's soul from the illusions of the ego.

Reflection and Intention:

✧ Take the piece of paper and write down any illusions or egoic patterns that you believe may be holding the deceased's soul back.
✧ Reflect on the ways in which these illusions may have limited their growth and prevented them from experiencing true spiritual liberation.
✧ Set the intention to release these illusions and free the deceased's soul from their grip.

Burning Ceremony:

✧ Hold the paper over the flame of the candle, allowing it to catch fire.
✧ Safely place the burning paper into the fire-safe container, watching as the flames consume the paper.

✧ As you observe the paper burning, imagine the illusions and egoic patterns dissolving away, leaving space for the true essence of the deceased's soul to shine forth.

Affirmation:

Repeat the following affirmation or create one of your own, speaking it aloud with conviction: "I release the illusions of the ego that bind the deceased's soul. May their true essence and divine nature be liberated and restored to its highest potential."

Gratitude and Closure:

✧ Express gratitude to the divine energies or deities for their presence and assistance in the liberation process.
✧ Blow out the candle, symbolizing the end of the spell and the completion of the liberation ritual.
✧ Take a moment to ground yourself, feeling your connection to the earth and the present moment.

Remember, the power of the spell lies in your intention and belief. By consciously releasing the illusions of the ego and setting the deceased's soul free, you create an opportunity for spiritual liberation and transformation. Trust in the process and have faith that the divine energies are supporting the soul's journey towards greater enlightenment and freedom.

70. Ritual for the communion with the spirits of the celestial gardens and blossoms

Items needed:

✧ A quiet and serene outdoor space or a room adorned with flowers and plants.
✧ Incense or scented candles with floral fragrances.
✧ Fresh flowers or petals.
✧ A small bowl or vessel of water.
✧ Optional: musical instruments or soothing music.

Instructions:

✧ Find a peaceful space where you can connect with nature or create a serene environment indoors.
✧ Light the incense or scented candles to fill the space with the fragrance of flowers, creating a sacred atmosphere.
✧ Arrange the fresh flowers or petals in a decorative manner, either in a vase or scattered around the ritual area.
✧ Place the bowl or vessel of water in the center of the space.
✧ Sit or stand comfortably near the flowers and close your eyes. Take a few deep breaths to center yourself.
✧ Visualize yourself surrounded by a beautiful celestial garden filled with vibrant blossoms. Feel the energy and presence of the spirits of the flowers and plants.
✧ Begin to offer your gratitude and reverence to the spirits of the celestial gardens. Speak from your heart, expressing your appreciation for their beauty, wisdom, and guidance.
✧ Dip your fingers in the bowl of water and gently sprinkle the water over the flowers as an offering to the spirits. You can also sprinkle a few drops on yourself as a symbol of purification and connection.
✧ Take a moment to silently listen and feel the presence of the spirits. Allow yourself to receive any messages, insights, or guidance they may offer.
✧ If you have musical instruments or soothing music, you can play them softly to further enhance the ambiance and create a harmonious connection.
✧ Spend as much time as you feel comfortable in this communion with the spirits of the celestial gardens. Allow yourself to be present in their presence and embrace their energy.
✧ When you feel ready, express your gratitude once again to the spirits for their presence and guidance. Bid them farewell with love and appreciation.

- ✧ Slowly open your eyes and take a few more deep breaths, grounding yourself back into the physical realm.
- ✧ You can leave the flowers and offerings in nature as a symbol of your connection and gratitude, or if indoors, you can place them in a special spot as a reminder of the communion you've shared.

Remember, this ritual is a way to connect with the spirits of the celestial gardens and blossoms. Approach it with reverence, sincerity, and an open heart, allowing yourself to be guided by the energy of nature and the spiritual realm.

71. Spell for the transmigration of the deceased's soul into the realm of eternal growth and evolution

"By the power of the eternal flame,
I call upon the cosmic forces, untamed.
From this earthly realm, I seek release,
Into the realm of eternal growth and peace.

Spirits of the ancient, guides of the way,
Guide this soul, beyond the mortal fray.
Into realms where growth knows no bounds,
Where evolution and wisdom truly astounds.

Through the veil of transition, we shall pass,
Leaving behind all remnants of the past.
Shedding old layers, embracing the new,
The soul's journey continues, strong and true.

As the phoenix rises from the ashes' pyre,
May this soul soar higher and higher.
Let growth be their companion, evolution their guide,
In the realm of eternity, let them abide.

With every step, let wisdom unfold,
As the soul's purpose and destiny are told.
May they learn, expand, and forever thrive,
In the realm of eternal growth, they shall arrive.

By the power of the cosmic divine,
I release this spell, may it align.
Transmigration of soul, in realms unseen,
Into eternal growth, where they shall convene.

So mote it be."

✧   Recite this spell with focused intention, speaking each word with clarity and conviction. Visualize the soul of the deceased transcending into the realm of eternal growth and evolution, free from limitations and obstacles. Feel the energy of growth and evolution surrounding you as you speak the spell.

Remember to approach this spell with respect and reverence, honoring the journey of the deceased's soul and their eternal evolution. May their path be filled with wisdom, growth, and endless possibilities.

72. Invocation of the god Ra for divine illumination and enlightenment in the afterlife

"Mighty Ra, radiant Sun,
I call upon your sacred flame, as the journey is begun.
In the realms of the afterlife, where darkness may reside,
I seek your divine illumination, as my guide.

Ra, bring forth your brilliance and light,
Illuminate the path, banishing all blight.
With your rays of wisdom, shine upon my soul,
Reveal the mysteries, make me whole.

Grant me the insight to see beyond the veil,
To understand the truths that never fail.
In the afterlife's realm, where secrets lie,
Empower my spirit, let knowledge amplify.

As the sun rises and sets, in eternal cycles of time,
May my spirit ascend, reaching heights sublime.
Open the doors to enlightenment's embrace,
In your divine radiance, let me find solace.

Ra, great god of illumination and might,
Guide me through the afterlife, shining bright.
Illuminate my path, with your celestial glow,
In your presence, may my soul forever grow.

Hail Ra, the radiant Sun,
In your name, my journey has begun.
Grant me divine enlightenment and sight,
In the afterlife's realm, let there be light.

So mote it be."

Recite this invocation with reverence and sincerity, calling upon the energy and power of Ra, the Sun god. Visualize his radiant light surrounding you, filling you with divine illumination and enlightenment. Feel his presence and guidance as you embark on the journey through the afterlife, navigating its mysteries with clarity and wisdom.

Remember to approach this invocation with respect and gratitude, honoring Ra as the bringer of light and knowledge. May his divine illumination guide you on your path of enlightenment in the afterlife.

73. Ritual of anointing with sacred essences for spiritual transformation and transcendence

Materials needed:

A small dish or bowl
Pure, high-quality essential oils or sacred plant essences of your choice
A candle or incense for ambiance
A quiet and sacred space

Steps:

✧ Prepare your sacred space by lighting the candle or incense and creating a peaceful atmosphere.
✧ Take a few moments to ground yourself and center your energy. Close your eyes, take deep breaths, and focus on quieting your mind.
✧ Place the dish or bowl in front of you, ready to hold the sacred essences.
✧ Select the essential oils or sacred plant essences that resonate with your intention for spiritual transformation and transcendence. Choose oils that carry the energies of expansion, elevation, and higher consciousness. Some examples may include frankincense, myrrh, sandalwood, lavender, rose, or any other essences that resonate with you.
✧ Take a few drops of each essence and carefully place them in the dish or bowl, creating a blend of their divine aromas.
✧ With reverence and intention, anoint yourself with the sacred essences. You may choose to anoint your forehead, temples, wrists, or any other areas of your body that feel significant to you. As you do so, visualize and affirm your intention for spiritual transformation and transcendence. Envision yourself shedding old limitations, expanding your consciousness, and transcending to higher realms of awareness.
✧ Take a moment to sit in stillness and absorb the energies of the sacred essences. Allow their scents to envelop you, permeating your being with their transformative vibrations.
✧ Express gratitude to the essences, acknowledging their power and the divine support they provide on your spiritual journey.
✧ Close the ritual by offering a final prayer or affirmation, expressing your commitment to your spiritual transformation and transcendence.

◇ Allow the candle or incense to burn out naturally, symbolizing the completion of the ritual.

◇ Remember, this ritual is a sacred and personal practice. Feel free to modify it to suit your individual preferences and needs. Trust your intuition and follow the guidance of your heart as you embark on this transformative journey with the support of the sacred essences.

74. Spell for the transformation of the deceased into a vessel of divine harmony and balance

Close your eyes and take a deep breath. Allow yourself to enter a state of calm and receptivity. Visualize the deceased's spirit standing before you, bathed in a soft, gentle light.

Recite the following spell:

"By the powers of the divine,
I call upon the energy sublime.
Transform this spirit, pure and true,
Into a vessel of harmony and balance anew.

Let discord fade and peace arise,
Within this soul, let harmony harmonize.
May balance be restored, both yin and yang,
In this vessel, let divine harmony rang.

From the chaos of life, let calm emerge,
Within this spirit, let tranquility surge.
Align with the rhythms of the cosmic dance,
Embodying balance, a divine circumstance.

As the soul transitions to the afterlife's shore,
May harmony be felt forevermore.
Bound by the threads of cosmic grace,
Embrace divine balance in this sacred space.

So mote it be."

Visualize the divine energy flowing into the deceased's spirit, filling them with a sense of harmony, balance, and peace. Feel the transformation taking place, as their essence becomes a vessel of divine harmony.

Express your gratitude to the divine forces and release the spell with love and trust, knowing that the deceased's spirit is now aligned with the harmonious and balanced energies of the universe.

Open your eyes and take a few moments to ground yourself. You have completed the spell for the transformation of the deceased into a vessel of divine harmony and balance.

75. Incantation to invoke the blessings of the celestial winds and breezes

Stand tall with arms outstretched, facing the open sky. Feel the gentle touch of the breeze upon your skin, connecting you to the unseen forces of the celestial winds. Take a deep breath and let the energy of the air fill your lungs.

Recite the following incantation:

"From the heavens above, I call upon thee,
Celestial winds, spirits so free.
Blessings of air, currents divine,
Flow through this space, in rhythm and time.

Whispering breezes, soft and mild,
Carry my voice, to every mile.
I invoke your power, ancient and vast,
Sweep away stagnation, a cleansing blast.

Through swirling vortex, gusts and gales,
Carry my wishes, to distant trails.
Bring forth inspiration, clarity of mind,
With each gentle zephyr, wisdom I find.

I am one with the winds, in harmony we dance,
Guided by your whispers, I take a chance.
Embrace me with your grace, serenity unfold,
In the sacred breezes, my spirit is bold.

May the winds of change, bring blessings anew,
Awakening my spirit, with each gust that blew.
I am open and receptive, to your gentle embrace,
In the blessings of the winds, I find solace and grace.

So mote it be."

Feel the energy of the celestial winds enveloping you, carrying your intentions and invoking their blessings. Embrace the power and guidance of the winds as they flow through your being.

Express your gratitude to the celestial winds for their presence and guidance in your life. Lower your arms and take a moment to ground yourself, feeling the connection to the earth beneath your feet.

You have invoked the blessings of the celestial winds and breezes through this incantation. Embrace their energy and allow their guidance to flow through your journey.

76. Ritual for the transfiguration of the deceased into a divine weaver of cosmic tapestries

Create a sacred space: Find a quiet and serene space where you can perform the ritual undisturbed. Clear the area of any clutter and create an altar at the center. Decorate it with symbols of the cosmos such as stars, planets, and galaxies.

Set your intention: Light a candle and take a moment to center yourself. Close your eyes and connect with the energy of the deceased. Set your intention to guide their soul towards the path of becoming a divine weaver of cosmic tapestries.

Sacred breathwork: Sit comfortably and take a few deep breaths. As you inhale, imagine drawing in the energy of the universe, filling yourself with cosmic light and wisdom. As you exhale, release any negativity or limitations that may hinder the transfiguration process.

Invocation of cosmic forces: Call upon the cosmic forces and celestial beings for their guidance and assistance in the transfiguration process. You can recite the following invocation:

"O cosmic weavers, guardians of the celestial tapestries,
I call upon your presence in this sacred rite.
Guide the spirit of [name of the deceased] in their journey,
From earthly form to the divine weaver they shall be."

Feel the presence of the cosmic forces surrounding you and the deceased, their energy intertwining with yours.

Symbolic weaving: Take a piece of fabric or yarn representing the cosmic tapestry. Begin weaving it slowly, symbolizing the weaving of the deceased's essence into the cosmic fabric. As you weave, visualize the deceased's spirit merging with the cosmic energies, becoming a weaver of divine creations.

Affirmation and release: As you complete the weaving, hold the fabric or yarn in your hands. Speak an affirmation, such as:

"I release [name of the deceased] to their cosmic destiny,
As a weaver of cosmic tapestries, they shall be free.

Their creations shall ripple through the universe,
Bringing beauty, harmony, and divine verse."

Closing and gratitude: Thank the cosmic forces, celestial beings, and the deceased for their presence in the ritual. Blow out the candle to symbolize the completion of the ritual.

Remember to honor the journey and individuality of the deceased's spirit as they embark on their path as a divine weaver of cosmic tapestries.

77. Spell for the reunion of the deceased's soul with their spiritual guides and guardians

✧ Create a sacred space: Find a quiet and peaceful space where you can perform the spell without interruption. Light candles and place them around the space to create a warm and inviting atmosphere.

✧ Center yourself: Take a few deep breaths to calm your mind and center your energy. Visualize a protective white light surrounding you, creating a sacred space for the spell.

✧ Invocation of spiritual guides and guardians: Stand at the center of the sacred space and open your heart and mind to the presence of the deceased's spiritual guides and guardians. Speak the following invocation:

"Divine guides and guardians of [name of the deceased],
I call upon your loving presence in this sacred space.
Guide the soul of [name of the deceased] with your wisdom and care,
Lead them to reunite with their eternal support, beyond time and space."

✧ Feel the energy of the spiritual guides and guardians filling the space, their love and guidance flowing towards you and the deceased.

✧ Offering and affirmation: Place a small offering, such as a flower or a crystal, on the altar. As you do, affirm your intention for the reunion of the deceased's soul with their spiritual guides and guardians. You can say:

"With this offering, I honor the bond between [name of the deceased]
And their spiritual guides and guardians.
May their reunion be filled with love, guidance, and divine connection."

✧ Open communication: Close your eyes and visualize the deceased's spirit surrounded by a warm, comforting light. Encourage the deceased to open their heart and mind to the presence of their spiritual guides and guardians. Invite them to communicate and reconnect on a soul level.

✧ Trust and surrender: Release any attachment or expectation and trust in the divine process of reunion. Surrender to the wisdom and timing of the spiritual realm, knowing that the deceased's soul will be guided and supported on their journey.

✧ Gratitude and closure: Express your gratitude to the spiritual guides and guardians for their presence and assistance in the spell. Thank them for their ongoing guidance and protection of the deceased's soul. Blow out the candles to symbolize the closure of the spell.

Remember to approach this spell with reverence and respect, allowing the spiritual guides and guardians to work in their own divine way. Trust that the reunion between the deceased's soul and their spiritual guides and guardians will unfold according to the highest good of all involved.

78. Invocation of the goddess Nephthys for protection and guidance in the afterlife

✧ Prepare your sacred space: Find a quiet and peaceful place where you can perform the invocation without interruption. Light candles or incense to create a sacred atmosphere.

✧ Center yourself: Take a few deep breaths to quiet your mind and center your energy. Allow yourself to enter a state of calm and receptivity.

✧ Call upon Nephthys: Stand or sit in the center of your sacred space and open your heart and mind to the presence of the goddess Nephthys. Speak the following invocation:

"Great and noble Nephthys, Lady of Protection and Guidance,
I call upon your divine presence in this sacred space.
Wrap me in your loving embrace and guide me on the path of the afterlife.
I seek your wisdom, your strength, and your protection."

✧ Feel the presence of Nephthys: Close your eyes and imagine a gentle, comforting presence surrounding you. Feel Nephthys' energy enveloping you, offering protection and guidance. Allow yourself to connect with her divine essence.

✧ State your intentions: Clearly state your intentions for protection and guidance in the afterlife. You can say:

"Nephthys, I humbly ask for your protection and guidance as I navigate the realms of the afterlife.
Watch over me, guide me through the challenges, and lead me towards enlightenment and eternal peace.
I trust in your loving care and wisdom."

✧ Express your gratitude: Take a moment to express your gratitude to Nephthys for her presence and assistance. Thank her for her protection, guidance, and blessings. Feel a sense of deep appreciation and connection.

✧ Close the invocation: Conclude the invocation by expressing your trust and faith in Nephthys' support. You can say:

"Thank you, great Nephthys, for your love, protection, and guidance.
May your presence remain with me always, in this life and the afterlife.
So mote it be."

✧   Take a moment of silence: Sit or stand quietly for a few moments, allowing the energy of the invocation to settle within you. Feel the presence of Nephthys surrounding you, bringing you a sense of peace and reassurance.

Remember to approach this invocation with sincerity, respect, and reverence for the goddess Nephthys. Trust in her guidance and protection as you navigate the realms of the afterlife.

79. Ritual of purification through the sacred movements of the eternal dance

Prepare your sacred space: Find a quiet and open space where you can move freely without any obstructions. Clear the area of any objects that may hinder your movements.

Set your intention: Before you begin the dance, take a moment to set your intention for purification. Focus on releasing any stagnant or negative energies from your body, mind, and spirit. Visualize yourself becoming cleansed and purified through the sacred movements of the dance.

Ground yourself: Stand with your feet hip-width apart and close your eyes. Take a few deep breaths, allowing your body to relax and your mind to quiet. Feel the connection between your feet and the earth beneath you. Imagine roots growing from the soles of your feet, grounding you deeply into the earth.

Begin the dance: Start with slow, deliberate movements, allowing your body to express itself freely. Let the energy flow through you as you sway, spin, twist, and stretch. Imagine that with each movement, you are releasing any impurities or negative energies that reside within you.

Connect with the sacred energy: As you dance, envision yourself surrounded by a radiant, purifying light. Feel the energy of the universe flowing through you, cleansing and purifying every cell of your being. Allow the dance to become a sacred ritual of transformation and purification.

Express your emotions: Let your movements reflect your emotions. If you feel sadness, allow your dance to express it. If you feel joy, let your dance embody it. Dance with authenticity and let your emotions flow through your body, allowing them to be released and transformed.

Chant or use music: You may choose to chant sacred mantras or use music that resonates with your intention. Allow the sound to guide your movements and deepen your connection with the divine energy.

Repeat and refine: Continue the dance for as long as you feel called to, allowing the purification process to unfold. You can repeat certain movements or explore new ones. Let your intuition guide you in the dance, and refine your movements as you go.

Closing and gratitude: When you feel complete, bring your dance to a gentle conclusion. Stand still with your feet rooted into the ground, take a few deep breaths, and express gratitude for the purification and transformation you have experienced. Offer thanks to the divine energies and the sacred dance itself.

Ground and integrate: Take a moment to ground yourself by placing your hands on the earth or taking a few moments of stillness. Allow the energy to settle and integrate into your being. Reflect on the experience and how you feel after the ritual of purification through the sacred dance.

Remember, this ritual is a personal and expressive practice. Let your body and intuition guide you in the movements. Trust in the power of the dance to purify and transform your energy.

80. Spell for the liberation of the deceased's soul from the limitations of the physical body

Find a quiet and sacred space: Create a peaceful environment where you can focus without any distractions. Light candles or incense to create a soothing atmosphere.

Ground and center yourself: Take a few deep breaths and visualize roots extending from your body, grounding you to the earth. Feel your connection with the divine energy surrounding you.

Clear your intention: State your intention clearly and sincerely. Declare your desire to assist the deceased soul in liberating from the confines of the physical body and transitioning into a state of freedom and transcendence.

Recite the spell: Speak the following words with conviction and belief:

"By the power of the divine,
I call upon the cosmic forces to align.
Release the soul from earthly ties,
Let it soar and transcend the skies.
Shed the limitations of mortal flesh,
Embrace the realm of the divine afresh.
Guide the departed with love and light,
Through the eternal realms, shining bright."

Visualize the liberation: Close your eyes and visualize the soul of the deceased being freed from the physical body. See it rising above, transcending the earthly plane, and being enveloped in a brilliant light of liberation and transcendence.

Send love and guidance: Extend your love and light to the departed soul. Visualize them surrounded by a protective and nurturing energy. Offer your guidance and support as they embark on their journey beyond the physical realm.

Express gratitude: Express your gratitude to the divine forces, spirits, or deities you believe in for their assistance in this liberation process. Thank them for their guidance, protection, and blessings.

Release and let go: Release the energy of the spell and trust that it will continue its work in the spiritual realms. Open your eyes, take a deep breath, and feel a sense of peace and fulfillment.

Remember, this spell is intended to be performed with respect and reverence for the deceased. It is important to honor their journey and allow them the freedom to choose their path in the afterlife. Trust in the divine wisdom and love that surrounds us all.

81. Incantation to awaken the dormant divine essence within the deceased's spirit

Find a quiet and sacred space: Create a peaceful environment where you can focus without any distractions. Light candles or incense to set the mood and create a sacred atmosphere.

Ground and center yourself: Take a few deep breaths and imagine roots extending from your body, grounding you to the earth. Feel your connection with the divine energy surrounding you.

Clear your intention: State your intention clearly and sincerely. Declare your desire to awaken the dormant divine essence within the deceased's spirit and facilitate their spiritual awakening.

Recite the incantation: Speak the following words with confidence and belief:

"By the powers of the divine and the eternal light,
I call upon the dormant essence to take flight.
Awaken, O spirit, from your slumber deep,
Rise from the shadows and your divine nature keep.
Unleash your power, let it shine bright,
Embrace your divinity, ignite your inner light."

Visualize the awakening: Close your eyes and visualize the dormant divine essence within the deceased's spirit awakening and expanding. See it as a radiant light growing brighter and more vibrant, filling their entire being with divine energy.

Send love and healing energy: Extend your love and healing energy to the deceased's spirit. Envision them surrounded by a warm, nurturing light that supports their awakening and encourages their spiritual growth.

Express gratitude: Express your gratitude to the divine forces, spirits, or deities you believe in for their assistance in this awakening process. Thank them for their guidance, wisdom, and blessings.

Release and let go: Release the energy of the incantation, knowing that it will continue to work in the spiritual realms. Open your eyes, take a deep breath, and feel a sense of peace and fulfillment.

Remember, this incantation is intended to be performed with respect and reverence for the deceased. It is important to honor their spiritual journey and allow them the freedom to unfold their divine essence at their own pace. Trust in the power of the divine and the inherent wisdom within each soul.

82. Ritual for the communion with the spirits of the celestial rivers and streams

Choose a sacred outdoor space: Find a serene location near a river, stream, or any flowing body of water. It could be a secluded spot in nature or a peaceful area in a park. Ensure that you have permission to access the area if it's not on public land.

Set up your sacred space: Create an altar or designated space where you can connect with the spirits of the celestial rivers and streams. Decorate it with natural elements such as river stones, seashells, water symbols, and fresh flowers.

Ground and center yourself: Take a moment to ground yourself by standing barefoot on the earth. Close your eyes, take deep breaths, and visualize roots growing from your feet, anchoring you to the ground. Allow your body and mind to relax, and open yourself to the energy of the surrounding nature.

Offerings and gratitude: Prepare offerings to express your gratitude and reverence for the spirits of the celestial rivers and streams. This could include a bowl of fresh water, flowers, fruits, or any other items that symbolize your appreciation. Place them on the altar or near the water.

Invocation and intention: Stand before the flowing water and speak your invocation with sincerity and respect. State your intention to commune with the spirits of the celestial rivers and streams, seeking their wisdom, guidance, and connection. You can use the following words or create your own:

"Spirits of the celestial rivers and streams,
I stand before you with reverence and dreams.
I seek your presence and sacred embrace,
To connect with your wisdom and divine grace.
I offer my gratitude and love this day,
May our communion bring blessings my way."

Meditation and connection: Sit comfortably near the water and enter into a meditative state. Close your eyes and allow the sound of the flowing water to guide you deeper into relaxation. Imagine yourself merging with the energy of the river, becoming one with its flow and rhythm. Feel the presence of the spirits surrounding you, offering their guidance and wisdom.

Receive messages and insights: In this meditative state, be open to receiving messages, insights, or symbols from the spirits of the celestial rivers and streams. Trust your intuition and allow their wisdom to flow through you. You may receive guidance, healing, or a deeper connection to the natural world.

Express gratitude and closure: When you feel complete, offer your gratitude to the spirits of the celestial rivers and streams for their presence and blessings. Thank them for their guidance, wisdom, and the connection you have established. Express your intention to carry their energy and teachings with you as you continue your spiritual journey.

Closing the ritual: Slowly bring your awareness back to the present moment. Thank the spirits once again and bid them farewell, knowing that their energy and connection will always be available to you. Take a few deep breaths, feel the earth beneath your feet, and gradually return to your normal state of consciousness.

Remember to approach this ritual with reverence and respect for the natural environment. Leave the area as you found it, taking care not to disturb or harm any living beings.

83. Spell for the transmigration of the deceased's soul into the realm of eternal serenity and peace

Ingredients:

✧ A white candle
✧ Lavender essential oil
✧ A small piece of amethyst or clear quartz crystal
✧ A quiet and peaceful space

Instructions:

✧ Find a calm and undisturbed space where you can perform the spell. Make sure you have all the ingredients within reach.

✧ Light the white candle, symbolizing purity and spiritual connection. Take a moment to focus your intention on the spell and the desired outcome of transmigration into the realm of eternal serenity and peace.

✧ Take the amethyst or clear quartz crystal in your hand and infuse it with your energy and intention. Visualize the soul of the deceased surrounded by a soft, serene light, gently guiding them towards the realm of eternal peace.

✧ Place a few drops of lavender essential oil on your fingertips and rub them together. Close your eyes and take a deep breath, inhaling the calming scent of lavender. As you exhale, imagine releasing any tension or negativity from within.

✧ Hold the crystal in front of the candle flame, allowing the light to pass through it. Visualize the light transforming into a beam of tranquility and peace, enveloping the soul of the deceased and guiding them to their eternal destination.

Recite the following spell or create your own, speaking with sincerity and intention:

"With this light and crystal clear,
I guide the soul, devoid of fear.
Transmigration to realms serene,
Eternal peace, forever seen.

From earthly ties, the spirit frees,
Soaring on gentle, calming breeze.
Serenity's embrace they find,
In realms of peace, forever kind.

As this candle burns so bright,
The soul ascends to realms of light.
Serenity and peace, we send,
A peaceful journey without end."

✦   Repeat the spell three times, each time infusing it with your intention and energy. Feel the power and peace of your words resonating within you.

✦   Gently place the crystal near the candle, allowing it to continue to radiate its energy. Sit in quiet reflection for a few moments, sending love and blessings to the deceased and their journey towards eternal serenity.

✦   When you are ready, extinguish the candle with gratitude, knowing that your spell has set in motion the transmigration of the deceased's soul into the realm of eternal serenity and peace.

✦   Leave the crystal in a safe and sacred space or carry it with you as a reminder of the spell and its intention. You can repeat this spell whenever you feel the need to connect with the soul of the departed and offer them guidance and peace.

Remember, when performing spells of this nature, it's important to approach them with respect, love, and a deep understanding of the spiritual journey of the deceased.

84. Invocation of the god Osiris for resurrection and rebirth in the afterlife

"Hail, mighty Osiris, Lord of the Underworld,
I call upon you with reverence and awe.
You, the divine judge and master of rebirth,
I seek your guidance in this sacred endeavor.

Osiris, hear my plea and lend me your strength,
Grant me the wisdom to understand the mysteries of life and death.
You who have journeyed through the Duat and emerged victorious,
Guide the departed soul on their path of resurrection.

By your divine power, Osiris, let life be restored,
May the deceased rise from the ashes like the phoenix.
With your blessings, let them shed the mortal coil,
And transcend into the realm of eternal existence.

O Osiris, the bringer of renewal and transformation,
We beseech you to embrace the departed with open arms.
Grant them passage through the gates of the afterlife,
Where they shall find solace and eternal peace.

May the soul of the departed find solace in your presence,
May they be granted a new beginning, free from earthly chains.
With your divine intervention, Osiris, let resurrection be realized,
And let the light of rebirth shine upon them once more.

In your name, Osiris, we invoke your power,
May your divine essence surround the departed soul.
Guide them through the trials of the afterlife,
And bestow upon them the gift of resurrection.

Hail, Osiris, Lord of the Underworld and the eternal cycle,
With reverence and gratitude, we honor your sacred presence.
Blessed be the departed, for in your realm they shall find eternal rest,
Resurrected and reborn in the everlasting embrace of your divine grace."

Note: When performing this invocation, it is important to approach it with respect, sincerity, and reverence for the god Osiris. Customize and adapt the invocation as needed to suit your personal beliefs and spiritual practice.

85. Ritual of anointing with sacred oils for spiritual healing and rejuvenation

Materials needed:

A small vial of sacred oil (such as frankincense, myrrh, lavender, or sandalwood)
A clean and quiet space
A candle
A small dish or bowl
Instructions:

Find a quiet space where you can perform the ritual without distractions. Light the candle and place it on a safe surface.

Take a few deep breaths to center yourself and enter a state of calm and receptiveness.

Hold the vial of sacred oil in your hands and focus your attention on it. Visualize the oil being infused with divine energy and healing vibrations.

Begin to anoint yourself with the sacred oil. Start by applying a small amount to your forehead, gently massaging it into your skin. As you do so, recite a personal affirmation or prayer for healing and rejuvenation. Repeat this process, anointing different parts of your body that may need healing, such as your heart, throat, wrists, and so on.

As you anoint yourself, imagine the healing properties of the oil seeping into your being, bringing balance, restoration, and rejuvenation to your body, mind, and spirit.

After anointing yourself, place a small amount of the sacred oil in the dish or bowl. Take a moment to offer gratitude and thanks for the healing energy that the oil represents.

Sit in quiet reflection for a few minutes, allowing the healing energy to integrate and flow through your entire being. You may choose to meditate, pray, or simply be present with the sensations and thoughts that arise.

Once you feel ready, extinguish the candle and take a moment to ground yourself. You can do this by placing your hands on the ground, taking deep breaths, or engaging in any grounding practice that resonates with you.

Note: Remember to choose an oil that resonates with you and your intention for healing and rejuvenation. You can modify this ritual to suit your personal beliefs and preferences. Additionally, ensure that you are not allergic to any of the oils used and perform a patch test if necessary.

86. Spell for the transformation of the deceased into a vessel of divine love and compassion

Materials needed:

A quiet and sacred space
A white candle
A small dish or bowl
A piece of paper
A pen or pencil
Rose quartz crystal

Instructions:

Find a quiet and sacred space where you can perform the spell without distractions. Light the white candle and place it on a safe surface.

Take a few moments to center yourself and connect with your intention of invoking divine love and compassion for the deceased. Focus your mind and heart on this intention.

Take the piece of paper and write down the name or description of the deceased. As you write, visualize the individual surrounded by a warm, glowing light of divine love and compassion.

Hold the paper in your hands and close your eyes. Take a deep breath and imagine a loving and compassionate energy flowing through you. See this energy filling the paper and infusing it with divine love and compassion.

Place the paper in the small dish or bowl and hold it over the flame of the candle. As the paper begins to burn, visualize the transformation taking place, with the deceased's spirit being enveloped by divine love and compassion.

As the paper turns to ashes, imagine the ashes being carried away by a gentle breeze, spreading the energy of love and compassion to the entire universe.

Take a moment to offer a prayer or affirmation, expressing your intention for the deceased to embody and radiate divine love and compassion in the afterlife.

If you have a rose quartz crystal, hold it in your hands and infuse it with the energy of love and compassion. You can place it near the candle or on the ashes of the burned paper as a symbol of the transformed energy.

Sit in quiet reflection for a few minutes, sending loving and compassionate thoughts to the deceased and to all beings. Allow yourself to feel the warmth and lightness in your heart as you connect with this energy.

When you feel ready, extinguish the candle and take a moment to ground yourself. You can do this by placing your hands on the ground, taking deep breaths, or engaging in any grounding practice that resonates with you.

Note: This spell is intended to invoke and amplify the energy of divine love and compassion for the deceased. Feel free to modify it according to your personal beliefs and preferences. Always perform spells with respect, intention, and a clear ethical framework.

87. Ritual for the transfiguration of the deceased into a divine guardian of sacred rituals

Materials needed:

An altar or sacred space
Candles (preferably white or silver)
Incense (such as frankincense or sage)
A representation of the deceased (such as a photograph or an object that symbolizes them)
Sacred symbols or objects related to rituals (such as a chalice, athame, or tarot cards)
A journal or piece of paper and a pen
Instructions:

Find a quiet and sacred space where you can perform the ritual undisturbed. Set up your altar or sacred space with the candles, incense, and sacred objects.

Light the candles and the incense, creating a serene and sacred atmosphere. Take a few moments to center yourself and connect with the divine energy.

Place the representation of the deceased on the altar or in front of you. Take a moment to focus on their presence and the intention of the ritual.

Hold your journal or piece of paper and pen in your hands. Close your eyes and take a few deep breaths, allowing yourself to enter a state of deep relaxation and connection.

Open your eyes and begin writing down your heartfelt intentions for the deceased's transfiguration into a divine guardian of sacred rituals. Speak directly to the deceased, expressing your desires and wishes for their spiritual journey.

Once you have written down your intentions, hold the paper close to your heart. Visualize the deceased surrounded by a radiant and divine light. See them transformed into a powerful guardian of sacred rituals, guiding and protecting others on their spiritual paths.

With gratitude and reverence, place the paper with your intentions on the altar or near the representation of the deceased. Thank them for their presence and their willingness to fulfill this sacred role.

Take a moment to sit in silence and reflection. Allow the energy of the ritual to permeate the space and your being. Feel a sense of connection and unity with the deceased and the divine.

When you are ready, close the ritual by expressing your gratitude and extinguishing the candles. Offer a final prayer or affirmation for the deceased's journey as a divine guardian of sacred rituals.

Note: This ritual can be adapted and personalized to suit your beliefs and preferences. Feel free to incorporate any additional elements or practices that resonate with you. Remember to approach the ritual with reverence and respect, and to always follow your intuition and inner guidance.

88. Spell for the reunion of the deceased's soul with their spiritual allies and helpers

Ingredients:

A quiet and sacred space
Candles (preferably white or blue)
Incense (such as lavender or sandalwood)
A representation of the deceased (such as a photograph or an object that symbolizes them)
Crystals or gemstones (such as amethyst or clear quartz)
A journal or piece of paper and a pen

Instructions:

Find a quiet and sacred space where you can perform the spell without interruption. Set up your candles, incense, crystals, and the representation of the deceased in a way that feels harmonious and respectful.

Light the candles and the incense, allowing their gentle flames and fragrances to create a sacred atmosphere. Take a moment to center yourself and connect with the spiritual energy around you.

Hold the representation of the deceased in your hands, close your eyes, and take a few deep breaths. Visualize their spirit surrounded by a warm and comforting light, radiating love and peace.

Speak aloud or silently call upon the spiritual allies and helpers of the deceased. Address them by name or simply as "Beloved Guides and Allies." Express your heartfelt intention to reunite the deceased's soul with their spiritual allies and helpers.

Take a crystal or gemstone in your hand and infuse it with your intention. Hold it up to the representation of the deceased, allowing the energy of the crystal to amplify your connection with the spiritual realm.

Open your journal or piece of paper and write down the names of the deceased's spiritual allies and helpers, or any messages or requests you have for them. Pour your heart into the writing, knowing that it will serve as a bridge between this realm and the spiritual realm.

Once you have finished writing, fold the paper or close the journal and hold it against your heart. Visualize the energy of the deceased's spiritual allies and helpers drawing closer, embracing the soul of the deceased with love and guidance.

Place the paper or journal near the representation of the deceased, or directly on the altar. Surround it with the crystals or gemstones, symbolizing the connection and support of the spiritual allies and helpers.

Take a moment to sit in silence and gratitude, feeling the presence of the spiritual allies and helpers. Express your deep gratitude for their guidance and assistance in the reunion of the deceased's soul with their spiritual allies and helpers.

When you feel ready, extinguish the candles and offer a final prayer or affirmation, releasing the energy of the spell into the universe. Trust that the reunion of the deceased's soul with their spiritual allies and helpers is now in motion.

Remember, this spell is meant to be performed with love, respect, and a genuine desire for the highest good of the deceased. Trust your intuition and adapt the spell as needed to align with your personal beliefs and practices.

89. Invocation of the goddess Ma'at for balance and harmony in the afterlife

O, Ma'at, goddess of balance and truth,
In this sacred moment, I call upon you.
Guide us through the realms of the afterlife,
Bring forth your divine presence, wise and bright.

With your wings spread wide, soar through the skies,
Bring harmony and justice, let them arise.
In the scales of judgment, let truth prevail,
As the deceased's soul embarks on this sacred trail.

May your feather of truth be the guide,
As the soul faces the tests on the other side.
Balance the heart, the deeds, and the soul,
Unveil the path to the eternal whole.

With your gaze, see beyond the veils,
Illuminate the darkness, where wisdom prevails.
Let justice be served with your gentle touch,
Restoring order, in this realm and such.

O, Ma'at, we honor your sacred name,
In this invocation, we kindle the flame.
Bring balance and harmony, now and forever,
In the afterlife's realm, may it endeavor.

May the scales of Ma'at always align,
As the deceased's spirit seeks to shine.
Guide them with your wisdom and grace,
In your presence, they find a sacred space.

We invoke your power, O goddess divine,
To bring balance and harmony, throughout time.
With deepest reverence and purest intent,
We welcome your presence, so potent.

O, Ma'at, goddess of balance and truth,
We thank you for gracing us in this sacred booth.

As the deceased's soul journeys on their way,
May your blessings protect and guide each day.

May the balance of Ma'at forever reside,
In the afterlife's realm, side by side.
Hail Ma'at, the goddess of balance and harmony,
In your embrace, we find eternal serenity.

Take a moment to reflect upon the invocation and offer your gratitude to the goddess Ma'at for her guidance and presence. Remember, this invocation is meant to be spoken with reverence and respect. Adapt it as needed to align with your personal beliefs and practices.

90. Ritual of purification through the sacred breath of the eternal winds

Find a quiet and serene space where you can perform the ritual undisturbed. It could be outdoors or indoors, as long as you feel connected to the energy of the wind.

Stand with your feet firmly planted on the ground, facing the direction from which the wind is blowing. Close your eyes and take a few deep breaths, allowing yourself to become fully present in the moment.

Visualize yourself surrounded by a gentle breeze, feeling the cool air against your skin. Imagine that this breeze carries with it the purifying power of the wind, capable of cleansing and rejuvenating your spirit.

Begin to focus on your breath. Inhale deeply, imagining that you are drawing in the pure energy of the wind. Feel it filling your lungs, purifying and revitalizing every cell in your body. As you exhale, visualize any negativity, impurities, or stagnant energy being released and carried away by the wind.

Repeat this breathing pattern several times, allowing the rhythm of your breath to sync with the natural flow of the wind. Feel the connection between your breath and the eternal winds, merging as one.

As you continue to breathe, let go of any tension, worries, or burdens that you may be carrying. Imagine the wind gently sweeping them away, leaving you feeling lighter, clearer, and more refreshed.

While still breathing deeply, set your intentions for purification. Focus on areas of your life or aspects of yourself that you wish to cleanse and purify. Whether it's emotional healing, releasing past traumas, or letting go of negative patterns, infuse your intentions into each breath.

Open yourself to receive the wisdom and guidance of the wind. Allow its whispers to caress your ears, carrying messages from the unseen realms. Listen attentively and trust the guidance that comes to you during this sacred connection with the eternal winds.

Take a few moments to simply stand and be present, embracing the energy of the wind. Feel its power, its freedom, and its ability to bring clarity and purification.

When you feel ready, express your gratitude to the wind for its cleansing presence. Thank the eternal winds for their role in this ritual of purification.

Remember, adapt this ritual to suit your personal preferences and beliefs. It's essential to approach the ritual with reverence and respect, honoring the sacredness of the wind and its purifying energy.

91. Spell for the liberation of the deceased's soul from the chains of karma

✧ Find a quiet and sacred space where you can perform the spell without any distractions. Light a white candle to create a peaceful ambiance.

✧ Close your eyes and take a few deep breaths, centering yourself and connecting with the divine energy around you. Visualize a golden light surrounding you, filling you with divine love and protection.

✧ Hold a clear quartz crystal in your hands, allowing its energy to resonate with your intention. Focus on the liberation of the deceased's soul from the chains of karma. See the chains breaking and dissolving, releasing the soul from any past karmic debts or limitations.

✧ Recite the following spell or create your own words, speaking with intention and conviction:

"By the power of the divine light,
I call upon the spirits' might.
Break the chains that bind the soul,
Release it now, make it whole.

Karma's hold, it shall undo,
Set the spirit free, anew.
With love and grace, let it be done,
Liberation for the departed one."

✧ Visualize the liberated soul rising above the chains of karma, ascending into a realm of pure light and freedom. See the soul surrounded by divine love, forgiveness, and compassion.

✧ Hold the crystal above the candle flame, allowing it to absorb the purifying energy. Visualize the flame cleansing and purifying the crystal, infusing it with the power to dissolve karmic bonds.

✧ Place the crystal on a small altar or sacred space, dedicating it to the liberation of the deceased's soul. Leave the candle burning as a symbol of the continuous release of karmic ties.

✧   Express your gratitude to the divine and the spirits for their assistance in this liberation. Thank them for their guidance and support.

✧   Allow the candle to burn down completely or snuff it out with a grateful heart. Keep the crystal on your altar as a reminder of the spell's intention and the ongoing liberation of the deceased's soul.

Remember, spells are a way to focus your intention and energy, but they should always be performed with respect and reverence. Adapt the spell as needed to align with your personal beliefs and practices.

92. Incantation to awaken the dormant inner wisdom within the deceased's spirit

✧ Find a quiet and sacred space where you can perform the incantation without any distractions. Light a purple or blue candle to symbolize wisdom and intuition.

✧ Close your eyes and take a few deep breaths, centering yourself and connecting with the divine energy around you. Visualize a gentle light surrounding you, representing the presence of wisdom and guidance.

✧ Place your hands over your heart or hold a clear quartz crystal in your hands, allowing its energy to resonate with your intention. Feel the connection with the deceased's spirit and their potential for inner wisdom.

✧ Recite the following incantation or create your own words, speaking with intention and reverence:

"Ancient spirits, wise and true,
Awaken the wisdom within you.
From realms unseen, ancient and deep,
Let knowledge and insight now seep.

Dormant wisdom, rise and shine,
Illuminate the depths divine.
Unveil the secrets, hidden and rare,
Let wisdom guide with love and care."

✧ Visualize a gentle awakening within the deceased's spirit, as if a flame of wisdom is ignited within them. See this inner wisdom growing and expanding, filling their spirit with knowledge, understanding, and clarity.

✧ Take a moment to meditate and listen in silence, opening yourself to receive any messages or insights from the awakened wisdom of the deceased's spirit.

✧ Express gratitude to the divine and the spirits for their assistance in awakening the dormant inner wisdom. Thank them for their guidance and support.

✧ Allow the candle to burn down completely or snuff it out with a grateful heart. Keep the crystal as a reminder of the awakened wisdom within the deceased's spirit.

Remember, this incantation is a way to focus your intention and energy, but it should always be performed with respect and reverence. Adapt the incantation as needed to align with your personal beliefs and practices.

93. Ritual for the communion with the spirits of the celestial rainbows and colors

Find a quiet and serene outdoor space where you can connect with nature and the elements. Ideally, perform this ritual during or shortly after a rain shower when rainbows are more likely to appear.

Stand or sit comfortably and take a few deep breaths to center yourself. Close your eyes and visualize a radiant rainbow stretching across the sky, filled with vibrant and shimmering colors.

Extend your arms outward, palms facing upward, as if to embrace the beauty and energy of the rainbow. Feel the connection between yourself and the celestial realms.

Begin by expressing gratitude to the spirits of the rainbows and colors, acknowledging their presence and the magic they bring to the world. Speak from your heart and let your words flow naturally.

Open yourself to receive the blessings and wisdom of the celestial rainbows and colors. Imagine the colors flowing into your being, filling you with their energy and vibrancy. Feel the harmonizing and uplifting effects of each color as it permeates your body and spirit.

Offer a small token or gesture of appreciation to the spirits, such as scattering flower petals or leaving a crystal or colorful ribbon at the base of a tree.

Spend some time in silent meditation, allowing yourself to be fully present in the moment. Listen for any messages or insights that the spirits of the rainbows and colors may have for you.

When you feel ready, slowly bring your awareness back to the physical world. Express gratitude to the spirits for their presence and guidance.

Take a moment to ground yourself by placing your hands on the earth or hugging a tree, feeling the connection with the natural world.

Reflect on the experience and consider how you can carry the energy and wisdom of the celestial rainbows and colors into your daily life. Allow their vibrancy and beauty to inspire and uplift you.

Remember, this ritual is a way to honor and connect with the spirits of the celestial rainbows and colors. Adapt it to suit your personal beliefs and preferences, and feel free to incorporate any additional elements or practices that resonate with you.

94. Spell for the transmigration of the deceased's soul into the realm of eternal joy and bliss

Gather the following items:

A white candle
A small bowl of water
A piece of paper and a pen
A small pouch or container

Your intention and focus
✧ Find a quiet and peaceful space where you can perform the spell without distractions. Light the white candle and place it before you.

✧ Take a few deep breaths to center yourself and calm your mind. Focus on your intention to facilitate the transmigration of the deceased's soul into the realm of eternal joy and bliss.

✧ Take the piece of paper and write down the name of the deceased or any specific intentions related to their soul's journey. Feel free to write any affirmations or blessings as well.

✧ Hold the paper in your hands and close your eyes. Visualize the soul of the deceased surrounded by radiant light and love. Envision them being gently guided to the realm of eternal joy and bliss, where they are embraced by peace, happiness, and fulfillment.

✧ Place the paper into the small pouch or container, symbolizing the safekeeping of the soul's intentions. You can also add any small tokens or symbols that represent joy and bliss to the pouch.

✧ Take the bowl of water and dip your fingers into it. Gently sprinkle the water over the pouch, infusing it with the purifying and blessing properties of water. Imagine the water purifying and energizing the intentions written on the paper.

✧ Hold the pouch or container in your hands and recite the following spell:

"In this sacred rite, I call upon divine light,
To guide [name of the deceased] to realms so bright.
Transmigration of soul, to joy and bliss it shall be,
In eternal embrace, may they find serenity.
With love and blessings, I release them to soar,
Into realms of happiness forevermore."

✧ Place the pouch or container in a safe and sacred space, such as an altar or a special place where it won't be disturbed. You can also choose to carry it with you as a personal reminder of your intention.

✧ Thank the divine forces, spirits, or deities you believe in for their presence and assistance in this spell.

✧ Allow the candle to burn out on its own, or safely extinguish it, knowing that the light and blessings of the spell will continue to guide the soul on its journey.

Remember, this spell is a symbolic representation of your intention and desire for the transmigration of the deceased's soul into a realm of eternal joy and bliss. It is important to approach it with sincerity, love, and respect. Adapt the spell as needed to align with your spiritual beliefs and practices.

95. Ritual of purification through the sacred waters of the eternal Nile

Materials needed:

A bowl or basin of clean water
Fresh rose petals or rosewater (optional)
Frankincense or sandalwood incense
A small white candle
A feather (symbolizing purification and truth)
Anointing oil (such as lavender or rose)
Instructions:

Find a quiet and peaceful space where you can perform the ritual undisturbed. Set up your materials on a clean altar or table.

Light the incense and the white candle, creating a serene and sacred atmosphere. Let the smoke of the incense fill the space, purifying the air.

Take a few deep breaths, centering yourself and clearing your mind. Visualize the powerful and sacred waters of the Nile, flowing pure and pristine.

Dip the feather into the bowl of water, and gently touch it to your forehead, saying:

"By the sacred waters of the eternal Nile,
I purify my mind, body, and soul.
May all impurities be washed away,
Leaving only purity and divine grace."

Take the anointing oil and apply a few drops to your palms. Rub your hands together, activating the oil with your intention and energy. Close your eyes and inhale the aroma, allowing it to calm and uplift your spirit.

With the anointing oil on your fingertips, trace a symbol of your choice on your chest, such as a spiral representing spiritual transformation, or a lotus flower symbolizing purity and enlightenment. As you trace the symbol, recite:

"In the sacred waters, I am cleansed,
Purified and reborn, my spirit enhanced.
From this moment forth, I walk the path divine,

Radiating love and light, in perfect harmony."

If you have fresh rose petals or rosewater, sprinkle a few drops or scatter the petals in the water as an offering to the divine. Roses are associated with love, beauty, and purity.

Place both of your hands over the bowl of water, and envision a soft, radiant light emanating from your palms. Feel the energy of the water being infused with your intention for purification and renewal.

Take a moment to express gratitude for the cleansing and rejuvenating properties of the sacred waters, and for the opportunity to partake in this ritual of purification.

To conclude the ritual, extinguish the candle and allow the incense to burn out on its own. You may choose to keep the water on your altar as a symbol of purification or dispose of it respectfully by pouring it onto the earth.

Remember, rituals are deeply personal, and you can always adapt and modify them to align with your beliefs and preferences. Trust your intuition and infuse the ritual with your own energy and intention for maximum efficacy.

96. Spell for the protection of the deceased's soul from malevolent forces

Materials needed:

A small white candle
Frankincense or sage incense
A black obsidian or protective crystal
A piece of white cloth or paper
A pen or marker
Instructions:

Find a quiet and peaceful space where you can perform the spell without interruptions. Set up your materials on a clean altar or table.

Light the white candle and the incense, creating a sacred and protected space. Let the smoke of the incense fill the area, purifying the energy and dispelling negativity.

Take the black obsidian or protective crystal in your hands and close your eyes. Focus on its energy, envisioning a shield of divine protection forming around you.

With the pen or marker, write the name of the deceased on the white cloth or paper. This represents the connection to the soul you are protecting.

Hold the cloth or paper in your hands and recite the following spell:

"By the power of light, by the strength of love,
I call upon the divine to watch from above.
Protect [name of deceased] from all harm and ill,
Safeguard their soul, let no malevolence spill."

Place the black obsidian or protective crystal on top of the cloth or paper with the name written on it. Visualize a powerful barrier of light surrounding the soul of the deceased, shielding them from any negative or malevolent forces.

Leave the candle and incense to burn out completely. As they burn, the energy of protection and purification will continue to surround and safeguard the deceased's soul.

Keep the cloth or paper with the name of the deceased and the black obsidian or protective crystal in a safe place, such as a special box or on your personal altar. You may also choose to carry the crystal with you as a symbol of protection.

Whenever you feel the need to reinforce the spell or send additional protection, you can light the white candle and incense, hold the crystal, and recite the spell again.

Remember, the intention and energy you put into the spell are of utmost importance. Trust your intuition and focus on the well-being and protection of the deceased's soul. Adapt the spell as needed to align with your personal beliefs and practices.

97. Ritual for the communion with the spirits of the sacred animals and totems

Items needed:

A quiet and serene space
An altar or sacred space
Representations or images of the sacred animals or totems you wish to commune with
Candles or incense for purification and focus
Offerings such as food, water, or herbs
Journal or paper and pen

Steps:

✧ Prepare your sacred space: Find a quiet and serene space where you can focus and connect with the spirits of the sacred animals and totems. Set up your altar or sacred space, placing the representations or images of the animals or totems on it. Light the candles or incense to purify the space and create a sacred atmosphere.

✧ Ground and center yourself: Take a few deep breaths and center yourself. Close your eyes and imagine roots growing from the soles of your feet, grounding you deep into the earth. Feel the stability and connection to the earth beneath you.

✧ Invocation: Light a candle or incense as an offering to the spirits. Stand or sit before your sacred space and speak an invocation to invite the spirits of the sacred animals and totems to join you. You can use the following example or create your own:

"Great spirits of the sacred animals and totems,
I call upon your wisdom and guidance.
I seek communion and connection with you,
To learn from your teachings and receive your blessings.
Join me in this sacred space, oh divine beings,
And let our energies intertwine and unite."

✧ Meditation and connection: Close your eyes and enter into a meditative state. Visualize the representations or images of the sacred animals or totems coming to life, moving and interacting with you. Feel their presence and the energy they carry. Allow yourself to connect with each spirit individually, observing their characteristics and qualities. Ask for their guidance and wisdom, and listen with an open heart and mind.

✧ Offering and gratitude: Offer your chosen offerings such as food, water, or herbs to the spirits of the sacred animals and totems. Express your gratitude for their presence and teachings. You can also write down any insights or messages you received during the meditation in your journal or on a piece of paper.

✧ Closing: Thank the spirits of the sacred animals and totems for their presence and guidance. Extinguish the candles or incense, symbolizing the end of the ritual. Take a moment to ground yourself and return to your normal state of awareness.

Remember to approach this ritual with reverence and respect for the spirits of the sacred animals and totems. Allow yourself to be open to their teachings and guidance, and continue to cultivate a relationship with them in your spiritual practice.

98. Spell for the transmigration of the deceased's soul into the realm of eternal knowledge

Items needed:

A quiet and sacred space
A white candle
A piece of paper or parchment
A pen or marker
A small container or cauldron for burning

Steps:

Prepare your sacred space: Find a quiet and sacred space where you can focus and perform the spell. Clear the space of any distractions and ensure you have privacy.

Light the white candle: Light the white candle and place it before you. This candle symbolizes purity, clarity, and the guiding light of knowledge.

Write the intention: Take the piece of paper or parchment and write down the following intention in your own words, focusing on the transmigration of the deceased's soul into the realm of eternal knowledge:

"By the power of the divine, I call forth the transmigration of [name of the deceased] into the realm of eternal knowledge. May their soul ascend to the highest realms of wisdom and understanding, where they shall be immersed in the eternal flow of knowledge. Let their spirit be free from all limitations and ignorance, and may they find solace and enlightenment in the realm of eternal knowledge."

Burn the intention: Carefully light the paper or parchment with the flame of the white candle, and place it into the small container or cauldron. As it burns, visualize the intention being released into the universe and reaching the realm of eternal knowledge. Feel the energy and power of the spell as the paper turns to ash.

Focus and channel energy: Close your eyes and focus on the flame of the white candle. Visualize the deceased's soul being enveloped in a radiant light, guiding them towards the realm of eternal knowledge. Send your energy and intention towards this visualization, channeling your thoughts and emotions into the spell.

Express gratitude: Express gratitude to the divine and the spirits for their guidance and assistance in this spell. Thank them for their presence and support.

Extinguish the candle: Safely extinguish the white candle, symbolizing the completion of the spell and the end of the ritual.

Note: This spell should be performed with utmost respect and reverence for the deceased. It is important to have the consent and intention of the deceased's loved ones before performing any rituals or spells on their behalf.

99. Ritual of anointing with sacred herbs for spiritual healing and transformation

Prepare a sacred space: Find a quiet and peaceful space where you can perform the ritual. Clear the space of any clutter and create an altar or a designated area where you will conduct the ritual.

Gather sacred herbs: Choose a selection of herbs that hold special meaning for you in terms of healing and transformation. Some commonly used herbs for this purpose include lavender for calming and purification, rosemary for clarity and protection, sage for cleansing and releasing negative energies, and rose petals for love and compassion.

Set your intention: Take a moment to center yourself and set your intention for the ritual. Focus on the specific areas of healing and transformation that you or the intended recipient of the ritual seek. This could be emotional healing, spiritual growth, releasing old patterns, or any other intention that resonates with you.

Prepare the anointing blend: Take a small bowl and mix the herbs together. As you do so, infuse the herbs with your intention and visualize them radiating with healing and transformative energy. You may also add a carrier oil such as jojoba oil or almond oil to create a blend that can be easily applied to the body.

Cleanse and bless the herbs: Hold your hands over the herb blend and offer a prayer or blessing, asking for the herbs to be charged with healing and transformative energy. You can also pass the herbs through the smoke of burning incense or a smudging bundle to cleanse and purify them.

Anointing ritual: Gently rub a small amount of the herb blend onto your fingertips or palms. Begin by anointing yourself, focusing on areas of the body that may benefit from healing and transformation. As you apply the blend, visualize the herbs infusing your being with their powerful properties, bringing about the desired healing and transformation.

Optional: If performing the ritual for someone else, you can invite them to participate by anointing them with the herb blend or applying it to specific areas of their body as needed. Offer them words of affirmation and support, expressing your intention for their healing and transformation.

Closing the ritual: Once you have completed the anointing, take a moment to express gratitude for the healing and transformation that is taking place. Offer a closing prayer or affirmation, sealing the intention and energy of the ritual.

Remember, rituals are personal and can be adapted to suit your own beliefs and practices. It's important to approach the ritual with reverence and respect for the sacredness of the herbs and their healing properties.

100.   Spell for the transformation of the deceased into a vessel of divine power and authority

Preparation: Find a quiet and sacred space where you can perform the spell. Set up an altar or a designated area to hold any tools or items you may need.

Invocation: Begin by lighting a white candle on the altar, representing purity and divine energy. Close your eyes and take a few deep breaths to center yourself. Call upon the presence of the deceased and the divine energies you wish to invoke for this transformation. You can address the deceased by name and ask for their willingness and permission to be transformed into a vessel of divine power and authority.

Symbol of Authority: Place an object or symbol of authority on the altar, such as a crown, a scepter, or a symbol representing power and leadership. This symbol will act as a focal point for the transformation.

Affirmation and Intention: Hold your hands over the symbol of authority and speak the following affirmation or create your own, expressing the intention for the transformation:

"By the power of the divine, I invoke the transformation of [name of the deceased] into a vessel of divine power and authority. May their spirit be infused with the strength, wisdom, and sovereignty of the divine realms. As they journey in the afterlife, may they wield their power with grace, benevolence, and righteous authority. So mote it be."

Repeat the affirmation several times, allowing the energy of your words to resonate and imbue the symbol with the intended transformation.

Symbolic Action: Perform a symbolic action to represent the transformation. This can include holding the symbol of authority in your hands and visualizing the divine energy infusing it with power, or gently touching the symbol to the forehead or heart area, symbolizing the transfer of divine authority to the deceased.

Gratitude and Closing: Express gratitude to the deceased and the divine energies for their presence and participation in the spell. Thank them for their willingness to embrace the transformation and for the power and authority they will now embody.

Blow out the candle to signify the end of the spell, knowing that the transformation has been set in motion.

Remember, this spell is intended to be performed with respect and reverence for the deceased and the divine energies involved. Always approach spellwork with a clear intention and focus, and remember to use your own words and adapt the spell to align with your personal beliefs and practices.

101.   Ritual for the transfiguration of the deceased into a divine messenger of the gods

Preparation:

✧ Find a quiet and sacred space where you can perform the ritual undisturbed.
✧ Set up an altar with representations or symbols of the gods or deities you wish to invoke.
✧ Place a picture or representation of the deceased at the center of the altar.
✧ Gather any items that hold personal significance for the deceased, such as jewelry or sentimental objects.

Purification:

✧ Begin by purifying yourself and the space. You can do this by lighting incense or sage and wafting the smoke around yourself and the altar.
✧ Take a moment to ground yourself and center your energy. Close your eyes, take a few deep breaths, and visualize any negativity or stagnant energy leaving your body.

Invocation:

✧ Light a candle or candles on the altar to symbolize the presence of divine light.
✧ Speak aloud your intention, stating that you are performing this ritual to facilitate the transfiguration of the deceased into a divine messenger of the gods.
✧ Call upon the specific gods or deities you wish to invoke, addressing them by name and expressing your desire for their guidance and assistance in this process.
✧ Share any personal prayers or messages for the deceased, expressing your love, gratitude, and wishes for their spiritual journey.

Anointing and Empowerment:

✧ Take a small amount of sacred oil or consecrated water and bless it with your intention.
✧ Gently anoint the picture or representation of the deceased with the oil or water, symbolizing the infusion of divine energy.
✧ As you anoint, visualize the deceased being enveloped in a radiant light, transforming and transcending into a divine messenger of the gods.

✧ Speak words of empowerment and affirmation, such as **"May the divine light and wisdom flow through you. May you carry the messages of the gods with grace and clarity."**

Communication and Release:

✧ Take a moment to sit in silence and connect with the energy of the deceased and the divine presence invoked.
✧ Allow any messages or insights to flow through you, sensing the presence of the divine messenger.
✧ Share any final words or blessings for the deceased, expressing your support and encouragement for their new role as a divine messenger.
✧ Release any attachment to the outcome and trust in the divine plan.

Closing:

✧ Express your gratitude to the gods and deities for their presence and assistance in the ritual.
✧ Extinguish the candles, symbolizing the end of the ritual.
✧ Close the ritual space in a way that aligns with your personal beliefs and practices, such as offering a final prayer or moment of reflection.

Remember to approach this ritual with respect, reverence, and a deep sense of love and honor for the deceased. Adapt the ritual as needed to align with your specific spiritual beliefs and practices.

102.   Spell for the reunion of the deceased's soul with their ancestral lineage

Preparation:

✧ Find a quiet and sacred space where you can perform the spell without interruption.
✧ Set up an altar or a special place where you can honor and connect with the deceased and their ancestral lineage.
✧ Gather items that represent your ancestors, such as photographs, family heirlooms, or objects with ancestral significance.

Centering and Intention:

✧ Take a moment to ground yourself and center your energy. Close your eyes, take a few deep breaths, and visualize yourself surrounded by a protective and loving energy.
✧ Set your intention for the spell. State that you are performing this spell to facilitate the reunion of the deceased's soul with their ancestral lineage, allowing them to find comfort, guidance, and connection.

Invocation:

✧ Light a candle or candles on the altar to symbolize the presence of ancestral spirits.
✧ Speak aloud your intention, addressing the ancestral spirits and stating your desire for their assistance in reuniting the deceased's soul with their ancestral lineage.
✧ Call upon specific ancestors or simply invite all benevolent and loving ancestral spirits to join you in this ritual.

Ancestral Connection:

✧ Take a moment to connect with the energy of the deceased and visualize them surrounded by a warm and loving light.
✧ Hold or touch the items representing the deceased's ancestors, feeling their presence and the connection to the ancestral lineage.
✧ Speak the names of the deceased's ancestors, honoring their memory and inviting them to embrace the departed soul as part of the lineage.

Communication and Healing:

✧ Open your heart and mind to receive any messages or insights from the ancestral spirits.
✧ Speak words of love and affirmation, expressing gratitude for the wisdom and guidance passed down through the generations.
✧ Share any personal messages or prayers for the deceased, expressing your wishes for their reunion with their ancestral lineage and the healing and support they may receive from it.

Release and Blessing:

✧ Express your gratitude to the ancestral spirits for their presence and assistance in the spell.
✧ Release any attachment to the outcome and trust in the divine plan.
✧ Close the ritual in a way that feels right to you, such as offering a final prayer, bowing
✧ in reverence, or speaking words of gratitude and closure.

Remember to approach this spell with love, respect, and reverence for your ancestors and the deceased. Adapt the spell as needed to align with your specific beliefs and practices.

103.   Invocation of the goddess Isis for protection and nurturing in the afterlife

Preparation:

✧ Find a quiet and sacred space where you can perform the invocation without interruption.
✧ Set up an altar or a special place where you can connect with the energy of Isis.
✧ Gather items that symbolize Isis, such as an image or statue of the goddess, candles, incense, and offerings.

Centering and Intent:

✧ Take a few moments to center yourself and clear your mind. Close your eyes, take deep breaths, and focus on your intention to connect with the energy of Isis for protection and nurturing in the afterlife.

Opening Invocation:

✧ Light the candles and the incense on your altar to create a sacred atmosphere.
✧ Stand or sit in front of the altar, facing the image or statue of Isis.
✧ Extend your arms in a welcoming gesture and speak the following invocation:

"Great goddess Isis, divine mother and protector,
I invoke your presence and your loving energy.
I call upon you to guide and nurture the souls of the departed,
Providing them with your comforting and protective embrace.
Hear my plea and grant them your divine shelter in the afterlife.
May they find solace and peace under your watchful gaze."

Connection and Communication:

✧ Take a moment to visualize the presence of Isis in front of you, emanating a loving and nurturing energy.
✧ Speak from your heart, expressing your specific desires for the protection and nurturing of the deceased in the afterlife.
✧ Share any personal messages or prayers for their well-being and ask for Isis's intercession on their behalf.

Offering and Gratitude:

✧ Present your offerings to the goddess, such as flowers, food, or other items that hold significance to you.
✧ Express your gratitude to Isis for her presence and protection, acknowledging her role as the divine mother and nurturer.
✧ Thank her for her guidance and support in ensuring the well-being of the departed souls.

Closing:

✧ Conclude the invocation by expressing your trust in Isis's power and her ability to fulfill your intentions.
✧ Offer a final prayer or blessing, asking for continued protection and nurturing for the departed souls in the afterlife.
✧ Take a moment to reflect on the connection you've established and the energy of Isis surrounding you.

Remember to approach this invocation with reverence and respect for the goddess Isis. Adapt the invocation as needed to align with your own beliefs and practices.

104.   Ritual of purification through the sacred fire of the eternal flame

Preparation:

✧ Find a safe and secluded outdoor location where you can perform the ritual. It can be a quiet corner of a garden or a sacred space specifically designated for this purpose.
✧ Create a sacred altar or area where you will light the eternal flame. Place items of significance such as candles, herbs, crystals, and any personal objects that hold spiritual meaning.

Lighting the Eternal Flame:

✧ Begin by centering yourself and connecting with the intention of purification and transformation.
✧ Light a sacred fire in a fire pit or cauldron, representing the eternal flame. You can use a candle if an open fire is not possible.
✧ As you light the flame, visualize it as a purifying and transformative force, capable of burning away impurities and illuminating the path of the deceased.

Invocation and Prayer:

✧ Stand before the eternal flame and speak an invocation or prayer, addressing the divine forces and spirits you wish to invoke for purification.
✧ Express your intention for the ritual, asking for the cleansing and release of any negative energies or attachments that may be lingering with the deceased.

Symbolic Offerings:

✧ Place symbolic offerings into the eternal flame as a representation of the release and purification process. These offerings can be written prayers, herbs, dried flowers, or other items that hold personal significance.
✧ Visualize the flame transforming these offerings into pure energy, carrying away any negativity or attachments.

Chanting and Affirmations:

✧ Engage in chanting or affirmations to amplify the energy of the ritual. You can use sacred words, mantras, or personal affirmations related to purification, release, and transformation.
✧ Repeat these chants or affirmations as you focus your attention on the eternal flame, allowing the vibrations to infuse the space and the energy of the deceased.

Visualization and Meditative Connection:

✧ Close your eyes and visualize the deceased standing in front of the eternal flame, surrounded by its purifying light.
✧ Imagine the flame enveloping and cleansing their spirit, releasing any lingering attachments and elevating their energy to a higher realm of purity and light.
✧ Hold this visualization for a few moments, sending your love, support, and intentions for their spiritual journey.

Closing and Gratitude:

✧ Express gratitude to the divine forces, spirits, and the eternal flame for their presence and assistance in the ritual.
✧ Allow the eternal flame to burn until it naturally extinguishes or safely extinguish it yourself, acknowledging the completion of the ritual.
✧ Take a few moments to ground yourself, offering gratitude for the opportunity to perform this sacred act of purification.

Remember to adapt and modify this ritual according to your personal beliefs and practices. It is essential to approach this ritual with reverence, intention, and respect.

105.   Spell for the liberation of the deceased's soul from earthly attachments

Create a Sacred Space:

✧ Find a quiet and undisturbed space where you can perform the spell. It can be indoors or outdoors, as long as you feel connected to the spiritual energy.

✧ Clear the space of any clutter and create a serene and sacred atmosphere. You may choose to light candles, burn incense, or use any other sacred tools that resonate with you.

Center Yourself:

✧ Take a few moments to center yourself and calm your mind. Close your eyes, take deep breaths, and focus on grounding your energy.

✧ Visualize a protective sphere of light surrounding you, creating a safe and sacred space for the spell.

Set Your Intention:

✧ Clearly state your intention to liberate the deceased's soul from earthly attachments. Speak from your heart and be specific about the attachments you wish to release.

"With love and compassion, I call upon the higher forces to assist in liberating the soul of [name of the deceased] from all earthly attachments that hinder their spiritual journey."

Visualization and Affirmations:

✧ Visualize the deceased's soul surrounded by a gentle, golden light. See this light growing brighter and more radiant with each passing moment.

✧ Speak affirmations that support the liberation of their soul, such as:

"I release you from the burdens of earthly attachments. Your spirit is free to soar and ascend to higher realms of light and love. All ties that bind you are dissolved, allowing you to embrace your true essence and divine purpose."

Symbolic Gesture of Release:

✧ Hold a symbolic object, such as a feather, in your hand. As you hold it, visualize the attachments being transferred to the object.
✧ Speak aloud the specific attachments you wish to release, such as fear, regret, attachment to material possessions, or unresolved emotions. As you name each attachment, imagine it being absorbed by the object you hold.

Release and Let Go:

Once you have spoken and visualized the release of the attachments, hold the symbolic object in your hand and declare, **"I release these attachments from the soul of [name of the deceased]. May they be freed and find their way to peace and enlightenment."**

Closing:

✧ Express gratitude to the higher forces, spirit guides, and any divine beings you invoked for their assistance in the liberation of the deceased's soul.
✧ Close the sacred space by thanking and releasing the energies that were present, stating, **"So mote it be"**

Remember, this spell is a way to focus your intention and send positive energy to support the liberation of the deceased's soul. It is important to perform it with sincerity, respect, and love.

106.   Ritual for the communion with the spirits of the celestial trees and plants

Choose a serene outdoor location where you can connect with nature. Find a spot surrounded by trees or plants that resonate with you.

Begin by grounding yourself. Stand barefoot on the earth, feeling the energy of the earth beneath your feet. Take a few deep breaths, allowing your body and mind to relax.

Light a sacred candle or incense to create a sacred space and invoke the presence of the spirits of the trees and plants. Offer a prayer or intention for your communion and connection with their energies.

Walk slowly and mindfully among the trees and plants, feeling their presence and energy. Observe their beauty, strength, and resilience. Allow yourself to become attuned to their wisdom and vibrations.

Find a comfortable place to sit or lean against a tree. Close your eyes and enter a meditative state. Imagine yourself surrounded by a radiant light, connecting you to the celestial realms.

Open your heart and mind to the messages and guidance of the tree and plant spirits. Listen for whispers, insights, and sensations that may come to you. Trust your intuition and the subtle signs of communication.

Engage in silent or spoken dialogue with the spirits of the trees and plants. Ask for their guidance, wisdom, and healing. Express your gratitude for their presence and willingness to connect with you.

Stay in this state of communion for as long as feels right to you. When you feel complete, thank the tree and plant spirits for their wisdom and support. Offer a small token of gratitude, such as a flower or a leaf, as an act of reciprocity.

Slowly bring yourself back to the present moment. Reflect on any insights or messages received during the communion. Write down your experiences and observations in a journal to revisit later.

Before leaving, express your gratitude once again to the spirits of the trees and plants, and extinguish the sacred candle or incense.

Remember, when communing with the spirits of the celestial trees and plants, approach them with respect, reverence, and an open heart. Cultivate a deep connection and appreciation for the natural world and the wisdom it holds.

107.   Spell for the transmigration of the deceased's soul into the realm of eternal peace

Create a peaceful and sacred space where you can focus your energy and intention. You can light candles, burn incense, or play calming music to set the ambiance.

Sit or stand in a comfortable position, taking a few moments to center yourself. Take deep breaths and release any tension or distractions.

Visualize a serene and tranquil environment, such as a peaceful garden or a tranquil beach. Imagine the soul of the deceased surrounded by this peaceful energy.

Begin chanting or reciting the following spell:

"By the power of love and light,
I call upon the eternal peace so bright.
Release all worries, let go of pain,
Embrace the serenity, the calm refrain.
May the soul find solace, free from strife,
Transmigrate into the eternal peace of life."

Repeat this chant several times, allowing the words to resonate deeply within you.

As you continue chanting, envision the soul of the deceased being embraced by the peaceful energy, feeling a sense of release and tranquility.

Offer your heartfelt prayers and intentions for the soul's journey into eternal peace. Express your wishes for their liberation from suffering and their ultimate transcendence into a state of complete peace and harmony.

Hold the image of the soul in eternal peace in your mind and heart, and affirm with conviction: "So mote it be."

Take a moment to express gratitude for the opportunity to perform this spell and for the soul's journey towards eternal peace.

Slowly release the energy you have raised, allowing it to disperse and return to the universe.

Close the ritual by offering a final prayer or blessing, acknowledging the power and presence of divine peace.

Remember, this spell is intended to support and facilitate the transmigration of the deceased's soul into the realm of eternal peace. It is important to perform it with love, respect, and pure intentions.

108.   Invocation of the god Ptah for creation and manifestation in the afterlife

Create a sacred space where you can focus your energy and connect with the divine. This can be a quiet room, an altar, or any space that feels spiritually significant to you.

Light a candle or incense as a symbolic representation of the divine presence.

Close your eyes, take a few deep breaths, and center yourself. Allow yourself to enter a state of calm and receptivity.

Begin by addressing the god Ptah with reverence and respect. You can say:

"Oh great and mighty Ptah, god of creation and manifestation,
I invoke your divine presence in this sacred space.
I humbly seek your guidance and blessings in the afterlife."

Express your intentions and desires for creation and manifestation in the afterlife. You can speak from the heart and use your own words or recite the following:

"Ptah, I ask for your divine assistance
in manifesting my dreams and desires in the afterlife.
Guide me in creating a reality of abundance, joy, and fulfillment.
Help me bring forth my true potential and purpose,
and allow my soul to express its creative essence.
Grant me the power to manifest my intentions
and shape my reality in alignment with divine will."

Take a few moments to visualize and imagine yourself in the afterlife, experiencing the manifestation of your desires and intentions. Feel the energy of Ptah's presence supporting and empowering you.

Offer gratitude to Ptah for his presence and assistance. You can say:

"Thank you, Ptah, for your divine presence and blessings.
I am grateful for your guidance and support
as I embark on my journey in the afterlife.
May my creations be aligned with your divine will.
So mote it be."

Take a few more deep breaths, allowing the energy of the invocation to settle within you. When you feel ready, open your eyes and acknowledge the completion of the invocation.

Remember, when invoking a deity, it is important to approach with reverence, sincerity, and respect. It is also essential to use your own words and intentions, as these rituals are meant to be personalized expressions of your spiritual connection.

109.   Ritual of anointing with sacred resins for spiritual elevation and enlightenment

Select a sacred resin that resonates with your intention. Examples of sacred resins commonly used for spiritual purposes include frankincense, myrrh, copal, and amber.

Prepare your sacred space by clearing any clutter and ensuring it is clean and peaceful. You can also play soft, soothing music or light candles to create a serene atmosphere.

Place the chosen resin in a heat-proof container such as a censer or incense burner. If using loose resin, you may need to place it on a charcoal disc or use an incense holder specifically designed for resins.

Light a charcoal disc and place it in the censer or incense burner. Wait for the charcoal to become hot and start to glow.

Once the charcoal is ready, carefully sprinkle a small amount of the sacred resin onto the glowing charcoal. As it starts to burn, the resin will release fragrant smoke and aromatic fumes.

As the smoke rises, close your eyes and take a few deep breaths. Set your intention for spiritual elevation and enlightenment. Visualize yourself surrounded by a radiant light and opening up to higher states of consciousness.

Hold your hands over the rising smoke and allow it to cleanse and purify your energy field. You can also gently fan the smoke towards your body, starting from your feet and moving upward, symbolizing the purification and elevation of your being.

As you do this, you can recite a personal affirmation or prayer that aligns with your intention. For example:

"With the sacred smoke and divine resin,
I elevate my spirit, mind, and soul within.
May I be blessed with enlightenment's grace,
and ascend to higher realms in sacred space."

Continue to focus on your intention and inhale the fragrant smoke deeply. Allow yourself to fully immerse in the experience and connect with the elevated energy.

When you feel the ritual is complete, express gratitude for the guidance and blessings received. You can say a simple thank you or express your gratitude in your own words.

Safely extinguish the charcoal and allow the sacred space to settle. You may choose to meditate or spend some quiet time reflecting on the experience.

Remember to handle the charcoal and burning resin with care to prevent any accidents or burns. It's also important to ensure proper ventilation in the space where you perform the ritual.

110.   Spell for the transformation of the deceased into a vessel of divine grace and mercy

Find a quiet and sacred space where you can focus without distractions. Light a white candle to symbolize purity, grace, and divine presence.

Take a few moments to center yourself and connect with your intention. Visualize the deceased surrounded by a radiant light and filled with love, compassion, and mercy.

Hold a piece of rose quartz in your hands, as this crystal is associated with unconditional love and compassion. Feel its energy and imagine it infusing the deceased with these qualities.

Recite the following spell or create your own heartfelt words:

"By the power of divine grace and mercy,
I call upon the sacred forces above.
May [Name of the deceased] be transformed,
A vessel of love and compassion, pure and true.

Let their spirit be bathed in divine light,
Guided by grace through eternal night.
May mercy flow from their being so fair,
Touching all souls with love and care.

As they journey through the realms above,
May they embody compassion and divine love.
Grant them the gift of grace, shining bright,
A beacon of mercy in eternal light."

As you recite the spell, visualize the words becoming a glowing energy that envelops the deceased, permeating their being with grace and mercy.

Hold the rose quartz near the candle flame, allowing the warmth and light to cleanse and bless the crystal. Then place the crystal near a photo or memento of the deceased.

Sit quietly for a few moments, envisioning the transformation taking place and feeling a sense of peace and serenity.

Express gratitude for the divine blessings bestowed upon the deceased. Thank the spiritual forces and deities that you invoked for their presence and assistance.

Safely extinguish the candle, but keep the rose quartz near the memorial or sacred space as a symbol of the ongoing transformation and connection to divine grace and mercy.

This spell can be performed on behalf of a deceased loved one to invoke the transformative power of divine grace and mercy within them. It is a way to honor their memory and support their journey in the afterlife. Remember to perform this spell with sincerity, respect, and love.

111. Incantation to invoke the blessings of the celestial music and melodies

"Ode to the Celestial Melodies"

Hark! Oh, heavens, hear my plea,
From celestial realms, I summon thee.
Bring forth your music, pure and divine,
Let it resonate within this shrine.

I call upon the melodies of the stars,
Harmonies that reach afar.
Strings of celestial spheres, play your tune,
In this sacred space, let your notes commune.

With every note, let healing unfold,
A symphony of love, powerful and bold.
Let celestial rhythms soothe the soul,
Awakening spirits, making us whole.

Melodies of joy, melodies of peace,
Let all worries and sorrows cease.
In this sacred moment, we align,
With the celestial music, divine.

O celestial choir, sing with grace,
Your harmonies, let us embrace.
Through your melodies, let wisdom flow,
Enveloping us in a celestial glow.

By the power of music, ancient and true,
I invite the celestial blessings anew.
May the music of the heavens above,
Fill this space with beauty and love.

As I speak this incantation, let the vibrations of my voice carry my intention to the celestial realms. May the blessings of the celestial music and melodies infuse this space, bringing harmony, healing, and spiritual upliftment. So be it.

Remember to perform this incantation with reverence and focus, allowing the words to resonate within you. You may choose to play gentle, soothing music in the background to enhance the atmosphere and create a sacred space for the celestial blessings to manifest.

112.   Ritual for the transfiguration of the deceased into a divine protector of sacred spaces

Preparation:

Find a quiet and peaceful space where you can perform the ritual undisturbed.
Gather sacred items such as candles, incense, crystals, and symbols representing protection and sacredness.
Take a few moments to center yourself and set your intention for the ritual.

Ritual Steps:

Light the candles and the incense, creating a serene and sacred atmosphere.
Sit or stand in the center of the space and close your eyes. Take a few deep breaths to calm your mind and connect with the spiritual realm.
Visualize a radiant light surrounding you, filling you with divine energy and strength.
Hold the sacred items in your hands, infusing them with your intention for protection and sacredness.
Begin to walk slowly and purposefully around the space, carrying the sacred items with you.

As you walk, recite the following incantation:

"In this sacred space, I stand,
A guardian of divine command.
With love and light, I do protect,
All who enter, I shall detect.

I call upon the sacred powers,
To shield this space, hour by hour.
From negativity and harm, I ward,
A sanctuary of light, I guard.

With every step I take, I bless,
This sacred space, I now address.
Divine protection, I invoke,
Within these walls, harmony evoke.

May this space be safe and pure,
A haven for all who endure.
I am the guardian, strong and true,
Protector of this sacred venue."

Continue to walk around the space, repeating the incantation and visualizing the space being infused with a vibrant shield of divine protection.
When you feel that the energy has been established and the space is properly protected, return to the center.
Offer gratitude to the divine forces and energies that have assisted you in this ritual.
Close the ritual by extinguishing the candles and offering a final word of thanks.

Remember to approach this ritual with respect and reverence. You are invoking divine energies and declaring your commitment to protect and honor the sacredness of the space. With each repetition of the ritual, the energetic bond between you and the space will grow stronger, enhancing its protection and sanctity.

113.   Spell for the reunion of the deceased's soul with their beloved pets and animal companions

Note: This spell is intended to honor and facilitate the reunion of the deceased with their beloved pets and animal companions in the afterlife. It is important to perform this spell with love, respect, and pure intentions.

Preparation:

Find a quiet and peaceful space where you can perform the spell without interruptions.
Gather a picture or representation of the deceased's beloved pet or animal companion.
Place a candle, preferably white or light blue, in a safe holder.

Spell Steps:

Light the candle, focusing on the flame as a symbol of divine presence and guidance.
Take a few deep breaths, grounding yourself in the present moment.
Hold the picture or representation of the deceased's beloved pet or animal companion in your hands.
Close your eyes and visualize a radiant and loving light surrounding you.
Invoke the divine energies by saying the following words:
"By the power of love and the bonds we share,
I call upon the divine to be aware.
With reverence and respect, I make this plea,
To reunite the souls, forever free.

[Pet's Name], dear one, wherever you may be,
I summon you now, to come and join me.
In the realms of spirit, let us meet,
Reunited in love, forever complete.

Cross the bridge, my faithful friend,
Together again, our journey won't end.
Guide their spirit through the divine light,
To the place where souls reunite.

By the power of love, I send this call,
May our spirits unite, one and all.
With open hearts and arms held wide,
Together we'll reside, forever side by side."

Envision the deceased's beloved pet or animal companion being embraced by the loving light, crossing the bridge to the afterlife, and being reunited with the deceased's spirit.

Hold the image or representation of the beloved pet close to your heart, expressing your love and gratitude for the connection and memories shared.

Offer a few moments of silent reflection or personal prayers to honor the reunion and express any additional thoughts or emotions.

When you feel ready, extinguish the candle, thanking the divine energies for their presence and assistance.

Place the picture or representation of the beloved pet in a safe and sacred space, allowing it to serve as a reminder of the eternal bond between the deceased and their cherished companion.

It is important to remember that this spell is a heartfelt intention to facilitate the reunion of souls. The actual reunion and experiences in the afterlife are beyond our direct control but can be supported by our love, prayers, and positive energy. Trust in the divine wisdom and know that the bond between the deceased and their beloved pet will always be cherished and honored.

114.   Invocation of the goddess Neith for wisdom and skill in the afterlife

Note: This invocation is intended to call upon the goddess Neith, revered for her wisdom and skill, to guide and empower the deceased in the afterlife. Neith is known as the goddess of weaving, warfare, and wisdom. Perform this invocation with reverence, focus, and a sincere desire to receive Neith's guidance and blessings.

Preparation:

Find a quiet and sacred space where you can perform the invocation without distractions.
Create a small altar or sacred space with a representation of the goddess Neith, such as a statue, picture, or symbol.
Light a candle and place it on the altar as a symbol of divine presence and illumination.
Have a small offering, such as a flower or incense, to present to Neith.

Invocation Steps:

Begin by grounding yourself and centering your energy. Take a few deep breaths and relax your body and mind.
Light the candle on the altar, allowing its flame to illuminate the space.
Stand before the altar and focus your attention on the representation of Neith.
Speak or recite the following invocation with respect and heartfelt intention:

"Hail, mighty Neith, goddess of wisdom and skill,
We seek your guidance, as our spirits fulfill.
In the realm beyond, where the souls reside,
Grant us your wisdom, as our journey we stride.

Neith, we call upon you, with reverence and trust,
To bless the deceased, who now rest with the just.
Bestow upon them your divine insight and grace,
Illuminate their path in the afterlife's embrace.

Oh, Neith, weavers of destiny's thread,
Guide their souls with wisdom, so they may tread,
The realms unknown, with courage and might,
Unveiling the mysteries, in the eternal night.

Grant them your skill in navigating the way,
Empower their spirits, by night and by day.
May they embody your wisdom, shining bright,
In the realms of the afterlife's eternal light.

Goddess Neith, we honor and adore,
Your guidance we seek, now and forevermore.
Accept this offering, given with love and respect,
As we invoke your presence, may our souls connect."

Take a moment to offer the small offering, such as a flower or incense, to the representation of Neith, expressing your gratitude and reverence.
Close your eyes and visualize the divine presence of Neith surrounding you and the deceased, offering wisdom, skill, and guidance in their journey through the afterlife.
Spend a few moments in silent reflection, allowing Neith's energy and wisdom to permeate your being and the sacred space.
When you feel ready, express your gratitude to the goddess Neith for her presence and guidance.
Extinguish the candle, symbolizing the completion of the invocation.
Leave the representation of Neith on the altar as a focal point for future connection and reverence.

Remember to approach this invocation with sincerity and an open heart. Trust in the wisdom and guidance of the goddess Neith, knowing that her presence will support the deceased in their journey through the afterlife, providing them with wisdom, skill, and divine protection.

115.   Ritual of purification through the sacred chants of the eternal hymns

Note: This ritual is designed to cleanse and purify the spirit through the power of sacred chants and hymns. The eternal hymns are believed to carry divine vibrations that can uplift and purify the soul. Perform this ritual in a serene and sacred space, where you can immerse yourself in the power of sound and intention.

Preparation:

Find a quiet space where you can perform the ritual without interruptions.
Create an altar or sacred space with items that hold spiritual significance to you, such as candles, crystals, or symbols of divinity.
Choose a selection of sacred chants or hymns that resonate with you. These can be from any spiritual tradition or culture.
Have a small bowl of purified water and a cleansing herb, such as sage or palo santo, nearby.

Ritual Steps:

Begin by grounding yourself and entering a state of calm and receptivity. Take a few deep breaths and focus your attention on the present moment.
Light the candles on your altar, creating a sacred ambiance and inviting divine presence.
Take a moment to hold the bowl of purified water and the cleansing herb in your hands, infusing them with your intentions for purification.
Use the cleansing herb to create smoke by lighting it and allowing it to smolder. Pass the smoke over your body, starting from your feet and moving upward, envisioning any negativity or stagnant energy being released and dissolved.
Set the cleansing herb aside and take a few moments to reflect on your intention for purification. This could be releasing negative emotions, clearing energetic blockages, or seeking spiritual clarity.
Begin playing the chosen sacred chants or hymns. Allow the sound vibrations to fill the space and resonate within your being. Focus on the lyrics and the essence of the chants, allowing them to uplift and purify your spirit.
As you listen to the sacred chants, you may choose to join in by singing or chanting along. Allow your voice to merge with the music, expressing your intentions for purification and spiritual transformation.

As you chant or listen to the sacred hymns, visualize a radiant light surrounding and permeating your being. See this light as a purifying force, washing away any impurities or negativity within you.

If you feel guided, you can also incorporate movements or gestures that align with the energy of the chants. This can enhance the ritual and deepen your connection to the divine vibrations.

Continue with the sacred chants for as long as it feels appropriate. Trust your intuition and the guidance of your spirit.

After the chants have concluded, sit or stand in silence, allowing the vibrations to settle and integrate within you. Offer gratitude for the purification and the blessings received.

If you wish, you can conclude the ritual by sipping the purified water from the bowl, symbolizing the internal cleansing and renewal of your spirit.

Take a few moments to offer thanks to the divine and close the ritual in a way that feels meaningful to you. This can be a prayer, a simple gesture, or any act of gratitude and reverence.

Leave the altar or sacred space set up for future spiritual practices and contemplation.

Remember, the power of sound and intention is potent. By engaging in this ritual regularly, you can strengthen your connection to the divine, cleanse your spirit, and invite greater clarity and harmony into your life.

116.   Spell for the liberation of the deceased's soul from the cycle of suffering

Note: This spell is intended to help release the deceased's soul from the cycle of suffering and bring about liberation and peace. Perform this spell with a sincere and compassionate heart, focusing on the intention of freeing the soul from all forms of suffering.

Preparation:

Find a quiet and sacred space where you can perform the spell without interruptions. Create an altar or sacred space with items that hold spiritual significance to you, such as candles, crystals, or symbols of liberation.
Have a small bowl of purified water and a white feather nearby.

Spell Steps:

Begin by grounding yourself and entering a state of calm and compassion. Take a few deep breaths and center your awareness on the present moment.
Light the candles on your altar, creating a sacred ambiance and inviting divine presence.
Hold the small bowl of purified water in your hands and infuse it with your intention for the liberation of the deceased's soul from suffering. Visualize the water being filled with pure, healing energy.
Take the white feather and gently fan it over the bowl of water, allowing the feather's energy to blend with the water's essence.
Close your eyes and focus on the image or memory of the deceased. Feel a deep sense of empathy and compassion for their suffering.

Begin reciting the following incantation, speaking from your heart:

"By the power of compassion and love divine,
I call upon the forces that transcend time.
In the name of liberation, I set you free,
From the cycle of suffering, you shall be."

Visualize the deceased's soul surrounded by a radiant light, illuminating their path to liberation. See them being released from all forms of suffering, attachments, and pain.

Dip your fingers into the bowl of purified water and sprinkle a few drops over the image or memory of the deceased, symbolizing the cleansing and purification of their soul.

Offer a heartfelt prayer or intention for the deceased's soul, expressing your wishes for their liberation and peace. You can speak from your own words or use the following as a guide:

"May your soul find release, may suffering cease,
In the realm of peace, may you find eternal ease.
May your spirit soar, unburdened and free,
In the embrace of liberation, may you forever be."

Sit in silence for a few moments, holding space for the energy of liberation and peace to permeate the ritual space.

When you feel ready, express your gratitude to the divine and close the spell in a way that feels meaningful to you. This can be a prayer, a simple gesture, or any act of gratitude and reverence.

Allow the candles to burn out on their own or extinguish them safely, knowing that the energy of liberation and peace will continue to work beyond the ritual.

Remember, the intention and energy you bring to this spell are key. By performing it with love, compassion, and a sincere desire for the liberation of the deceased's soul, you contribute to their journey towards freedom from suffering.

117.   Incantation to awaken the dormant spiritual senses within the deceased's spirit

Note: This incantation is intended to help awaken the dormant spiritual senses within the deceased's spirit, allowing them to perceive and engage with the spiritual realm. Perform this incantation with reverence and focus, inviting the divine energies to activate the spiritual senses of the departed.

Preparation:

Find a quiet and sacred space where you can perform the incantation without interruptions.
Create an altar or sacred space with items that hold spiritual significance to you, such as candles, crystals, or symbols of spiritual awakening.
Have a small bowl of purified water and a bell or chime nearby.

Incantation Steps:

Begin by grounding yourself and entering a state of receptivity and openness. Take a few deep breaths and center your awareness on the present moment.
Light the candles on your altar, creating a sacred ambiance and inviting divine presence.
Hold the small bowl of purified water in your hands and infuse it with your intention to awaken the deceased's spiritual senses. Visualize the water becoming charged with vibrant energy.
Stand or sit comfortably and hold the bell or chime in front of you.
Close your eyes and connect with the energy of the deceased. Visualize their spirit awakening and becoming aware of the presence of the divine.
Gently ring the bell or chime three times, allowing the sound to reverberate through the space and resonate within the spirit of the deceased.

Recite the following incantation with clarity and conviction:

"By the power of the sacred sound and divine light,
I call upon the dormant senses to ignite.
Awaken the spirit, open the inner eye,
Perceive the unseen, let the senses fly."

Visualize the deceased's spirit being bathed in a radiant light, illuminating their spiritual senses and awakening their ability to perceive and interact with the spiritual realm.

Take a moment to silently or verbally invite the deceased to embrace their awakened spiritual senses. Speak from your heart, expressing your intentions for their spiritual growth and exploration.

Dip your fingers into the bowl of purified water and sprinkle a few drops over the image or memory of the deceased, symbolizing the purification and activation of their spiritual senses.

Sit in silence for a few moments, holding space for the energy of awakening and perception to settle within the ritual space.

When you feel ready, offer a prayer or intention for the deceased's spiritual journey, expressing your hopes for their continued awakening and spiritual expansion.

Thank the divine energies and the deceased for their presence and close the incantation in a way that feels appropriate to you. This can be a simple gesture, a moment of silence, or any act of gratitude and reverence.

Allow the candles to burn out on their own or extinguish them safely, knowing that the energy of awakened spiritual senses will continue to work beyond the incantation.

Remember, your sincere intention and the focused energy you bring to this incantation are crucial. By performing it with reverence and love, you contribute to the awakening of the deceased's spiritual senses, enabling them to navigate and explore the spiritual realm with clarity and perception.

118.   Ritual for the communion with the spirits of the celestial mountains and peaks

This ritual is designed to establish a connection with the spirits of the celestial mountains and peaks, drawing upon their wisdom, strength, and elevated energies. By performing this ritual, you can attune yourself to the higher vibrations of these sacred natural formations. Here is a step-by-step guide:

Preparation:

Choose a quiet and serene location where you can perform the ritual undisturbed. It could be outdoors near a mountain or peak, or indoors in a space where you feel connected to nature.
Gather materials that symbolize the energy of mountains, such as rocks, crystals, or images depicting mountain landscapes.
Have a journal or notebook and writing utensil nearby to record any insights or experiences during the ritual.
Dress comfortably and consider wearing earth tones or colors that resonate with mountain energy.

Ritual Steps:

Begin by grounding yourself. Take a few deep breaths, focusing on your connection with the Earth. Feel yourself rooted and centered.
Set up your sacred space with the materials you've gathered, arranging them in a way that represents the energy and beauty of mountains.
Light a candle or incense as a symbol of purification and creating a sacred atmosphere.
Close your eyes and visualize yourself standing at the foot of a majestic mountain or peak. Feel the vastness and power emanating from it. Imagine a bridge of light forming between you and the mountain, creating a connection.

Extend your arms in front of you, palms facing upward, and recite the following invocation or create one of your own:

"O mighty spirits of the celestial mountains and peaks,
I call upon your wisdom and strength, so unique.
Grant me your guidance, your elevated view,
As I seek communion and connection with you."

Take a few moments to meditate and quiet your mind. Focus on the energy of the mountain and allow yourself to be receptive to any messages or insights that may arise.

When you feel ready, open your eyes and begin to explore the items in your sacred space. Take each one in your hands and feel its texture, weight, and energy. Reflect on how it relates to the energy of mountains.

Choose one item that resonates strongly with you and hold it close to your heart. Allow its energy to merge with yours, symbolizing the connection you're establishing with the spirits of the mountains.

Sit quietly with your chosen item and listen to any guidance or messages that come to you. You may experience visualizations, emotions, or a deep sense of knowing.

If you feel inspired, write down your experiences, insights, or any guidance received in your journal.

Express gratitude to the spirits of the mountains for their presence and guidance. Thank them for the connection you've established.

Close the ritual in a way that feels authentic to you. This can be a simple gesture, prayer, or affirmation expressing your gratitude and sealing the energetic connection. If you lit a candle or incense, extinguish it safely, acknowledging that the connection with the spirits of the mountains will continue beyond the physical ritual.

Remember, the purpose of this ritual is to establish a communion and connection with the spirits of the celestial mountains and peaks. Approach it with reverence, respect, and an open heart. Through this ritual, you can tap into the wisdom and strength of these natural formations, gaining insights and guidance for your spiritual journey.

119.   Spell for the transmigration of the deceased's soul into the realm of eternal light and truth

This spell is intended to assist the deceased's soul in transitioning into the realm of eternal light and truth, where it can find enlightenment, peace, and divine understanding. By performing this spell, you can invoke the energies of light and truth to guide the soul's journey. Here is a spell you can use:

You will need:

A white candle
A small mirror
A clear quartz crystal
A piece of paper
A pen or marker
Instructions:

Find a quiet and sacred space where you can perform the spell without interruptions. Light the white candle and place it in front of you.
Take a moment to center yourself and focus on your intention to assist the deceased's soul in finding its way to the realm of eternal light and truth.
Hold the mirror in your hands and gaze into it, visualizing a radiant and pure light emanating from it. Feel the energy of divine truth and enlightenment.
Place the mirror next to the candle, allowing the reflection of the flame to merge with the energy of the mirror.

Hold the clear quartz crystal in your hand and speak the following incantation:

"By the light that shines so bright,
I call upon the realm of eternal light.
Guide the soul with truth and grace,
To find its eternal resting place."

Place the crystal next to the mirror and candle, aligning it with the energy of light and truth.
Take the piece of paper and write the name of the deceased or a message of love and guidance for their journey. Visualize their soul being enveloped in the light of truth as you write.

Fold the paper and hold it in your hands, infusing it with your intentions and love.

Speak the following affirmation:

"I release your soul to the realm of light,
May truth and love guide your flight.
May you find peace and understanding deep,
In the realm of eternal light, you shall keep."

Place the folded paper in front of the candle and allow it to be illuminated by the flame.
Sit in silence and envision the deceased's soul being surrounded by a beautiful, radiant light, as it is guided towards the realm of eternal light and truth.
Express gratitude to the divine forces, the deceased, and any spiritual guides or guardians who may be assisting in this journey.
Allow the candle to burn out completely, symbolizing the completion of the spell.

Note: This spell is intended as a supportive and symbolic ritual to assist the deceased's soul in its transition. It is important to remember that the journey of the soul is unique and personal. This spell should be performed with respect, love, and an understanding that ultimately, the soul's destiny rests in divine hands.

Please ensure that you conduct this spell with the utmost reverence and intention, honoring the memory and spiritual journey of the deceased.

120.　Ritual of anointing with sacred crystals for spiritual clarity and insight

To perform a ritual of anointing with sacred crystals for spiritual clarity and insight, follow these steps:

Preparation:

Choose a quiet and sacred space where you can perform the ritual undisturbed. Gather the following items: a selection of sacred crystals that resonate with you and your intentions for clarity and insight, a small dish or cloth to hold the crystals, and a clear and focused mind.

Cleansing and Clearing:

Begin by cleansing and clearing your sacred space. You can use methods such as smudging with sage or palo santo, lighting incense, or using sound tools like bells or singing bowls. This will help remove any negative or stagnant energies.

Intention Setting:

Sit in a comfortable position and take a few deep breaths to center yourself. Set your intention for the ritual, focusing on clarity and insight in your spiritual journey. Visualize yourself surrounded by a pure and radiant light.

Crystal Selection:

Take a moment to connect with your collection of sacred crystals. Allow your intuition to guide you in selecting the crystals that resonate with your intention. Some crystals that are known for enhancing clarity and insight include Clear Quartz, Amethyst, Selenite, Labradorite, and Lapis Lazuli. Choose the ones that speak to you the most.

Anointing:

Take each crystal, one by one, and hold it in your hand. Close your eyes and visualize the crystal's energy merging with your own. Feel its vibrations and the clarity it brings to your mind and spirit.
With a gentle and deliberate motion, rub the crystal against your forehead, also known as the third eye area. As you do this, repeat a personal affirmation or mantra

that aligns with your intention. For example, you can say, "I am open to receiving divine clarity and insight."

Continue this process with each crystal you have chosen, focusing on your intention and allowing the energy of the crystals to merge with your own.

Gratitude and Closure:

Once you have anointed each crystal, take a moment to express gratitude for the guidance and wisdom they will bring to your spiritual journey. Offer thanks to the crystals themselves, the divine energies they represent, and any spiritual guides or higher powers you connect with.

Place the anointed crystals in a special and safe place, such as an altar or a sacred box, where you can return to them whenever you need clarity and insight.

Remember, this ritual is a personal and sacred practice. Feel free to modify it to suit your preferences and spiritual beliefs. The key is to approach it with reverence, intention, and an open heart.

121.   Spell for the transformation of the deceased into a vessel of divine transformation

To perform a spell for the transformation of the deceased into a vessel of divine transformation, follow these steps:

Preparation:

Choose a serene and sacred space where you can perform the spell without interruptions.
Gather the following items: a white candle, a small dish of salt, a clear quartz crystal, and a photo or representation of the deceased.
Cleansing and Purification:

Begin by purifying the space. Light the white candle and sprinkle a pinch of salt around the area, moving in a clockwise direction. This helps cleanse the space of any negative energies.

Invocation:

Sit in a comfortable position in front of the candle. Take a few deep breaths to center yourself and enter a focused state of mind.
Hold the clear quartz crystal in your hands, close your eyes, and visualize a radiant white light surrounding you. Imagine this light expanding and enveloping the entire space.

Connection with the Deceased:

Hold the photo or representation of the deceased in your hands. Gently close your eyes and take a moment to connect with their energy and presence.
Speak aloud or in your mind, addressing the deceased by name. Express your intentions for their transformation into a vessel of divine transformation. You can say something like, "I call upon [Name of the deceased]. May your spirit be transformed into a vessel of divine transformation, embracing the wisdom and power of the divine."

Charging the Crystal:

Place the clear quartz crystal in front of the candle, allowing it to absorb the candle's flame and energy. Visualize the crystal radiating with a bright light, symbolizing the divine transformation the deceased will undergo.

Affirmations:

Repeat affirmations or statements that reflect the desired transformation. For example, you can say, **"Through divine grace, [Name of the deceased] is transformed into a vessel of profound change and spiritual growth. May their spirit ascend to higher realms and embrace their true divine potential."**

Closing:

Take a few moments to express gratitude for the deceased and their journey of transformation. Thank them for the lessons they have learned and the light they will continue to shine.

Allow the candle to burn down completely or extinguish it safely, signaling the completion of the spell.

Remember, this spell is a personal and sacred practice. You can adapt it to fit your beliefs and preferences. The most important aspect is to approach it with reverence and an open heart, honoring the journey of the deceased and their potential for divine transformation.

122. Ritual for the transfiguration of the deceased into a divine guardian of sacred wisdom

Items needed:

A quiet and sacred space
A candle
Incense (preferably frankincense or sage)
A small bowl of water
A symbol of wisdom (such as an owl figurine or a written affirmation)
Optional: any personal items or mementos associated with the deceased

Steps:

Find a quiet and sacred space where you can perform the ritual undisturbed.

Light the candle and the incense, placing them in front of you. These represent the presence of divine light and purification.

Take a moment to center yourself and connect with your intention of transfiguring the deceased into a divine guardian of sacred wisdom.

Hold the small bowl of water in your hands and imagine it being filled with divine wisdom and knowledge. Visualize the water shimmering with a radiant light.

Gently dip your fingers into the bowl of water and sprinkle a few drops over the symbol of wisdom, infusing it with the essence of the divine.

If you have any personal items or mementos associated with the deceased, you can also sprinkle a few drops of the water over them, symbolizing the transfer of wisdom and connection.

Take a few deep breaths and speak the following affirmation:

"By the power of sacred wisdom,
I invoke the transfiguration of [name of the deceased].
May their spirit be transformed into a guardian of divine knowledge,
A beacon of wisdom and insight.

May they guide and protect those who seek truth and enlightenment.
May their presence be felt in the realm of sacred wisdom.
So mote it be."

Sit in silent meditation for a few minutes, allowing the energy of the ritual to settle and integrate. Visualize the deceased being transformed into a radiant guardian of wisdom, radiating light and offering guidance to those in need.

When you feel ready, extinguish the candle and let the incense burn out naturally. Keep the symbol of wisdom in a special place as a reminder of the transfiguration ritual and the connection with the deceased as a guardian of sacred wisdom.

123.   Spell for the reunion of the deceased's soul with their spiritual lineage

Items needed:

A quiet and sacred space
A white candle
A small mirror
A symbol representing the deceased's spiritual lineage (e.g., a family heirloom, a photo, or a written affirmation)
Optional: any personal items or mementos associated with the deceased's spiritual lineage

Steps:

Find a quiet and sacred space where you can perform the spell without interruption.

Light the white candle, placing it in front of you. This candle symbolizes purity and illumination.

Place the small mirror in front of the candle, reflecting its light and energy.

Take a moment to center yourself and connect with your intention of reuniting the deceased's soul with their spiritual lineage.

Hold the symbol representing the deceased's spiritual lineage in your hands, and if you have any personal items or mementos associated with their lineage, hold them as well. Feel the energy and connection to their lineage flowing through these objects.

Gaze into the mirror, allowing its reflective surface to symbolize the bridge between the realms. Visualize the deceased's soul standing before you, bathed in the gentle light of the candle and mirror.

Speak the following affirmation or create your own, directing your words to the deceased's soul:

"By the power of love and divine connection,
I call upon the spirits of [deceased's spiritual lineage].
May the soul of [deceased's name] be guided and reunited
With the ancestors and spiritual lineage of their past.

May the bond between them be strengthened and restored,
And may their collective wisdom and support be felt.
As above, so below. So mote it be."

Hold the symbol of their spiritual lineage close to your heart, imagining the energy of the deceased's soul merging with the energy of their ancestors. Feel the love and connection flowing between them.

Take a few moments to sit in silence, allowing the energy to settle and the connection to strengthen.

When you feel ready, extinguish the candle, acknowledging the completion of the spell. Keep the symbol of their spiritual lineage in a special place or wear it as a reminder of the reunion and connection between the deceased's soul and their spiritual lineage.

Note: This spell is intended as a symbolic and personal ritual. Adjust the steps and language according to your beliefs and intentions. You can incorporate additional elements or practices that hold significance for you and the deceased's spiritual lineage. Trust your intuition and follow your heart in creating a meaningful and heartfelt reunion.

124. Ritual of purification through the sacred dances of the eternal rhythm

Prepare a sacred space where you can perform the ritual undisturbed. Light candles or incense to create a serene atmosphere. Wear comfortable clothing that allows freedom of movement.

Begin by grounding yourself and centering your energy. Take deep breaths, allowing any tension or distractions to fade away.

Stand in the center of the sacred space, feeling the connection between your feet and the earth. Close your eyes and visualize a circle of radiant light surrounding you.

Start moving your body to the rhythm of the eternal music that flows within you. Let the music guide your movements, allowing your body to express itself freely. Feel the energy flowing through your limbs, awakening your spirit.

As you dance, imagine that with each movement, you are shedding away any negative energies or impurities that may have attached themselves to your being. Visualize these energies being released and dissipated into the surrounding space, leaving you purified and cleansed.

Let your dance become a prayer of purification, a sacred offering to the divine. Allow your body to flow with grace and intention, surrendering to the rhythm and energy that moves through you.

With each step, spin, and gesture, envision yourself being cleansed, purified, and renewed. Feel the lightness and clarity washing over you, as if you are being bathed in the purest of waters.

Continue the dance for as long as it feels right, letting the energy build and intensify. Allow yourself to be fully present in the moment, surrendering to the transformative power of the dance.

When you feel complete, gradually slow down your movements and come to a stillness. Stand with your feet planted firmly on the ground, feeling the energy settling within you.

Take a few deep breaths, acknowledging the purification and renewal that has taken place. Express gratitude to the divine and to yourself for engaging in this sacred ritual.

Finally, offer a closing prayer or affirmation, expressing your intention to carry the purified energy with you into your daily life.

Remember, the sacred dances of the eternal rhythm can be performed whenever you feel the need for purification and renewal. Allow the music and movement to guide you, and let the dance be a sacred expression of your connection with the divine.

125.   Spell for the liberation of the deceased's soul from the illusions of the material world

Note: This spell is intended for ritual purposes and should be performed with respect and reverence.

You will need:

A quiet and sacred space
A black candle
A white candle
A piece of paper and a pen
A small cauldron or fire-safe container
Begin by creating a sacred space where you can perform the spell undisturbed. Clear the area and set up your candles in a safe place. Place the black candle on the left and the white candle on the right.

Sit quietly and take a few deep breaths to center yourself. Close your eyes and visualize the deceased's soul surrounded by a golden light, free from the illusions of the material world.

Light the black candle, representing the illusions and attachments of the material world. As you light the candle, say:

"I call upon the divine forces to reveal the truth,
Release the deceased from the illusions that bind.
May their soul be liberated, free to soar and find
The eternal essence that transcends space and time."

Take the piece of paper and the pen, and write down any specific illusions or attachments that you wish to release on behalf of the deceased. Be specific and concise in your words.

Fold the paper carefully and hold it between your hands. Visualize the illusions and attachments represented on the paper, and imagine them dissolving into nothingness.

Light the white candle, representing purity and spiritual liberation. Hold the folded paper over the flame, allowing it to catch fire. Safely place the burning paper into the cauldron or fire-safe container.

As the paper burns, visualize the release of the illusions and attachments. See the deceased's soul being liberated and rising above the constraints of the material world, embracing their true essence.

Say the following affirmation:

"I release you from the illusions that bind,
May your soul find freedom, peace of mind.
Transcend the earthly attachments, rise above,
Embrace the eternal truth, boundless love."

Sit in quiet contemplation for a few moments, feeling the energy of liberation and release filling the space.

When you feel ready, extinguish the candles, starting with the black candle to symbolize the fading of illusions. Express gratitude to the divine and to the deceased for their journey and the opportunity to assist in their liberation.

Remember to honor the privacy and consent of the deceased and their loved ones when performing this spell. Approach the ritual with sensitivity and respect, focusing on the highest good for all involved.

126.   Incantation to awaken the dormant spiritual powers within the deceased's spirit

Note: This incantation is intended for ritual purposes and should be performed with respect and reverence.

You may recite the following incantation while visualizing the deceased's spirit being infused with divine energy and awakening their dormant spiritual powers:

"By the power of the eternal flame,
I call upon the ancient names.
Awaken, spirit, from slumber deep,
Rise now, from your eternal sleep.

From realms beyond the mortal plane,
I summon forth your power, unchained.
With every word, with every breath,
Awaken now, embrace life's breadth.

Ignite the fire within your soul,
Let your spiritual powers take control.
From the depths of time, they emerge,
Awakening gifts, ancient and pure.

Awaken now, O spirit divine,
Unveil the treasures that are thine.
Unlock the doors to cosmic sight,
Illuminate with your radiant light.

By the grace of the sacred source,
May your spirit soar, guided by course.
Awaken, awaken, oh dormant power,
Unleash your gifts, this very hour.

So mote it be."

Visualize the deceased's spirit being filled with vibrant energy, awakening their dormant spiritual powers and embracing their true essence. Feel the presence of divine guidance and support surrounding the spirit as they embark on a journey of spiritual awakening.

Remember to approach this incantation with sincerity and reverence, holding the intention for the highest good of the deceased's spirit.

127. Ritual for the communion with the spirits of the celestial stars and constellations

Note: This ritual is meant to establish a connection with the spirits of the celestial stars and constellations. Perform it with reverence and a sincere intention to commune with these higher realms.

Materials Needed:

A quiet and open space, preferably outdoors under a clear sky
Candle(s) or lantern(s)
Incense (such as frankincense or sandalwood)
Paper and pen
Optional: Telescope or stargazing equipment
Instructions:

Choose a night with clear skies for your ritual. Find a peaceful and quiet space where you can have an unobstructed view of the stars and constellations above.

Prepare your ritual space by lighting the candle(s) or lantern(s). Place them around the area to create a sacred ambiance.

Light the incense and let its fragrant smoke fill the air, purifying the space and preparing it for spiritual communion.

Take a moment to ground yourself and center your energy. Close your eyes, take deep breaths, and connect with the present moment.

Open your eyes and gaze at the vast expanse of the starry sky above you. Allow yourself to be immersed in the beauty and wonder of the celestial realm.

Take the paper and pen and write down any questions or intentions you have for the spirits of the stars and constellations. This can include seeking guidance, wisdom, or simply a desire to connect and understand the cosmic forces at play.

Speak your intentions aloud, addressing the spirits of the stars and constellations. Express your reverence and willingness to receive their wisdom and guidance.

Spend some time in silent meditation, allowing yourself to be receptive to any messages or insights that may come to you. Be open to signs, symbols, or feelings that may arise during this communion.

If you have a telescope or stargazing equipment, you can use it to observe specific stars or constellations that hold significance to you. Take your time to appreciate their beauty and contemplate their cosmic energy.

When you feel ready, express your gratitude to the spirits of the stars and constellations for their presence and wisdom. Thank them for the insights received and for any guidance they may continue to provide.

Extinguish the candle(s) or lantern(s) and let the incense burn out naturally, symbolizing the completion of the ritual.

Take a moment to ground yourself once again, feeling connected to both the earthly and celestial realms. Reflect on the experience and consider journaling any messages or insights you received during the ritual.

Remember, this ritual is a sacred act of connection with the celestial realm. Approach it with reverence, an open heart, and a willingness to receive the wisdom and guidance that the spirits of the stars and constellations may offer.

128.   Spell for the transmigration of the deceased's soul into the realm of eternal love and unity

Note: This spell is intended to assist the soul of the deceased in transitioning into a realm of eternal love and unity. Perform this spell with utmost respect and sincerity, honoring the departed soul's journey.

Materials Needed:

A quiet and sacred space
A white candle
An image or representation of the deceased (such as a photograph or personal item)
Fresh flowers
A small bowl of water
Optional: Incense (such as rose or lavender)
Instructions:

Find a peaceful and sacred space where you can perform the spell without interruptions. It could be indoors or outdoors, as long as you feel a sense of tranquility and connection.

Set up a small altar or space dedicated to the deceased. Place the white candle in the center and light it, symbolizing the presence of divine light and love.

Arrange the image or representation of the deceased in front of the candle. Surround it with fresh flowers, symbolizing purity, beauty, and life.

If using incense, light it and let its smoke fill the air, creating a sacred atmosphere and inviting the presence of spiritual energies.

Take a moment to center yourself and connect with the intention of facilitating the transmigration of the deceased's soul into the realm of eternal love and unity.

Gently hold the small bowl of water and focus your attention on it. Visualize the water as a purifying and transformative agent, capable of carrying the soul into a realm of infinite love and unity.

Speak the following incantation, or create your own heartfelt words:

"Soul of the departed, now set free,
Into the realm of love and unity.
I invoke the power of eternal light,
To guide your journey through day and night.
May love surround you, now and forever,
Embracing you in its divine endeavor."

As you recite the incantation, imagine the love and unity of the divine enveloping the deceased's soul, providing a sense of comfort, peace, and belonging.

Lower the small bowl of water towards the image or representation of the deceased, as if offering it as a vessel for the soul's transmigration. Allow a few drops of water to fall onto the image or representation, symbolizing the soul's journey into eternal love and unity.

Take a moment to sit in silence, allowing the energy of the spell to settle and permeate the space. You may offer additional prayers or intentions, expressing your love and support for the departed soul.

When you feel ready, express your gratitude to the divine and the spirits for their presence and assistance in this spell. Thank them for their love, guidance, and protection.

Allow the candle to burn out naturally or extinguish it with gratitude. Leave the flowers as an offering on the altar, letting them wither and return to the earth as a symbol of the cycle of life.

Remember, this spell is a sacred act of love and support for the deceased. Perform it with sincerity, reverence, and an open heart. Trust in the power of love and unity to guide the soul into a realm of eternal peace and harmony.

129.   Invocation of the god Amun-Ra for divine protection and guidance in the afterlife

Note: This invocation is intended to seek the protection and guidance of the powerful deity Amun-Ra in the afterlife. Perform this invocation with reverence, sincerity, and respect for the ancient Egyptian tradition.

Instructions:

Find a quiet and sacred space where you can perform the invocation without interruptions. Ensure you have a suitable altar or space dedicated to Amun-Ra. You may choose to have an image or statue of Amun-Ra as a focal point.

Light a candle or incense as an offering to Amun-Ra. The flame or smoke symbolizes the presence of divine light and energy.

Take a few deep breaths to center yourself and create a connection with the divine. Allow any distractions or worries to fade away as you focus on the intention of seeking Amun-Ra's protection and guidance.

Stand before the altar or sit in a comfortable position. Place your hands on your heart and close your eyes. Visualize a radiant golden light surrounding you, filling you with warmth and strength.

Begin the invocation by addressing Amun-Ra with respect and reverence:

"Oh mighty Amun-Ra, the great and powerful,
I call upon you in this sacred hour.
Lord of the heavens and the eternal sun,
Guide and protect me as my journey is begun."

State your intention clearly and humbly. You may use the following or modify it to suit your specific needs:

"Amun-Ra, I seek your divine protection,
In the afterlife's vast and mysterious reflection.
Guard me with your mighty wings unfurled,
As I navigate this spiritual world."

Express your gratitude and admiration for Amun-Ra, acknowledging his wisdom, strength, and guidance:

"I honor your wisdom, Amun-Ra, divine and true,
Your strength and guidance I humbly pursue.
Thank you for your eternal love and light,
Illuminating my path with your celestial might."

Take a moment to sit in silence, allowing the energy of the invocation to resonate within you. Feel the presence of Amun-Ra surrounding you, offering protection and guidance.

When you feel ready, offer any additional prayers, thoughts, or intentions to Amun-Ra. Seek his continued presence and assistance in your spiritual journey.

Conclude the invocation with gratitude and respect:

"I offer this candle/incense as a symbol of my devotion,
To Amun-Ra, the source of eternal motion.
Thank you, Amun-Ra, for your divine grace,
May your protection guide me in this sacred space."

Allow the candle or incense to burn out naturally or extinguish it with gratitude. Leave the altar as a dedicated space for future connection with Amun-Ra. Remember, when invoking Amun-Ra, approach with reverence, sincerity, and an open heart. Trust in his divine protection and guidance as you navigate the afterlife, and express gratitude for his presence in your spiritual journey.

130.   Ritual of anointing with sacred incense for spiritual elevation and connection

Note: This ritual is designed to elevate your spiritual connection and create a sacred atmosphere using the power of sacred incense. Ensure that you have a safe and well-ventilated space to perform this ritual.

Materials needed:

High-quality sacred incense (such as frankincense, myrrh, sage, or palo santo)
Incense burner or heat-resistant dish
Matches or a lighter
A small bowl of salt or sand
Optional: A feather or fan for dispersing the smoke
Instructions:

Choose a quiet and undisturbed space where you can perform the ritual. Clear the space of any clutter and ensure you have a comfortable place to sit or stand.

Prepare your sacred incense by selecting the type that resonates with your spiritual practice or intention. Take a moment to hold the incense in your hands and set your intention for the ritual. Visualize the smoke carrying your prayers and intentions to the spiritual realm.

Light the incense using a match or lighter, allowing the flame to engulf the tip of the incense stick or resin. Blow out the flame gently, allowing the incense to smolder and release fragrant smoke.

Place the lit incense in the incense burner or heat-resistant dish, ensuring it is stable and secure. If using loose resin, sprinkle a small amount onto the burning charcoal or heat source.

Take a few deep breaths to center yourself and prepare for the ritual. Allow your mind to settle, and let go of any distractions or worries.

Hold your hands over the smoke of the burning incense, palms facing upward. As the smoke rises, visualize it cleansing and purifying your energy, bringing you into a state of heightened awareness and connection.

If desired, use a feather or fan to gently waft the smoke towards yourself, enveloping your body and aura in the sacred fragrance. As you do this, imagine the smoke permeating every cell of your being, creating a sacred space within and around you.

As the incense continues to burn, offer your prayers, intentions, or affirmations. You can speak them aloud or silently in your mind. Feel the words being carried by the rising smoke, connecting you to the divine and opening channels of communication.

Spend as much time as you desire in this sacred space, allowing the incense to elevate your spiritual connection. You can meditate, reflect, journal, or engage in any other spiritual practice that resonates with you.

When you feel ready to conclude the ritual, express gratitude for the experience and the energy of the sacred incense. Thank the spiritual forces or deities you invoked for their presence and guidance.

Safely extinguish the incense by gently pressing the burning end into the bowl of salt or sand until the smoke ceases. Allow the incense burner or dish to cool before handling it.

Take a moment to ground yourself by connecting with the earth. You can stand barefoot on the ground, place your hands on the earth, or visualize roots extending from your body and grounding you firmly.

Remember, the ritual of anointing with sacred incense is a powerful way to enhance your spiritual practice and deepen your connection with the divine. Allow yourself to fully immerse in the experience, trusting that the sacred smoke is elevating your spiritual vibration and facilitating a stronger connection to the spiritual realm.

131.   Incantation to invoke the blessings of the celestial birds and their songs

(You can recite this incantation while visualizing the beauty and grace of celestial birds, and their songs resonating through the heavens.)

Aves eximiae, volatiles divinae,
Celestialis pinnis aureis ornatae,
Ad me venite, ales celestes,
Vestris cantibus divinis benedictionem afferentes.

O pulchrae avium, spirantes harmoniam,
Vestrae cantiones aetheris resonant,
Ad me venite, per caeli lucem,
Liberate me in canticis vestris.

Melodiae vestrae faciant cor meum elevatum,
Per auras vitales me transportant,
O aves coeli, per astra volantes,
Benedictiones vestras mihi tribuite.

Sicut alarum vobis pinnarum,
Ales sacrae, spiritum meum suscitat,
Per vestrum canticum, ad divinam connexum,
Celestialis spiritus me pervadit.

Vos, aves astrales, divinum significate,
Per vobis aethereis et sonis vocis,
Ad me venite, donum afferentes,
De celo descendentem in gratia.

Coniunctio divina per cantus vestros fiat,
Inter mundanum et caeleste reconciliatio sit,
O aves celestiales, per auras volantes,
Vobis tribuo honorem et devotum servitium.

Sic fiat, sic fiat, sic fiat!

Translation:

Exquisite birds, celestial creatures,
Adorned with golden wings,
Come to me, celestial birds,
Bringing divine blessings with your songs.

O beautiful birds, breathing harmony,
Your songs resonate through the heavens,
Come to me, through the light of the sky,
Liberate me with your divine melodies.

May your melodies lift my heart,
Transport me through vital airs,
O birds of the sky, flying through the stars,
Bestow your blessings upon me.

Like the wings of your feathers,
Sacred bird, arouse my spirit,
Through your song, connect me to the divine,
Let the celestial spirit permeate me.

You, astral birds, signify the divine,
Through your ethereal wings and voices,
Come to me, bringing a gift,
Descending from heaven in grace.

Let the divine union be realized through your songs,
May reconciliation between the earthly and celestial occur,
O celestial birds, flying through the airs,
I offer you honor and devout service.

So be it, so be it, so be it!

132.   Ritual for the transfiguration of the deceased into a divine guide of sacred paths

(Perform this ritual in a quiet and sacred space. You will need candles, incense, a representation of the deceased, and any other objects or symbols that hold significance.)

Preparation:

Set up the sacred space with candles and incense.
Place the representation of the deceased in the center.
Take a few deep breaths to center yourself and enter a calm state of mind.
Invocation:

Light the candles and incense, symbolizing the presence of divine energy.
Close your eyes and visualize a gentle light surrounding you and the representation of the deceased.
Begin the invocation by calling upon the divine forces and ancestors:
"Divine spirits and sacred ancestors,
I call upon you with reverence and respect.
Gather around us and lend your guidance and wisdom.
Hear my plea and assist in the transfiguration of [Name of the deceased]."

Reflection and Intent:

Reflect on the qualities and attributes that you wish the deceased to embody as a divine guide of sacred paths.
Focus on their wisdom, compassion, strength, and the ability to guide others on their spiritual journeys.
Hold the intention of the deceased's transfiguration into a divine guide.

Affirmation and Prayer:

Open your eyes and address the representation of the deceased directly.
Speak the following affirmation, imbued with your sincere intention and love:
"Beloved [Name of the deceased],
In this sacred moment, I honor your spirit.
I invoke the divine transformation within you,
That you may become a guide of sacred paths,
Leading others with wisdom, compassion, and grace.

May you embrace your divine purpose and fulfill it with love.
Guide those who seek your assistance on their spiritual journeys.
I affirm your transfiguration and the divine light within you."

Offering and Blessing:

Offer a heartfelt message or prayer to the deceased, expressing your gratitude and love.
You may also choose to place an object or symbol representing their new role as a divine guide near the representation.
Send your blessings and well-wishes to the deceased, knowing that they will continue to serve a higher purpose.

Closing:

Thank the divine spirits and ancestors for their presence and guidance.
Extinguish the candles and let the incense burn out naturally.
Take a moment to ground yourself, breathe deeply, and return to a calm state.
Remember that rituals are deeply personal and can be adapted to your beliefs and practices. The intention, love, and respect with which you perform the ritual are essential.

133.   Spell for the reunion of the deceased's soul with their spiritual teachers and mentors

(Perform this spell in a peaceful and sacred space. You will need candles, a representation of the deceased, and any objects or symbols that remind you of their spiritual teachers and mentors.)

Preparation:

Set up the sacred space with candles, ensuring a calm and peaceful atmosphere.
Place the representation of the deceased in the center.
Gather objects or symbols that represent their spiritual teachers and mentors.
Invocation:

Light the candles, symbolizing the presence of divine light and guidance.
Close your eyes and take a few deep breaths to center yourself.
Visualize a warm and loving light surrounding you and the representation of the deceased.
Begin the invocation by calling upon the spiritual teachers and mentors:
"Divine guides and mentors, wise and loving souls,
I call upon you with reverence and gratitude.
Gather around us and aid in the reunion of [Name of the deceased].
Hear my plea and assist in their journey of reunion and enlightenment."

Reflection and Intent:

Reflect on the profound impact and guidance the spiritual teachers and mentors had on the deceased during their lifetime.
Focus on the lessons learned, the wisdom imparted, and the love shared between them.
Hold the intention of facilitating the reunion of the deceased's soul with their beloved spiritual teachers and mentors.
Affirmation and Prayer:

Open your eyes and address the representation of the deceased directly.
Speak the following affirmation, infused with your sincerity and love:
"Beloved [Name of the deceased],
I invoke the reunion of your soul with your spiritual teachers and mentors,

Those who guided you with wisdom, compassion, and grace.
May the divine light of their presence surround and guide you,
As you continue your journey of growth and enlightenment.
I affirm your reunion and the deep connection between your souls."

Offering and Blessing:

Offer a heartfelt message or prayer to the deceased's spiritual teachers and mentors, expressing gratitude for their guidance.
Place the objects or symbols representing their spiritual teachers and mentors near the representation of the deceased.
Send your blessings and well-wishes to the deceased, knowing that their reunion will bring them comfort and wisdom.
Closing:

Express your gratitude to the spiritual guides and mentors for their presence and support.
Allow the candles to burn out naturally or extinguish them with gratitude.
Take a moment to ground yourself, breathe deeply, and release any residual energy.
Remember, this spell is a personal and heartfelt expression. Adapt it to align with your own beliefs and practices. The key is to infuse it with genuine love, gratitude, and reverence.

134. Invocation of the goddess Bastet for joy and protection in the afterlife

(Perform this invocation in a quiet and sacred space. You may have an altar with an image or representation of the Goddess Bastet, as well as offerings such as flowers, incense, or candles.)

Preparation:

Create a peaceful and sacred space where you can focus your energy and connect with the divine.
Set up your altar with the representation of the Goddess Bastet and any offerings you have chosen.
Grounding and Centering:

Take a few deep breaths to center yourself and clear your mind.
Feel your connection to the Earth beneath you, grounding yourself in its stability and strength.
Opening Invocation:

Begin by lighting the candles or incense on your altar, symbolizing the presence of the divine.
Close your eyes and visualize a warm and gentle light surrounding you, inviting the presence of the Goddess Bastet.
"Great Goddess Bastet, feline deity of joy and protection,
I call upon you with reverence and love.
Enter this sacred space and grace me with your presence.
Guide me on this journey to connect with you in the afterlife.
I seek your joy and protection, O Divine Bastet."

Connection and Communication:

Open your heart and mind to the presence of the Goddess Bastet.
Speak from your heart and express your intentions, desires, and gratitude.
"Goddess Bastet, hear my voice and know my soul.
I seek your joy in the afterlife, that which brings lightness to the spirit.
Protect me and guide me through the challenges that lie ahead.
Surround me with your loving energy and shield me from harm.
I am grateful for your presence and the blessings you bestow upon me."

Offering and Devotion:

Present your offerings to the Goddess Bastet, whether they be flowers, incense, or any other symbolic gifts.
Express your gratitude for her guidance and protection in the afterlife.
"Goddess Bastet, I offer these gifts to honor your divine essence.
May they be a reflection of my devotion and gratitude.
I thank you for your joy and protection, which I humbly receive."

Closing:

Take a moment to bask in the energy and presence of the Goddess Bastet.
Offer a final prayer or expression of gratitude.
"Goddess Bastet, I honor you and bid you farewell for now.
May your joy and protection be with me always.
I carry your blessings in my heart and soul.
Thank you, O Divine Bastet, for your presence and love."

Grounding and Integration:

Take a few deep breaths and visualize yourself firmly rooted to the Earth.
Feel the energy of the sacred space grounding and integrating within you.
When you are ready, slowly open your eyes and return to the present moment.
Remember, this invocation is a personal and heartfelt connection with the Goddess Bastet. Feel free to adapt it to your own beliefs and practices, and always approach it with respect, sincerity, and love.

135. Ritual of purification through the sacred symbols of the eternal hieroglyphs

(Perform this ritual in a quiet and sacred space. You may have an altar with representations or images of the ancient Egyptian hieroglyphs, or you can draw or print out copies of the hieroglyphs to work with.)

Preparation:

Create a peaceful and sacred space where you can focus your energy and connect with the divine.
Set up your altar with the representations or images of the ancient Egyptian hieroglyphs.
Grounding and Centering:

Take a few deep breaths to center yourself and clear your mind.
Feel your connection to the Earth beneath you, grounding yourself in its stability and strength.
Opening Invocation:

Light candles or incense on your altar, symbolizing the presence of the divine.
Close your eyes and visualize a soft and glowing light surrounding you, inviting the energy of the ancient Egyptian hieroglyphs.
"Oh, ancient symbols of the eternal hieroglyphs,
I call upon your power and wisdom.
Enter this sacred space and cleanse me with your sacred essence.
Guide me on this journey of purification and renewal.
I honor your presence and seek your guidance."

Selection of Hieroglyphs:

Focus your attention on the representations or images of the ancient Egyptian hieroglyphs.
Allow your intuition to guide you in choosing the hieroglyphs that resonate with your intention for purification.
Visualization and Chanting:

Take one hieroglyph at a time and visualize its symbol and meaning.
Chant or recite the name or sound associated with each hieroglyph, feeling its vibration and energy cleansing your being.

Symbolic Cleansing:

Using a feather, a smudging tool, or your hand, lightly sweep or trace the hieroglyphs on your body or in the air around you, symbolically cleansing and purifying yourself.
Affirmation and Intentions:

As you work with each hieroglyph, affirm your intentions for purification and renewal.
Visualize the cleansing energy of the hieroglyphs purifying your mind, body, and spirit.
Closing:

Take a moment to thank the ancient Egyptian hieroglyphs for their presence and power in your ritual.
Offer a final prayer or expression of gratitude.
"Oh, ancient symbols of the eternal hieroglyphs,
I thank you for your cleansing and purifying energy.
May your wisdom and power guide me on my spiritual path.
I carry your blessings within me as I continue my journey.
Thank you for your presence and guidance."

Grounding and Integration:

Take a few deep breaths and visualize yourself firmly rooted to the Earth.
Feel the energy of the sacred space grounding and integrating within you.
When you are ready, slowly open your eyes and return to the present moment.
Remember, this ritual is a personal and symbolic connection with the ancient Egyptian hieroglyphs. Feel free to adapt it to your own beliefs and practices, and always approach it with respect, sincerity, and reverence for the ancient traditions.

136.   Spell for the liberation of the deceased's soul from the limitations of the physical body

(Perform this spell in a quiet and sacred space. You may have an altar with representations or images of the elements or symbols that resonate with liberation.)

Preparation:

Create a peaceful and sacred space where you can focus your energy and connect with the divine.
Set up your altar with representations or images that symbolize liberation and transcendence.

Grounding and Centering:

Take a few deep breaths to center yourself and clear your mind.
Feel your connection to the Earth beneath you, grounding yourself in its stability and strength.

Opening Invocation:

Light candles or incense on your altar, symbolizing the presence of the divine.
Close your eyes and visualize a radiant light surrounding you, inviting the energy of liberation.
"I call upon the forces of the Universe,
To release the soul from its earthly ties.
Let the limitations of the physical body be undone,
And may the spirit soar freely in the realms beyond.
I invite the power of liberation to flow through me,
As I set the deceased soul on its journey of freedom."

Visualization and Intention:

Focus your attention on the representations or images that symbolize liberation and transcendence.
Visualize the deceased's soul breaking free from the confines of the physical body, becoming radiant and weightless.
Chanting or Affirmation:

Repeat a chant or affirmation that resonates with liberation and release. For example:
"From earthly bounds, you now depart,
Soar beyond the limits of flesh and heart.
Let the spirit rise, unbound and free,
Liberated from all that once held thee."

Repeat the chant or affirmation several times, allowing the words to reverberate within you.

Release and Letting Go:

Symbolically release the limitations by visualizing them being dissolved and transformed into light.
Extend your hands towards the representation or image on your altar, offering your intention for liberation.

Closing:

Take a moment to thank the forces of liberation for their presence and assistance in the spell.
Offer a final prayer or expression of gratitude.
"I give thanks to the forces of liberation,
For aiding the departed on their journey.
May their spirit be forever free,
Transcending the limitations of mortality.
With gratitude and reverence, I close this spell."

Grounding and Integration:

Take a few deep breaths and visualize yourself firmly rooted to the Earth.
Feel the energy of the sacred space grounding and integrating within you.
When you are ready, slowly open your eyes and return to the present moment.
Remember, this spell is a personal and symbolic connection with the forces of liberation. Feel free to adapt it to your own beliefs and practices, and always approach it with respect, sincerity, and reverence for the spiritual journey of the deceased.

137. Incantation to awaken the dormant spiritual insights within the deceased's spirit

(Perform this incantation in a peaceful and sacred space. You may have candles, crystals, or other objects that symbolize spiritual awakening.)

Preparation:

Create a serene and focused environment by clearing the space of any distractions. Place objects or symbols that represent spiritual awakening on an altar or in front of you.

Grounding and Centering:

Take a moment to ground yourself by standing or sitting comfortably.
Close your eyes and take several deep breaths, allowing your body to relax.

Opening Invocation:

Light a candle or hold a crystal, connecting with its energy and symbolism.
Speak the following invocation:
"In the realm of spirit, I call upon divine light,
Awaken the dormant insights, shining bright.
From the depths of the soul, let wisdom arise,
Illuminate the path, beyond mortal guise."

Visualization and Intent:

Visualize a gentle light glowing within the deceased's spirit, gradually growing brighter and expanding.
See this light spreading throughout their being, illuminating their consciousness with spiritual insights.

Chanting or Affirmation:

Repeat a chant or affirmation that resonates with spiritual awakening and insight. For example:
"Awaken the insights, hidden deep within,
Unveil the wisdom, let the journey begin.
From darkness to light, from slumber to sight,

Arise, spirit, in knowledge and in might."

Repeat the chant or affirmation several times, allowing the words to reverberate within you.

Connection and Transmission:

Extend your hands towards the representation or symbol of the deceased's spirit. Imagine a gentle flow of energy from your hands, transmitting the intention for awakening.

Silence and Receptivity:

Sit in silence for a few moments, allowing the energy and intention to settle and integrate.
Be open to receiving any insights, messages, or guidance that may come through.

Closing:

Express gratitude to the divine and the deceased's spirit for their presence and willingness to receive insight.
Offer a final prayer or expression of appreciation.
"With gratitude and reverence, I thank the divine,
For awakening insights in the deceased's spirit, sublime.
May the wisdom unfold, guiding their eternal flight,
In the realms of spirit, shining with divine light."

Grounding and Integration:

Take a few deep breaths, feeling your connection with the Earth beneath you.
Slowly open your eyes, bringing yourself back to the present moment.
Remember, this incantation is a symbolic and energetic connection with the dormant spiritual insights within the deceased's spirit. Customize it to align with your own beliefs and practices, always approaching it with respect, love, and the sincere intention to support the spiritual growth and awakening of the deceased.

138.   Ritual for the communion with the spirits of the celestial clouds and rainbows

(Perform this ritual outdoors or in a space where you can observe the sky and weather phenomena.)

Preparation:

Choose a time when the sky is clear or when there are visible clouds and rainbows. Find a comfortable spot where you can have an unobstructed view of the sky.

Grounding and Centering:

Stand with your feet firmly planted on the ground.
Close your eyes, take a few deep breaths, and allow yourself to become present in the moment.

Opening Invocation:

Raise your arms outstretched towards the sky, palms facing upward.
Speak the following invocation:
"O spirits of the celestial realms,
I call upon you with reverence and love.
Bless me with your presence and wisdom,
As I seek communion with your divine essence."

Connection with the Sky:

Observe the sky, taking in the beauty of the clouds, the vastness of space, and the colors of the rainbow (if present).
Feel a deep connection with the celestial realms, sensing the energy and presence of the spirits within the clouds and rainbows.
Breath and Visualization:

Take a slow, deep breath, imagining that you are drawing in the energy and essence of the celestial realms.
Visualize this energy entering your body, filling you with light, peace, and a sense of expansiveness.

Intention and Communication:

State your intention clearly in your mind or aloud, expressing your desire to commune with the spirits of the celestial clouds and rainbows.
Open your heart and mind to receive any messages, insights, or guidance that may be shared with you.

Contemplation and Reflection:

Continue to observe the sky, allowing your gaze to wander among the clouds and rainbows.
Reflect on the symbolism and significance they hold for you personally, and consider any thoughts or feelings that arise.
Gratitude and Farewell:

Express your gratitude to the spirits of the celestial realms for their presence and the communion you have shared.
Lower your arms, feeling a sense of completion and connection with the natural world around you.

Closing:

Take a moment to ground yourself by feeling your feet firmly on the ground.
Offer a final prayer, blessing, or expression of gratitude to the spirits and the universe.
"With gratitude and reverence, I thank the spirits of the celestial realms,
For their presence, wisdom, and the communion we have shared.
May their energy and essence continue to guide and inspire me,
As I walk my path in harmony with the natural world."

Remember, this ritual is a symbolic and energetic connection with the spirits of the celestial clouds and rainbows. Customize it to align with your own beliefs and practices, always approaching it with respect, love, and the sincere intention to connect with the divine essence present in the natural world.

139.   Spell for the transmigration of the deceased's soul into the realm of eternal harmony

(Perform this spell with a calm and focused mind, preferably in a quiet and serene environment.)

Preparation:

Create a sacred space by clearing any clutter and ensuring a peaceful ambiance.
Light a white or blue candle to represent purity and harmony.
Place a bowl of water nearby to symbolize cleansing and purification.

Grounding and Centering:

Sit comfortably and take a few deep breaths to calm your mind and body.
Visualize roots extending from your feet, anchoring you deep into the earth, grounding and stabilizing your energy.

Opening Invocation:

Speak the following invocation or create your own heartfelt words:
"In this sacred moment, I call upon the divine forces of harmony,
I seek the transmigration of [Name of the deceased] into the realm of eternal harmony.
May their soul find peace, balance, and serenity in this sacred journey.
As I speak these words, may the universe align to guide them on their path."

Connection and Intent:

Focus your attention on a photo or representation of the deceased.
Hold the image or object in your hands and envision a radiant light surrounding it.
Set your intention clearly, stating that you are facilitating the transmigration of their soul into the realm of eternal harmony.

Affirmation of Harmony:

Speak the following affirmation or create your own words of affirmation:

"With love and intention, I release [Name of the deceased] from all earthly attachments,
I guide their soul to the realm of eternal harmony.
May they find peace, balance, and unity with the divine essence.
As their soul journeys onward, may harmony be their guiding light."

Visualization and Release:

Close your eyes and imagine the soul of the deceased surrounded by a gentle and luminous light.
Visualize this light expanding and enveloping their essence, gradually lifting them up and away from earthly concerns.
Imagine their soul moving gracefully and effortlessly into a realm of perfect harmony, where peace and serenity prevail.

Blessing and Farewell:

Extend your gratitude and blessings to the soul of the deceased for the time shared together.
Express your wish for their continued journey in the realm of eternal harmony, free from suffering and discord.
Closing:

Offer a moment of silence to honor the sacredness of the ritual and the soul's transition.
Extinguish the candle as a symbolic completion of the spell.

Remember, this spell is a sacred act of intention and connection. Adjust the wording and elements to align with your beliefs and practices. Approach this spell with love, respect, and the sincere desire for the deceased to find eternal harmony.

140.   Invocation of the god Horus for divine vision and guidance in the afterlife

(Perform this invocation with reverence and a focused mind, preferably in a quiet and sacred space.)

Preparation:

Find a quiet and serene space where you can connect with the divine.
Light a white or gold candle to represent the presence of Horus.
Place a symbol or image of Horus before you as a focal point for your invocation.

Centering and Grounding:

Take a few deep breaths and allow yourself to become present in the moment.
Feel your connection to the earth beneath you, grounding and stabilizing your energy.

Opening Invocation:

Speak the following invocation or create your own heartfelt words:
"Horus, mighty falcon-headed god,
I call upon you in this sacred space and time.
Guide my vision and illuminate my path,
In the afterlife and beyond, be my guiding light."

Connection and Invocation:

Gaze upon the image or symbol of Horus and feel a connection with his divine energy.
Place your hands on your heart or raise them towards the image as a gesture of reverence.

Invocation of Horus:

Speak the following invocation or create your own words to invoke Horus:
"Horus, lord of the heavens and the earthly realms,
I seek your presence and divine guidance.
Bestow upon me your divine vision and insight,
That I may navigate the realms of the afterlife with clarity and purpose."

State Your Intentions:

Clearly state your intentions and desires for divine vision and guidance in the afterlife. Express your trust in Horus to guide and protect you on your spiritual journey.

Offerings and Gratitude:

Offer words of gratitude and appreciation to Horus for his presence and assistance. If you wish, you can also offer a small offering such as incense, a feather, or a piece of jewelry as a symbol of your devotion.

Closing:

Express your gratitude once again for Horus's guidance and presence.
Take a moment to sit in silence and feel the energy of Horus surrounding you.
When you are ready, extinguish the candle as a symbolic completion of the invocation.

Remember, this invocation is a sacred act of connecting with the divine energy of Horus. Adjust the words and elements to resonate with your beliefs and practices. Approach this invocation with reverence, openness, and a sincere desire for divine vision and guidance in the afterlife.

141.   Ritual of anointing with sacred oils for spiritual empowerment and transformation

(Perform this ritual with reverence and intention in a sacred space where you can focus your energy.)

Preparation:

Gather the following items: sacred oils of your choice (such as frankincense, myrrh, sandalwood, lavender, or rose), a small bowl or dish to hold the oils, and a white or beeswax candle.
Find a quiet space where you can perform the ritual without interruptions.
Light the candle as a symbol of divine presence and guidance.

Centering and Grounding:

Close your eyes, take a few deep breaths, and bring your awareness to the present moment.
Visualize roots extending from your feet into the earth, grounding and connecting you to its energy.

Invocation of Intent:

Hold your hands over the bowl of sacred oils and state your intention for spiritual empowerment and transformation.
Speak from your heart, expressing your desire for growth, healing, and alignment with your higher self.

Blessing of the Oils:

Gently pour a small amount of each sacred oil into the bowl, one by one, as you offer a few words of blessing for each oil.
Acknowledge their sacred properties and the energy they carry for your spiritual journey.

Anointing Ritual:

Dip your finger or a small cotton swab into the bowl of sacred oils.
Begin at your forehead and draw a horizontal line across your third eye, symbolizing awakening and spiritual insight.

Continue anointing with the oils, following the natural flow of energy in your body, such as your temples, throat, heart, wrists, and palms.
As you anoint each area, visualize the oil infusing your being with divine empowerment, wisdom, and transformation.
Affirmations and Intentions:

As you anoint each area, repeat affirmations or intentions that resonate with your desired spiritual transformation.
For example, "I am empowered to walk my spiritual path with courage and clarity" or "I embrace transformation and release all that no longer serves my highest good."

Express Gratitude:

Take a moment to express gratitude for the sacred oils, the divine energies, and any spiritual guides or higher beings who are supporting your journey.

Closing:

Extinguish the candle as a symbol of completion and release.
Allow the anointed oils to remain on your skin, absorbing their energy and symbolism.
Take a few more deep breaths, centering yourself and feeling the transformative energy within.

Remember, this ritual is a sacred act of self-empowerment and transformation. Adjust the oils, affirmations, and intentions to align with your personal beliefs and goals. Approach this ritual with reverence, focus, and an open heart, allowing the sacred oils to support your spiritual journey.

142. Spell for the transformation of the deceased into a vessel of divine knowledge and understanding

(Perform this spell with reverence and intention in a quiet and sacred space.)

Preparation:

Find a comfortable space where you can focus your energy without interruptions.
Light a white or blue candle to represent the divine wisdom and illumination you seek.
Place a small dish or bowl filled with water in front of the candle.

Centering and Grounding:

Close your eyes, take a few deep breaths, and bring your awareness to the present moment.
Visualize roots extending from your feet into the ground, grounding and connecting you to the Earth's energy.
Invocation of Intent:

Stand or sit in front of the candle and water, and speak your intention aloud.
State your desire for the deceased's soul to be transformed into a vessel of divine knowledge and understanding.

Connection with the Divine:

Hold your hands over the water, feeling its energy and connection to the universal flow of wisdom and understanding.
Call upon the divine energies, such as the goddess Ma'at or the god Thoth, known for their association with knowledge and truth.

Chant or Incantation:

Begin to chant or recite the following incantation, focusing your energy and intention on the transformation of the deceased's soul:
"From realms beyond, where wisdom lies,
I call upon the divine to rise.
Transform this soul, in light and grace,

Into a vessel of knowledge's embrace.
Let wisdom flow, like rivers deep,
Understanding awakens from eternal sleep."

Repeat the incantation several times, allowing its words to resonate within you and permeate the space.

Visualize the Transformation:

Close your eyes and visualize the deceased's soul surrounded by a radiant light.
See their essence expanding and absorbing divine knowledge and understanding.

Express Gratitude:

Thank the divine energies for their presence and assistance in the transformation of the deceased's soul.
Express gratitude for the wisdom and understanding that will be gained.

Closing:

Blow out the candle, symbolizing the completion of the spell.
Allow the water to sit undisturbed as a symbol of the transformative energies.
Remember, this spell is a sacred act of calling upon the divine energies to facilitate the transformation of the deceased's soul. Adjust the words, deity names, or visualization to align with your personal beliefs and practices. Approach this spell with respect, focus, and an open heart, allowing the divine energies to guide the process of transformation and understanding.

143. Incantation to invoke the blessings of the celestial sun and its radiant energy

(Perform this incantation outdoors during a clear day when the sun is visible. Stand facing the sun and feel its warmth and energy.)

Sun, source of light and life divine,
I call upon your radiant shine.
Bless me with your celestial power,
Illuminate my path every hour.

With each ray that touches my skin,
I feel your energy deep within.
Infuse me with your warmth and might,
Fill me with your radiant light.

Sun, mighty orb of golden hue,
Guide me, protect me, make me new.
Grant me strength and vitality,
As I bask in your luminosity.

From dawn to dusk, your presence I feel,
Your energy, a potent zeal.
With gratitude, I embrace your rays,
And walk in your bright, illuminating ways.

Sun, I invoke your blessings true,
Fill my life with joy and breakthrough.
Illuminate my path with your divine grace,
And bring blessings to every place.

As I stand under your celestial fire,
Fill me with passion and inspire.
Sun, I honor you, radiant and bright,
Guide me with your glorious light.

So mote it be.

Note: Remember to exercise caution and not look directly at the sun. Perform this incantation while facing the sun, but do not stare at it directly. Use your intuition to adjust the wording or personalize the incantation to align with your beliefs and intentions.

144. Ritual for the transfiguration of the deceased into a divine guardian of sacred secrets

(Prepare a sacred space with candles, incense, and any personal items that hold significance. Begin the ritual at a time and place where you can focus without interruption.)

Ground and center yourself: Close your eyes, take deep breaths, and visualize roots growing from the soles of your feet, anchoring you to the earth. Feel your connection to the divine and the energy of the universe.

Set your intention: Light a candle and state your intention clearly. For example: "I invoke the sacred transformation of [Name] into a divine guardian of sacred secrets. May their spirit be elevated and empowered to protect and preserve the wisdom and knowledge of the ages."

Invoke the divine: Call upon the deities or spiritual entities you resonate with for their guidance and assistance in this transfiguration ritual. You can address them by name or simply invite their presence and support.

Offerings and gratitude: Prepare an offering, such as a small bowl of water, flowers, or food, to express your gratitude and reverence for the divine beings you invoked. Place the offering on your altar or in a designated sacred space.

Sacred anointing: Take a small amount of sacred oil or perfume and anoint your fingers. Gently touch the forehead, heart, and hands of the deceased, symbolizing the transformation of their mind, spirit, and actions into a guardian of sacred secrets. As you anoint, recite a prayer or affirmation that reflects your intention for their transfiguration.

Divine blessing: Raise your hands above the deceased's resting place and visualize a beam of divine light descending upon them. Envision this light surrounding them, filling them with divine wisdom, protection, and the ability to safeguard sacred knowledge. Speak words of blessing and empowerment, acknowledging their new role as a guardian of sacred secrets.

Closing the ritual: Express gratitude to the deities, spirits, and the deceased for their presence and participation in the ritual. Extinguish the candle, but leave the sacred space undisturbed for a while to allow the energy to settle.

Note: This ritual can be adapted to suit your personal beliefs and practices. Feel free to Always approach rituals with respect and reverence, keeping the intentions pure and focused on the highest good.

145.   Spell for the reunion of the deceased's soul with their spiritual companions and allies

(Prepare a quiet and sacred space where you can focus without interruptions. Have candles, incense, and any personal items that hold significance.)

Center and ground yourself: Close your eyes, take deep breaths, and envision roots growing from your feet, grounding you to the earth. Feel your connection to the divine and the energy of the universe.

Set your intention: Light a candle and state your intention clearly. For example: "I invoke the reunion of [Name]'s soul with their beloved spiritual companions and allies. May their souls be guided, supported, and surrounded by love and light."

Invocation: Call upon the spirits, guides, and allies that were significant to the deceased during their lifetime. Address them by name or simply invite their presence and support in this sacred reunion.

Offering and gratitude: Prepare a small offering, such as a bowl of water, flowers, or food, to express your gratitude and honor the spiritual companions and allies you invoked. Place the offering on your altar or in a designated sacred space.

Sacred chant or prayer: Begin chanting or reciting a prayer that honors the deceased and their spiritual companions. Let your words flow from your heart, expressing love, gratitude, and a sincere desire for their reunion. Allow the vibrations of your voice to create a sacred space of connection and harmony.

Visualization and invitation: Envision the deceased's soul surrounded by a radiant light, and imagine their spiritual companions and allies appearing around them. See them joining hands or forming a circle, uniting in love and support. Send out an invitation for their reunion, calling the deceased's soul to join their beloved allies in this realm of spiritual connection.

Blessing and affirmation: Speak words of blessing and affirmation, acknowledging the reunion of the deceased's soul with their spiritual companions and allies. Affirm that they are now surrounded by love, guidance, and support on their continued spiritual journey.

Closing the spell: Express gratitude to the spirits, guides, and allies for their presence and participation in the spell. Extinguish the candle, but leave the sacred space undisturbed for a while to allow the energy to settle.

Remember, this spell is meant to be adapted to your personal beliefs and practices. Feel free to Approach it with respect and sincerity, always focused on the highest good for all involved.

146.   Invocation of the goddess Nephthys for protection and healing in the afterlife

(Prepare a quiet and sacred space where you can focus without interruptions. Have candles, incense, and any personal items that hold significance.)

Center and ground yourself: Close your eyes, take deep breaths, and envision roots growing from your feet, grounding you to the earth. Feel your connection to the divine and the energy of the universe.

Set your intention: Light a candle and state your intention clearly. For example: "I invoke the presence and blessings of the goddess Nephthys to provide protection and healing for [Name] in their journey through the afterlife. May Nephthys envelop them in her compassionate embrace and guide them towards spiritual wholeness."

Invocation: Call upon the goddess Nephthys, addressing her with reverence and respect. Speak from your heart, inviting her presence and requesting her protection and healing powers. You may use the following or create your own:

"Great Nephthys, Lady of the Night,
Divine Protector and Healer of Souls,
I humbly invoke your presence and grace.
Wrap your wings of comfort around [Name],
Guide them through the afterlife's unknown paths,
Shield them from harm and turmoil,
And heal their wounds, body, mind, and spirit."

Offering and gratitude: Prepare a small offering, such as incense, flowers, or a symbol that represents Nephthys, to express your gratitude and honor her presence. Place the offering on your altar or in a designated sacred space.

Sacred chant or prayer: Begin chanting or reciting a prayer that invokes the essence and qualities of Nephthys. Let your words flow from your heart, expressing gratitude and a sincere desire for her protection and healing. Allow the vibrations of your voice to create a sacred space of connection and receptivity.

Visualization and connection: Envision a warm, gentle light surrounding the deceased, representing the loving embrace of Nephthys. See her wings enveloping them, providing a sense of comfort and security. Visualize her healing energies flowing through their being, bringing peace and restoration.

Blessing and affirmation: Speak words of blessing and affirmation, acknowledging Nephthys' presence and her role as protector and healer. Affirm that the deceased is held in her loving care, and that she guides them towards spiritual wholeness and transformation.

Closing the invocation: Express gratitude to Nephthys for her presence and assistance. Extinguish the candle, but leave the sacred space undisturbed for a while to allow the energy to settle.

Remember, this invocation is meant to be adapted to your personal beliefs and practices. Feel free to Approach it with respect and sincerity, always focused on the highest good for all involved.

147.   Ritual of purification through the sacred breath of the eternal winds

(Prepare a quiet and open space where you can comfortably stand or sit. Have candles, incense, and any personal items that hold significance.)

Center and ground yourself: Close your eyes, take deep breaths, and focus on your breath. Allow yourself to become fully present in the moment. Feel your connection to the earth beneath you and the vastness of the sky above you.

Set your intention: Light a candle and state your intention clearly. For example: "I invoke the cleansing and purifying power of the eternal winds to cleanse my body, mind, and spirit. May the breath of the divine wash away any negativity or impurities, leaving me refreshed and renewed."

Breath awareness: Begin by focusing on your breath. Take slow, deep breaths, allowing the air to fill your lungs and then releasing it fully. With each inhalation, envision pure, fresh air entering your body, carrying with it revitalizing energy. With each exhalation, imagine releasing any stagnant or negative energy.

Invocation: Call upon the power of the eternal winds, addressing them with reverence and respect. Speak from your heart, inviting their presence and requesting their cleansing and purifying energies. You may use the following or create your own:

"Sacred winds, carriers of purity and transformation,
I call upon your ancient wisdom and gentle strength.
Blow away the stagnant energy that lingers within me,
Cleanse my body, mind, and spirit with your sacred breath.
Carry away all negativity, leaving only pure light and love in its wake."

Visualize the winds: With your eyes still closed, visualize a gentle breeze surrounding you. Feel the coolness and freshness of the wind against your skin. Envision it penetrating your being, clearing away any impurities and refreshing every cell of your body.

Breath as the wind: As you continue to breathe deeply, imagine that with each inhalation, you are drawing in the pure, cleansing energy of the winds. Feel it filling every part of your being, revitalizing and rejuvenating you. With each exhalation, release any tension, negativity, or heaviness, allowing it to be carried away by the wind.

Chant or affirmations: If desired, you can incorporate chanting or affirmations into the ritual. Choose words or phrases that resonate with you and express your desire for purification and renewal. Repeat them with intention and conviction, allowing the vibration of your voice to align with the energy of the winds.

Gratitude and closing: Express gratitude to the eternal winds for their presence and cleansing power. Thank them for their assistance in purifying your body, mind, and spirit. Extinguish the candle, but continue to bask in the renewed sense of lightness and clarity that the ritual has brought forth.

Remember, this ritual is meant to be adapted to your personal beliefs and practices. Feel free to Approach it with reverence and sincerity, always focusing on the purification and rejuvenation of your being.

148. Spell for the liberation of the deceased's soul from the burdens of the past

(Prepare a quiet and sacred space where you can focus your energy. Have candles, incense, and any personal items that hold significance.)

Center and ground yourself: Close your eyes, take deep breaths, and center your energy. Feel the connection between your physical body and the earth beneath you. Allow yourself to let go of any distractions or worries.

Set your intention: Light a candle and state your intention clearly. For example: "I invoke the divine power of liberation and release to free the soul of [name of the deceased] from the burdens of the past. May their spirit be liberated, allowing them to move forward on their journey of growth and transformation."

Call upon the divine: Address the divine source that resonates with your beliefs. Whether it's a higher power, a specific deity, or the universal energy, speak with reverence and trust. You may use the following or create your own:

"Divine presence, hear my plea,
Release the burdens that bind, set the spirit free.
Unshackle the chains of the past's heavy weight,
Allow [name of the deceased] to soar to their destined fate.
Liberate their soul from the pain and strife,
Grant them freedom and a new lease on life."

Visualize the release: Envision the burdens of the past as heavy weights or chains that are attached to the deceased's soul. See these burdens being lifted, one by one, until the soul is completely free and unencumbered. Visualize the soul soaring upwards, breaking free from the constraints of the past.

Affirmation of liberation: Repeat affirmations that resonate with the intention of liberation and release. You may use the following or create your own:

"From the past, you are set free,
Embracing the present, your soul can be.
Burdens released, chains untied,
A new path of light and growth you shall stride.

Into the realms of possibility and grace,
You are liberated, in this sacred space."

Gratitude and closing: Express gratitude to the divine for their presence and assistance in liberating the soul of the deceased. Thank them for their guidance and support. Take a moment to bask in the energy of liberation and release, knowing that the deceased's soul is now free to embark on a new journey of growth and transformation.

Remember, this spell is intended to be adapted to your personal beliefs and practices. Approach it with reverence and sincerity, always focusing on the liberation and release of the deceased's soul from the burdens of the past.

149.   Incantation to awaken the dormant spiritual potentials within the deceased's spirit

(Prepare a quiet and sacred space where you can focus your energy. Have candles, incense, and any personal items that hold significance.)

Center and ground yourself: Close your eyes, take deep breaths, and center your energy. Feel the connection between your physical body and the earth beneath you. Allow yourself to let go of any distractions or worries.

Set your intention: Light a candle and state your intention clearly. For example: "I call upon the divine power within and around me to awaken the dormant spiritual potentials within the spirit of [name of the deceased]. May their inner gifts and abilities be activated, allowing their spirit to shine brightly."

Call upon the divine: Address the divine source that resonates with your beliefs. Whether it's a higher power, a specific deity, or the universal energy, speak with reverence and trust. You may use the following or create your own:

"Spirit divine, awaken and arise,
Unleash the dormant powers that lie inside.
Ignite the flame of their inner light,
Reveal their gifts, shining bright.
From the depths of their spirit's core,
Let their potentials blossom and soar."

Visualize the awakening: Envision the spirit of the deceased surrounded by a radiant and vibrant energy. See this energy flowing into their being, awakening and activating their dormant spiritual potentials. Imagine their spirit becoming brighter and more illuminated as their gifts and abilities awaken.

Affirmation of awakening: Repeat affirmations that resonate with the intention of awakening dormant potentials. You may use the following or create your own:

"Awaken, spirit, to the gifts you possess,
Unleash your power, your true essence.
From within, let your talents unfold,
As you embrace your purpose, bold.

Let your spirit shine with radiant grace,
Awakening your potentials in this sacred space."

Gratitude and closing: Express gratitude to the divine for their presence and assistance in awakening the dormant spiritual potentials within the deceased's spirit. Thank them for their guidance and support. Take a moment to honor the awakened potentials and the journey of growth and expansion that lies ahead for the spirit.

150.   Ritual for the communion with the spirits of the celestial rain and dew

(Prepare a quiet and sacred space where you can focus your energy. Have candles, incense, and any personal items that hold significance.)

Center and ground yourself: Close your eyes, take deep breaths, and center your energy. Feel the connection between your physical body and the earth beneath you. Allow yourself to let go of any distractions or worries.

Set your intention: Light a candle and state your intention clearly. For example: "I call upon the divine power within and around me to awaken the dormant spiritual potentials within the spirit of [name of the deceased]. May their inner gifts and abilities be activated, allowing their spirit to shine brightly."

Call upon the divine: Address the divine source that resonates with your beliefs. Whether it's a higher power, a specific deity, or the universal energy, speak with reverence and trust. You may use the following or create your own:

"Spirit divine, awaken and arise,
Unleash the dormant powers that lie inside.
Ignite the flame of their inner light,
Reveal their gifts, shining bright.
From the depths of their spirit's core,
Let their potentials blossom and soar."

Visualize the awakening: Envision the spirit of the deceased surrounded by a radiant and vibrant energy. See this energy flowing into their being, awakening and activating their dormant spiritual potentials. Imagine their spirit becoming brighter and more illuminated as their gifts and abilities awaken.

Affirmation of awakening: Repeat affirmations that resonate with the intention of awakening dormant potentials. You may use the following or create your own:

"Awaken, spirit, to the gifts you possess,
Unleash your power, your true essence.
From within, let your talents unfold,
As you embrace your purpose, bold.
Let your spirit shine with radiant grace,
Awakening your potentials in this sacred space."

Gratitude and closing: Express gratitude to the divine for their presence and assistance in awakening the dormant spiritual potentials within the deceased's spirit. Thank them for their guidance and support. Take a moment to honor the awakened potentials and the journey of growth and expansion that lies ahead for the spirit. Remember, this incantation is meant to be tailored to your personal beliefs and practices. Approach it with sincerity and reverence, always focusing on the awakening and activation of the dormant spiritual potentials within the deceased's spirit.

151.   Spell for the transmigration of the deceased's soul into the realm of eternal joy and bliss

(Prepare a serene and sacred space for this spell. Light candles, burn incense, and have any personal items that hold significance.)

Center yourself: Take a few deep breaths and allow yourself to enter a calm and peaceful state. Focus your mind on the intention of guiding the deceased's soul to the realm of eternal joy and bliss.

Set your intention: Light a candle to symbolize the soul's journey and state your intention clearly. For example: "With love and compassion, I call upon the divine to guide and assist the soul of [name of the deceased] in their transmigration to the realm of eternal joy and bliss. May their soul be liberated from all attachments and find true happiness and peace."

Invoke divine assistance: Call upon the divine source that resonates with your beliefs. It may be a higher power, angels, or spiritual guides. Speak with reverence and trust. You can use the following invocation or create your own:

"Spirit guides and angels of light,
Hear my plea on this sacred night.
Guide the soul of [name of the deceased] with care,
To the realm of joy and bliss, so fair.
Release their burdens, free their heart,
Grant them eternal joy, never to depart."

Visualize the soul's journey: Close your eyes and imagine the soul of the deceased surrounded by a gentle and comforting light. See this light growing brighter and expanding, enveloping the soul and carrying it towards the realm of eternal joy and bliss. Visualize the soul being embraced by love and experiencing a profound sense of peace and happiness.

Affirmation of transmigration: Repeat affirmations that resonate with the intention of the soul's transmigration into the realm of joy and bliss. You can use the following or create your own:

"Soul of [name of the deceased], be released and set free,

Transcend the earthly bounds, to pure ecstasy.
Let go of all sorrows and past strife,
Embrace eternal joy, in the realm of life.
With open heart and spirit light,
Enter the realm of bliss, shining bright."

Gratitude and closing: Express gratitude to the divine for their presence and assistance in guiding the deceased's soul to the realm of eternal joy and bliss. Thank them for their loving guidance and support. Take a moment to honor the soul's journey and the boundless joy and bliss that awaits.

Remember, this spell can be adapted to suit your personal beliefs and practices. Modify it, add or remove elements, and make it your own. Approach it with reverence and sincerity, always focusing on guiding the deceased's soul to the realm of eternal joy and bliss.

152. Invocation of the god Thoth for wisdom and knowledge in the afterlife

(Prepare a sacred space for this invocation. Light candles, burn incense, and have any symbols or representations of Thoth present.)

Center yourself: Take a moment to ground yourself and clear your mind. Breathe deeply and let go of any distractions or concerns. Feel your connection to the divine and the presence of Thoth.

Offerings and reverence: Place offerings that symbolize your respect and reverence for Thoth before you. This could be a written prayer, a small statue or image of Thoth, or an item that represents knowledge and wisdom. Offer your words of respect and gratitude to Thoth, acknowledging his role as the god of wisdom and knowledge.

Invocation: Speak the following invocation or create your own heartfelt words to invoke Thoth:

"Great Thoth, Lord of Wisdom and Knowledge,
I call upon you in this sacred hour.
Guide me with your divine intellect,
Illuminate my path with your profound insight.

In the afterlife's realm of mysteries,
May your presence be felt by [name of the deceased].
Grant them wisdom to navigate the unknown,
And understanding to transcend limitations.

O Thoth, holder of the sacred scrolls,
Unveil the secrets of the universe,
Bestow your wisdom upon [name of the deceased],
That their soul may soar with enlightenment.

In the realm beyond, let knowledge be their guide,
And may they attain the highest truths.
Grant them the keys to unlock the mysteries,
And let their spirit ascend to new heights.

Thoth, I humbly seek your divine guidance,

For [name of the deceased] on their eternal journey.
May they be surrounded by your wisdom and knowledge,
Forever enlightened in the afterlife's embrace."

Open yourself to Thoth's presence: Take a moment to meditate in silence, opening your heart and mind to receive Thoth's wisdom and guidance. Allow yourself to feel his presence and the knowledge he imparts.

Gratitude and closing: Express gratitude to Thoth for his wisdom and guidance. Thank him for his presence during this invocation. Take a moment to reflect on the blessings of wisdom and knowledge that Thoth bestows upon the deceased.

Remember, this invocation can be adapted to suit your personal beliefs and practices. Modify it, add or remove elements, and make it your own. Approach it with sincerity and respect, always seeking Thoth's wisdom and knowledge for the benefit of the deceased.

153.   Ritual of anointing with sacred herbs for spiritual healing and rejuvenation

(Prepare a sacred space for this ritual. Gather the necessary sacred herbs and oils, such as lavender, rosemary, sage, or any herbs that hold significance for you.)

Set your intention: Take a moment to reflect on your intention for this ritual. Is it for personal healing and rejuvenation or for someone else? Clarify your intention and hold it in your mind throughout the ritual.

Cleanse and purify: Begin by smudging yourself and the space with sacred herbs, such as sage or palo santo. Allow the smoke to cleanse your energy and the environment, clearing away any negativity or stagnant energy.

Prepare the anointing oil: Mix a carrier oil, such as jojoba or almond oil, with a few drops of your chosen essential oils or infused herbal oils. Focus on selecting herbs and oils that promote healing, rejuvenation, and spiritual well-being. As you mix the oils, infuse them with your intention and the healing properties you seek.

Center and ground: Take a few moments to center yourself and connect with the Earth. Stand barefoot on the ground or sit in a comfortable position. Close your eyes, breathe deeply, and imagine roots extending from your body into the Earth, grounding you and establishing a connection to its healing energy.

Invocation: Speak or silently recite an invocation to the divine or your chosen deity, asking for their presence and assistance in this healing and rejuvenation ritual. You can use your own words or adapt the following:

"Divine (or Deity's name), I invite your presence and guidance in this sacred ritual of healing and rejuvenation. I ask for your blessings and assistance in restoring balance, vitality, and spiritual well-being. May the sacred herbs and oils used in this ritual bring forth their healing properties and nourish my body, mind, and spirit. May this act of anointing be a catalyst for transformation and renewal. With gratitude, I open myself to receive your divine healing energy."

Anointing: Take a small amount of the prepared anointing oil in your hands. Rub them together to warm the oil and infuse it with your energy. Begin by anointing yourself, starting from your forehead and moving down the body, focusing on areas that require healing or rejuvenation. As you apply the oil, visualize the herbs and oils working their magic, bringing healing energy to every cell of your being. If you are performing this ritual for someone else, follow the same process, but with their consent and anoint them with gentle, loving intention.

Affirmations and gratitude: As you anoint yourself or the person you are performing the ritual for, repeat affirmations or prayers that reinforce your intention for healing and rejuvenation. Express gratitude for the healing energies present and the divine assistance you have invoked.

Closing: Once you have completed the anointing, take a few moments to sit in stillness and integrate the healing energies. Express gratitude to the divine or your chosen deity for their presence and support in this ritual. Ground yourself by connecting with the Earth once again, feeling its stability and strength beneath you.

Release and integration: Release any remaining tension or negativity from your body and energy field. Visualize it dissolving and being absorbed by the Earth. Take a few deep breaths, inhaling positive energy and exhaling any remaining stress or discomfort.

Gratitude and closure: Offer gratitude to the sacred herbs, oils, and the divine for their healing energies and the transformation you have experienced. Close the ritual with words of thanks and honor. You may choose to leave any remaining anointing oil on your skin or gently wash it off, depending on your preference.

154. Spell for the transformation of the deceased into a vessel of divine power and authority

(Note: This spell is intended to be performed by someone on behalf of the deceased.)

Create a sacred space: Set up a sacred space where you will perform the spell. Arrange items that hold spiritual significance to you, such as candles, crystals, symbols, or personal mementos of the deceased.

Ground and center: Take a few deep breaths and center yourself. Imagine roots growing from the soles of your feet, anchoring you deep into the Earth. Feel yourself connected and grounded.

Call upon the divine: Invoke the presence and assistance of the divine energies that resonate with power and authority. You may choose to call upon a specific deity or simply ask for the presence and guidance of divine power and authority. Use your own words or recite a prayer such as:

"Divine power and authority, I call upon your presence in this sacred space. Guide me in this ritual as I seek to transform the spirit of (name of the deceased) into a vessel of divine power and authority. Grant them the strength and authority to navigate the realms of the afterlife with confidence and purpose. May their spirit shine with divine light and radiate with divine power."

Connect with the deceased: Visualize the spirit of the deceased in your mind's eye. Imagine them standing before you, surrounded by a golden light. Feel their presence and their desire for transformation.

Speak the spell: Speak the following spell or adapt it to your own words, speaking with conviction and intention:

"Spirit of (name of the deceased), I call upon the power and authority of the divine to transform you into a vessel of divine power and authority. May your spirit be infused with the strength and wisdom to navigate the realms of the afterlife. Embrace your divine essence and step into your true power. As you transcend earthly limitations, may you shine with the radiance of divine authority. So mote it be."

Visualize the transformation: Envision the spirit of the deceased being enveloped in a golden light, as their energy and essence are elevated and transformed. See them radiating with a newfound sense of power and authority.

Offer blessings and gratitude: Express gratitude to the divine energies and the spirit of the deceased for their presence and participation in the spell. Offer blessings and well-wishes for the journey of the transformed spirit in the afterlife.

Close the ritual: Thank the divine energies for their assistance and guidance. Ground yourself once again by connecting with the Earth and releasing any excess energy.

Release the space: Safely extinguish any candles or incense used in the ritual. Close the sacred space, knowing that the transformation spell has been cast and the spirit of the deceased has been infused with divine power and authority.

Remember, performing this spell is an act of reverence and should be approached with sincerity and respect. Always seek the highest good for the deceased and their journey in the afterlife.

155.   Incantation to invoke the blessings of the celestial rainbows and colors

(You can recite this incantation during a meditation or ritual to connect with the energies of celestial rainbows and colors.)

I call upon the celestial rainbows and colors,
Ethereal manifestations of divine beauty,
With hues that dance and shimmer with grace,
Bringing blessings from the celestial realms.

From red to violet, the colors arise,
Each holding its own magic and surprise,
A tapestry of light, a bridge to the divine,
With each shade, a blessing shall be mine.

Rainbow of red, ignite my passion and desire,
Infuse my spirit with love's eternal fire.
Orange, bring me joy and creativity's flow,
Inspire my soul, let my inner light glow.

Yellow, fill me with warmth and radiant energy,
Illuminate my path, grant clarity to see.
Green, nurture my heart, bring healing and growth,
Connect me to nature, where divinity is most.

Blue, calm my mind, bring peace and serenity,
Guide me with truth and wisdom for eternity.
Indigo, open my third eye, expand my insight,
Unveil the mysteries, let intuition take flight.

Violet, connect me with spirituality divine,
Transcendence and enlightenment, may I find.
In every shade and hue, the blessings flow,
Celestial rainbows, your energies bestow.

With gratitude and reverence, I embrace your light,
Guiding me through the day and into the night.
Celestial rainbows, I honor and invite,
Bless me with your magic, forever shining bright.

As I speak these words with heartfelt intent,
I merge my spirit with the celestial ascent.
Blessings of the rainbows, I welcome thee,
Divine energies, fill me, set my spirit free.

By the power of celestial rainbows and colors,
May blessings shower upon me, now and forever.

So mote it be.

156.   Ritual for the transfiguration of the deceased into a divine messenger of the gods

Note: This ritual is a symbolic representation of the transfiguration process. Adapt it to your specific beliefs and practices.

Materials needed:

A sacred space or altar
Representation of the deceased (photo, personal item, or symbol)
Candles (preferably white or gold)
Incense (frankincense or sandalwood)
Offering of fruit or flowers
Pen and paper

Preparation:

Find a quiet and sacred space where you can perform the ritual undisturbed.
Set up your altar with the representation of the deceased, candles, incense, and offering.
Take a few deep breaths to center yourself and enter a calm and focused state of mind.

Invocation:

Light the candles and the incense, invoking the presence of the divine.
Call upon the gods or goddesses of your belief system, inviting their guidance and blessings.
State your intention clearly, such as: "I invoke the divine presence to witness and assist in the transfiguration of [name of the deceased] into a divine messenger of the gods."

Reflection and Connection:

Take a moment to reflect on the qualities and virtues you wish the deceased to embody as a divine messenger. Write them down on the paper.
Hold the representation of the deceased in your hands and visualize their spirit being infused with divine light and wisdom. Feel a connection with their essence.

Affirmation and Transfiguration:

Speak aloud an affirmation or prayer, affirming the transfiguration process. For example: "By the power of the divine, I now transfigure [name of the deceased] into a divine messenger of the gods. May their spirit be elevated, enlightened, and empowered to carry divine messages of love, wisdom, and guidance."

Offering and Gratitude:

Place the offering of fruit or flowers on the altar, dedicating it to the divine and the deceased.
Express your gratitude to the gods, goddesses, and the deceased for their presence and assistance in this transfiguration process.

Closing:

Extinguish the candles and incense, symbolizing the completion of the ritual.
Take a moment to sit in silence, feeling the energy of the ritual and the connection with the divine and the deceased.
Close the ritual with a closing prayer or words of gratitude.

Remember, this ritual is a symbolic representation, and its purpose is to create a sacred space for intention and connection.

157. Invocation of the goddess Isis for protection and nurturing in the afterlife

Note: This invocation is a symbolic representation of seeking the protection and nurturing energy of the goddess Isis. Adapt it to your specific beliefs and practices.

Materials needed:

A sacred space or altar
Representation of the goddess Isis (statue, picture, or symbol)
Candles (preferably blue or white)
Incense (lotus or myrrh)
Offering of water or milk
Pen and paper

Preparation:

Find a quiet and sacred space where you can perform the invocation undisturbed.
Set up your altar with the representation of the goddess Isis, candles, incense, and offering.
Take a few deep breaths to center yourself and enter a calm and focused state of mind.

Invocation:

Light the candles and the incense, invoking the presence of the goddess Isis.
Call upon Isis, addressing her with respect and devotion. State your intention clearly, such as: "I invoke the presence of the benevolent goddess Isis to grant me protection and nurturing in the afterlife."

Reflection and Connection:

Take a moment to reflect on the qualities and attributes of the goddess Isis. Consider her protective nature, nurturing energy, and wisdom.
Write down any specific aspects of protection or nurturing you seek from Isis on the paper.

Affirmation and Invocation:

Hold the representation of the goddess Isis in your hands and speak aloud an affirmation or prayer, invoking her presence and seeking her protection and nurturing. For example: "O benevolent goddess Isis, I humbly invoke your divine presence. Please wrap me in your protective wings, guiding and nurturing me through the journey of the afterlife. Grant me strength, comfort, and wisdom. I open my heart to receive your love and protection."

Offering and Gratitude:

Place the offering of water or milk on the altar, dedicating it to the goddess Isis. Express your gratitude to Isis for her presence and assistance in providing protection and nurturing in the afterlife.

Closing:

Extinguish the candles and incense, symbolizing the completion of the invocation. Take a moment to sit in silence, feeling the energy of the invocation and the connection with the goddess Isis.
Close the invocation with a closing prayer or words of gratitude.

Remember, this invocation is a symbolic representation, and its purpose is to create a sacred space for intention and connection. Adapt it to your beliefs and preferences, adding or modifying any steps as necessary.

158.   Ritual of purification through the sacred fire of the eternal flame

Note: Fire is a powerful symbol of transformation and purification in many spiritual traditions. This ritual utilizes the energy of fire for purification purposes. Please ensure you follow fire safety guidelines and take necessary precautions when working with fire.

Materials needed:

A safe and designated space for the ritual, preferably outdoors or in a well-ventilated area
A fireproof container or cauldron
Sacred herbs or incense for smudging (such as sage, cedar, or frankincense)
Matches or a lighter
A written statement or representation of what you wish to release or purify
Protective gloves (optional)

Preparation:

Choose a safe and secluded area where you can perform the ritual undisturbed. Ensure there are no flammable objects nearby.
Set up the fireproof container or cauldron in the center of your ritual space.
Place the sacred herbs or incense nearby, ready for use.
Take a few moments to center yourself and set your intention for the purification ritual.

Lighting the Sacred Fire:

Take the matches or lighter and light the sacred herbs or incense, allowing them to smolder and release smoke.
Use the smoking herbs or incense to cleanse yourself and the ritual space by wafting the smoke around your body and in the area. Visualize the smoke purifying and cleansing any negative energies.

Writing and Releasing:

Take the written statement or representation of what you wish to release or purify. Hold it in your hands and connect with the energy and emotions associated with it.

Speak aloud or silently affirm your intention to release and let go of these energies or attachments.

When you feel ready, place the written statement or representation into the fireproof container or cauldron.

Purification by the Eternal Flame:

Carefully light the fire in the fireproof container using matches or a lighter. Take precautions to ensure safety and avoid accidental fires.

As the flame grows, visualize the fire as the eternal flame of purification and transformation.

Hold your hands over the flame (without touching it) and imagine the flame's energy purifying and transmuting any negative or stagnant energies within you.

Feel the warmth and power of the fire, allowing it to cleanse and purify your being on all levels.

Release and Let Go:

As the fire burns, focus on releasing and letting go of the energies or attachments represented by the written statement or representation.

Visualize the fire transforming these energies into pure light and releasing them into the universe.

Feel a sense of liberation and freedom as you let go of what no longer serves you.

Gratitude and Closing:

Express gratitude to the sacred fire and the elements for their participation in the ritual.

Take a moment to silently or aloud express your gratitude for the purification and release you have experienced.

Allow the fire to burn out completely in a safe manner or use a fire extinguisher if necessary.

Close the ritual with a grounding practice, such as deep breathing or meditation, to restore balance and center yourself.

Remember, fire can be dangerous, and safety should be your utmost priority. Always exercise caution and follow fire safety guidelines when working with open flames. Adapt this ritual to fit your beliefs and preferences, making any necessary modifications or additions.

159.   Spell for the liberation of the deceased's soul from earthly attachments

Note: This spell is intended to help release the deceased's soul from any lingering earthly attachments and facilitate its journey into the spiritual realms. It is important to perform this spell with respect, love, and intention.

Materials needed:

A quiet and sacred space
A white candle
A piece of paper
A pen or marker
A fireproof container or cauldron
Matches or a lighter

Preparation:

Find a quiet and undisturbed space where you can perform the spell.
Set up the fireproof container or cauldron in the center of your space.
Light the white candle and place it near the container.
Centering and Intentions:
Take a few deep breaths to center yourself and enter a calm state of mind.
Focus your intention on the liberation of the deceased's soul from earthly attachments.
Visualize a bright and radiant light surrounding you and the candle, creating a sacred space.

Writing and Releasing:

Take the piece of paper and the pen or marker.
Write down any specific earthly attachments or burdens that you believe may be holding the deceased's soul back.
Take a moment to reflect on each attachment and acknowledge its presence.

Letting Go:

Hold the paper in your hands and feel the energy of the attachments.
Speak aloud or silently affirm your intention to release these attachments and set the deceased's soul free.

Visualize each attachment dissolving and disappearing, transforming into pure light and releasing its hold on the deceased's soul.

Burning and Transformation:

Carefully place the paper into the fireproof container or cauldron.
Use matches or a lighter to ignite the paper, allowing it to burn.
As the paper burns, visualize the attachments being consumed by the flames and transforming into pure energy.
Feel the release and liberation of the deceased's soul as the attachments are transformed and dissolved.

Closing and Gratitude:

Watch the flames until the paper has burned completely.
Express gratitude to the fire and the elements for their participation in the spell.
Thank the deceased's soul for its presence and acknowledge its journey of liberation and freedom.
Extinguish the candle, symbolizing the completion of the spell.

Closure and Grounding:

Take a moment to ground yourself by connecting with the earth beneath you.
Breathe deeply and visualize any excess energy flowing down into the earth, grounding and stabilizing you.

Remember, this spell is performed with respect and love. It is essential to approach it with pure intentions and a sincere desire to assist the deceased's soul on its spiritual journey. Adapt this spell as necessary to align with your beliefs and preferences, ensuring that it resonates with your spiritual practices.

160.   Incantation to awaken the dormant spiritual gifts within the deceased's spirit

Note: This incantation is intended to awaken and activate the dormant spiritual gifts and abilities within the deceased's spirit, allowing them to fully embrace and utilize their innate powers in the afterlife. Perform this incantation with reverence, intention, and respect for the deceased.

Begin by creating a calm and sacred space where you can focus your energy and intention. Light a white candle to represent purity and spiritual illumination. Take a few moments to center yourself and connect with the energy of the deceased.

Recite the following incantation:

"Spirit of the departed, hear my plea,
Awaken the gifts that slumber within thee.
Unleash the power that lies dormant and still,
Let it surge and flow, your spirit to fulfill.

With divine guidance, let your senses ignite,
Open the gates to the spiritual sight.
Let intuition blossom, clear and bright,
Guiding your journey with wisdom's light.

Unleash the magic that dwells deep inside,
Manifesting your gifts, let them be your guide.
Embrace your purpose with passion and grace,
Awakened and empowered in this sacred space.

May your spirit soar, unbounded and free,
In harmony with the divine, eternally.
Let your gifts unfold, a radiant display,
In the realms beyond, where spirits play.

So mote it be."

Visualize the spirit of the deceased being surrounded by a radiant light, as their dormant spiritual gifts awaken and come to life. Envision them embracing their newfound abilities and stepping into their full spiritual potential.

Take a moment to express gratitude for the awakening of their gifts and the blessings they will bring to their spiritual journey. Allow the candle to burn down completely as a symbol of the energy and intention released into the universe.

Remember to approach this incantation with respect and love, focusing on the highest good for the deceased. Adapt and modify the incantation as needed to align with your personal beliefs and practices, ensuring that it resonates with your intentions and the spirit of the deceased.

161.   Ritual for the communion with the spirits of the celestial trees and plants

Note: This ritual is designed to facilitate a deep and sacred connection with the spirits of trees and plants in the celestial realms. It allows for a communion of energy, wisdom, and healing between the deceased and these divine beings. Perform this ritual with reverence, gratitude, and respect for nature.

You will need:

A quiet and peaceful outdoor space, preferably near trees or plants.
Incense or dried herbs associated with the earth element, such as sage, cedar, or frankincense.
A small bowl or container of fresh water.
Optional: Crystals or gemstones associated with nature and the plant kingdom, such as moss agate or tree agate.
Optional: Offerings for the spirits, such as flowers, fruits, or seeds.
Instructions:

Find a serene outdoor space where you can sit or stand comfortably. Choose a spot near trees or plants, allowing yourself to be surrounded by their presence.

Light the incense or herbs, allowing the smoke to rise and fill the air. Take a few deep breaths, inhaling the scent and letting it calm your mind and focus your intention.

Hold the bowl of water in your hands, visualizing it being infused with the essence and energy of the celestial trees and plants. Set your intention for communion and connection with the spirits of nature.

If you have chosen to bring crystals or gemstones, hold them in your other hand or place them around you, creating a sacred and harmonious energy field.

Close your eyes and enter a state of deep relaxation. Visualize yourself surrounded by a radiant light, connected to the earth and the heavens. Feel the presence of the spirits of the celestial trees and plants gathering around you, their energy merging with yours.

Offer words of reverence and gratitude to the spirits, expressing your desire to commune with them and learn from their wisdom. Speak from your heart, allowing your words to flow naturally.

Take a moment to listen and observe. Pay attention to any messages, feelings, or sensations that arise. Allow yourself to be open and receptive to the guidance and teachings of the spirits.

When you feel ready, dip your fingertips into the water and gently touch the earth, symbolizing the connection between the celestial realms and the physical plane. Offer any physical offerings you have brought, placing them at the base of a tree or near a plant.

Express gratitude to the spirits for their presence and wisdom. Offer thanks for the communion and connection you have experienced.

Slowly and gently, bring your awareness back to the present moment. Take a few deep breaths, grounding yourself and feeling the energy of the earth beneath your feet.

Conclude the ritual with a final expression of gratitude and a closing statement, such as "May the blessings of the celestial trees and plants guide and inspire me on my spiritual journey. So mote it be."

Remember to always approach nature with respect and reverence. Be mindful of the environment and leave no trace of your presence. Adapt and modify this ritual as needed to align with your personal beliefs and practices, allowing it to resonate deeply with your intention and connection to the spirits of the celestial trees and plants.

162.   Spell for the transmigration of the deceased's soul into the realm of eternal peace

Note: This spell is intended to facilitate the transmigration of the deceased's soul into a state of eternal peace and tranquility. It helps release any lingering attachments or burdens, allowing the soul to transition to a higher realm of existence. Perform this spell with reverence, love, and the utmost respect for the departed.

You will need:

A quiet and sacred space where you can focus without interruptions.
A white candle to represent purity and spiritual illumination.
A small piece of paper and a pen or a feather.
Optional: An image or personal item of the deceased to enhance the connection.
Instructions:

Set up your sacred space by arranging the candle and any optional items in a manner that feels meaningful and comforting to you.

Light the white candle, representing the divine light and guidance for the soul's journey.

Take a few deep breaths to center yourself and invoke a sense of inner peace. Allow yourself to be fully present in the moment.

Hold the small piece of paper in your hand or hold the feather, symbolizing the ethereal nature of the soul.

Close your eyes and visualize the presence of the departed soul. Feel their energy surrounding you with love and trust.

Focus your intention on the transmigration of the soul into the realm of eternal peace. Envision a serene and luminous path unfolding before the soul, leading them to a realm of harmony and bliss.

Speak the following incantation with sincerity and conviction:

"By the power of divine love and light,

I call upon the eternal peace in sight.
May [name of the deceased] transcend all strife,
And journey to the realm of eternal life.

Let go of earthly ties and burdens deep,
Embrace the serenity of endless sleep.
Guide their soul with gentle grace,
To find solace in the heavenly embrace."

Take a moment to reflect on the memories and love you shared with the deceased. Offer words of farewell, expressing your love, gratitude, and support for their journey.

Imagine the soul of the departed gradually becoming lighter and freer, as if their essence is lifted and carried away on a gentle breeze.

When you feel ready, carefully burn the piece of paper or release the feather into the air, symbolizing the release and transmigration of the soul.

Sit in quiet contemplation for a few moments, allowing the energy of the ritual to settle. Feel the peace and serenity enveloping the space.

Thank the divine forces and the departed soul for their presence and participation. Extinguish the candle, knowing that the energy and intention of the spell will continue to guide the soul on its journey.

Remember that this spell is a way to offer support and love to the departed soul, but ultimately the journey of the soul is guided by higher powers and the individual's spiritual path. May this spell bring comfort and peace to you and the departed, facilitating their transition into the realm of eternal peace.

163.   Invocation of the god Ptah for creation and manifestation in the afterlife

Note: The following invocation is intended to call upon the divine presence of Ptah, the Egyptian god associated with creation and craftsmanship. This invocation seeks Ptah's guidance and assistance in the afterlife to facilitate the process of creation and manifestation. Perform this invocation with respect, sincerity, and a focused intention.

You will need:

A quiet and sacred space where you can concentrate without interruptions.
An altar or a dedicated space where you can place a representation or image of Ptah.
If you don't have a physical representation, you can create one with your imagination.
Optional: Offerings such as flowers, incense, or food to honor Ptah.
Instructions:

Find a peaceful space where you can perform the invocation without distractions. Ensure that the space is clean and conducive to a spiritual practice.

Set up your altar or dedicate a space to Ptah. If you have a physical representation or image of Ptah, place it on the altar. If not, visualize Ptah's presence in your mind's eye, imagining his attributes and qualities.

Take a moment to center yourself and enter a state of calm and reverence. Take a few deep breaths and allow yourself to connect with the energy of the divine.

Light any candles or incense you may have as an offering and to create a sacred atmosphere.

Stand or sit comfortably in front of the altar. Close your eyes and bring your attention to your heart center. Visualize a golden light emanating from your heart, representing your divine essence.

With sincerity and reverence, recite the following invocation:

"Great Ptah, Master of Creation,
Divine Craftsman and Artisan of the gods,
I call upon your presence in this sacred space.
Guide me in the realm of the afterlife,
Where creation and manifestation are boundless.

I seek your wisdom and guidance,
To bring forth the power of creation within me.
Grant me the ability to shape my reality,
And manifest my desires in alignment with divine will.

Ptah, I honor your creative essence,
Your hands that shaped the world and all within it.
Help me understand the mysteries of existence,
And use the power of creation for the highest good.

In this sacred union of spirit and matter,
I invoke your presence, Ptah, in the afterlife.
Guide me, inspire me, and empower me,
To manifest my true purpose and divine potential."

Take a moment to feel the presence of Ptah around you. Allow yourself to be open to any messages, insights, or guidance that may come during this invocation.

Express your gratitude to Ptah for his presence and guidance. You may offer your physical offerings at the altar or express your gratitude through words and thoughts.

Spend a few moments in quiet reflection, absorbing the energy and blessings of the invocation.

When you feel ready, slowly conclude the invocation. Thank Ptah once again for his presence and assistance. You may choose to leave the offerings on the altar for some time as a symbol of your gratitude.

Remember that invoking Ptah is a way to connect with the divine energies associated with creation and manifestation. It is through your own efforts, actions, and alignment with divine will that you can bring forth positive and transformative changes in your life, both in the afterlife and in the present realm.

164.   Ritual of anointing with sacred resins for spiritual elevation and enlightenment

This ritual involves the use of sacred resins, such as frankincense, myrrh, copal, or other resinous substances that have been traditionally associated with spiritual elevation and enlightenment. These resins have been used for centuries in various spiritual and religious practices for their purifying and elevating properties. The ritual of anointing with sacred resins can help create a sacred space, purify the energy, and enhance spiritual connection and awareness.

You will need:

Sacred resins (e.g., frankincense, myrrh, copal)
Charcoal tablets or a resin burner
A heatproof container or incense holder
A lighter or matches
Optional: Essential oils or carrier oils for blending
Instructions:

Choose a quiet and dedicated space where you can perform the ritual without interruptions. Ensure that the space is well-ventilated and safe for burning resins.

Prepare your sacred resins and charcoal tablets. If using larger resin pieces, break them into smaller chunks or grind them into a powder for easier burning.

Set up your heatproof container or incense holder. Place a charcoal tablet inside the container and ignite it with a lighter or matches. Allow the charcoal to fully ignite and turn ash-gray before proceeding.

Once the charcoal is ready, sprinkle a small amount of the chosen resin onto the hot surface of the charcoal. As the resin begins to burn and release fragrant smoke, focus your intention on spiritual elevation and enlightenment. Visualize the smoke carrying your intentions and prayers upward towards the divine.

As the sacred resin burns, you may choose to anoint yourself or others present with the smoke. Extend your hands or use a feather or fan to gently waft the smoke over your body, starting from the crown of your head and moving downward, envisioning the smoke purifying and elevating your energy.

While anointing with the smoke, you can recite affirmations or prayers that resonate with your spiritual goals. Speak from your heart and express gratitude for the spiritual elevation and enlightenment you seek.

If desired, you can also blend a few drops of essential oils or carrier oils with the sacred resins to create a personalized anointing oil. This can add an extra layer of intention and fragrance to the ritual. Apply a small amount of the oil mixture to your wrists, temples, or other pulse points as a symbolic anointing.

Allow the resin to burn completely, or if you prefer to end the ritual before that, you can extinguish the charcoal tablet by placing it in a heatproof container filled with sand or water. Ensure that the charcoal is fully cooled before discarding.

Take a few moments to reflect and integrate the experience. Notice any sensations, thoughts, or insights that may arise during or after the ritual. Trust in the transformative power of the ritual and embrace the potential for spiritual elevation and enlightenment.

Remember, the ritual of anointing with sacred resins is a personal and sacred practice. Tailor it to your own beliefs and preferences. The intention and focus you bring to the ritual are key. Regularly incorporating this ritual into your spiritual practice can deepen your connection with the divine, purify your energy, and open the path for spiritual elevation and enlightenment.

165.   Spell for the transformation of the deceased into a vessel of divine grace and mercy

This spell is intended to facilitate the transformation of the deceased into a vessel of divine grace and mercy, allowing them to embody and radiate these qualities in the afterlife. It can be performed as part of a funeral or memorial service, or as a personal ritual to honor and bless the departed soul.

You will need:

A quiet and sacred space
A white candle
Incense (such as sandalwood or frankincense)
A small bowl of water
A photo or representation of the deceased (optional)
Your heartfelt intention and focus
Instructions:

Find a peaceful and undisturbed space where you can perform the spell. It can be indoors or outdoors, as long as it allows for a sense of sacredness and tranquility.

Set up your ritual space by placing the white candle, the incense, and the bowl of water in a central location. If you have a photo or representation of the deceased, you can place it nearby as a focal point.

Light the white candle as a symbol of purity and divine presence. Take a moment to center yourself and connect with your intention of invoking grace and mercy for the deceased.

Light the incense, allowing the fragrant smoke to fill the space. As the smoke rises, visualize it carrying your prayers and intentions to the divine realms, seeking the blessings of grace and mercy for the departed soul.

Dip your fingertips into the bowl of water and gently touch your forehead, heart, and palms, symbolizing purification and the intention to invoke divine qualities. You can silently or verbally express your intention, speaking from your heart.

Direct your focus towards the photo or representation of the deceased, or simply visualize their presence in your mind's eye. Imagine them surrounded by a soft, radiant light, symbolizing divine grace and mercy enveloping their being.

Recite the following spell or create your own heartfelt words:

"In this sacred space, I call upon the divine,
To guide and transform [name of the deceased] in their journey divine.
May their spirit be filled with grace and mercy's embrace,
Radiating love, compassion, and kindness in every place.
As they traverse the realms of the afterlife's domain,
May divine blessings and forgiveness be their eternal gain."

Spend a few moments in silent contemplation, allowing the energy of your intention and the spell to permeate the space. Trust that the divine grace and mercy you invoked will touch and uplift the deceased soul.

When you feel ready, express gratitude for the opportunity to honor and bless the departed soul. Allow the candle and incense to burn out naturally or extinguish them safely if needed.

Take some time for personal reflection or meditation, and if desired, write down any insights or experiences that arise during or after the spell.

Remember, this spell is a deeply personal and spiritual practice. Customize it to suit your beliefs and relationship with the deceased. The power of intention, love, and the connection with the divine are the driving forces behind the transformation. By invoking divine grace and mercy, you contribute to the spiritual growth and well-being of the departed soul in the afterlife.

166. Incantation to invoke the blessings of the celestial music and melodies

This incantation is designed to invoke the blessings and harmonizing influence of the celestial music and melodies, bringing forth a sense of tranquility, inspiration, and connection with the divine. It can be recited during meditation, ritual, or any other practice aimed at attuning oneself to the higher frequencies of the universe.

Close your eyes, take a few deep breaths, and center yourself before beginning the incantation. Allow yourself to feel the presence of the celestial realms and the ethereal melodies that flow through them. When you feel ready, recite the following incantation:

"O celestial realms, where music dwells,
I call upon your harmonies and spells.
With every note, a sacred message is sent,
From the heavens above to the earth, it is sent.

In the symphony of stars and celestial spheres,
I find solace, peace, and ancient wisdom near.
Melodies flow like rivers of light,
Guiding my spirit through the darkest night.

Celestial music, weave your enchanting spell,
Awakening my soul, like a sacred bell.
Elevate my being to higher planes,
Where divine harmonies forever reign.

With every chord and celestial tune,
I attune myself to the eternal commune.
Let the vibrations of your melodies seep,
Into my being, nurturing, soothing, and deep.

O celestial music, bless me with your grace,
Fill my heart and soul, every sacred space.
Align me with the rhythm of the cosmic dance,
Where harmony and divinity forever enhance.

I surrender to your ethereal melodies divine,
Merging with the symphony, as I intertwine.

In unity, oneness, and serenade sublime,
I find peace, love, and harmony, for all of time.

Thank you, celestial music, for your sacred art,
May your blessings forever fill my heart.
As I listen and attune to your celestial symphony,
I embrace the divine within, eternally."

Take a moment to breathe and absorb the vibrations of the incantation. Visualize yourself surrounded by celestial light and immersed in the soothing melodies of the universe. Feel the harmonizing energy flowing through your entire being, aligning you with the higher frequencies of love, peace, and inspiration.

When you feel ready, express gratitude for the celestial music and its blessings. Open your eyes and continue your practice or enjoy the newfound sense of connection and serenity that the incantation has invoked.

Remember, the power of this incantation lies in your intention and receptivity. Allow yourself to be open to the subtle vibrations and messages that the celestial music carries. Embrace the beauty and healing it offers, knowing that the celestial realms are always there, ready to bestow their harmonious gifts upon those who seek them.

167.   Ritual for the transfiguration of the deceased into a divine protector of sacred spaces

This ritual is designed to honor and empower the deceased, transforming their spirit into a guardian and protector of sacred spaces. By invoking their presence and infusing them with divine energy, their essence becomes a force of protection and blessings for sacred places. This ritual can be performed in a specific location or as a general invocation to sanctify any sacred space.

Materials needed:

A representation of the deceased (a photograph, a personal item, or a symbolic object)
Incense or sacred herbs for cleansing and purification
Candles (preferably white or blue) to symbolize purity and divine energy
An offering (flowers, fruits, or any meaningful item)
Procedure:

Choose a quiet and sacred space where you will perform the ritual. Light the incense or sacred herbs and allow the fragrance to fill the space, purifying it and creating a sacred atmosphere.

Place the representation of the deceased in the center of the sacred space, facing the direction you wish them to protect. This can be a photograph of the deceased or any item that symbolizes their presence and essence.

Light the candles and place them around the representation of the deceased, creating a circle of light. As you light each candle, visualize divine energy and protection emanating from it.

Stand before the representation of the deceased and take a few deep breaths to center yourself. Reflect on the qualities and virtues of the deceased that you wish to invoke and honor during the ritual.

Begin to recite the following invocation:

"O spirit of [name of the deceased], I call upon you now,
To be a guardian and protector of this sacred space, somehow.
Infuse your essence with divine light and might,
To watch over and bless this place both day and night.

Through this ritual, I honor your memory and soul,
And ask that you embrace this new divine role.
As a guardian and protector, strong and true,
May your presence radiate and imbue.

[Name of the deceased], let your spirit soar high,
As you safeguard this sacred space, I testify.
Protect it from harm, negativity, and ill,
May only love, light, and divinity fulfill.

I offer this [name the offering] as a token of gratitude,
For your presence here, your protection pursued.
Bless this space with your divine grace,
Creating a sanctuary in this sacred place.

Guide those who enter with wisdom and love,
Showering blessings from the realms above.
May your spirit interweave with the sacred land,
Creating harmony and peace, hand in hand.

I thank you, [name of the deceased], for your eternal embrace,
For becoming a divine guardian in this sacred space.
As I complete this ritual, your presence I feel,
Blessings and protection, forever real."

Take a moment to sit or stand in silence, allowing the energy to settle and the presence of the deceased to envelop the space. Offer your own personal prayers, thoughts, or messages to the deceased, expressing your gratitude and intentions for their guardianship.

When you feel ready, extinguish the candles and leave the sacred space in a state of reverence. You may choose to keep the representation of the deceased in the sacred space permanently or return it to its original place, knowing that their presence will continue to protect and bless the space.

Remember, this ritual is a symbolic act of honoring and invoking the divine qualities of the deceased as a protector of sacred spaces. The power lies in your intention and belief in the sacred bond between the deceased and the space. Trust that their essence will continue to watch over and safeguard the sanctity of the space, bringing blessings and harmony to all who enter.

168.   Spell for the transformation of the deceased into a vessel of divine light and wisdom

Note: This spell is intended to facilitate the transformation of the deceased into a vessel of divine light and wisdom. It is important to approach this spell with reverence and respect for the deceased and their journey.

Materials needed:

A quiet and sacred space
A candle (preferably white or gold)
Matches or a lighter
A photo or representation of the deceased (optional)
A piece of paper and a pen or a small piece of parchment
A small bowl or container
Instructions:

Find a quiet and sacred space where you can perform this spell without interruptions. Create a serene atmosphere by clearing the space of any clutter and ensuring a sense of calmness.

Place the candle in a safe holder at the center of your workspace. Light the candle using matches or a lighter, invoking the divine presence and the light of wisdom.

If you have a photo or representation of the deceased, place it near the candle. If not, you can simply visualize the presence of the deceased in your mind.

Take a few deep breaths and center yourself. Allow your mind to settle and your heart to open. Focus your attention on the candle flame, acknowledging it as a symbol of divine light and wisdom.

On the piece of paper or parchment, write the name of the deceased. If you have any specific intentions or prayers for their transformation, write them down as well. Feel free to express your love, gratitude, and any messages you wish to convey.

Hold the paper in your hands and visualize the deceased surrounded by a radiant

169.   Spell for the reunion of the deceased's soul with their beloved pets and animal companions

This spell is designed to facilitate the reunion of the deceased with their beloved pets and animal companions in the afterlife. It is a heartfelt invocation that seeks to bring comfort, love, and eternal companionship between the departed soul and the animals that were dear to them in life.

Materials needed:

A photograph or representation of the deceased
A photograph or representation of the beloved pet or animal companion
Candles (preferably white or green) to symbolize purity and connection with nature
Incense or sacred herbs for cleansing and purifying the space
An offering (such as a small bowl of water or a favorite treat of the beloved pet)
Procedure:

Find a quiet and peaceful space where you can perform the spell. Light the incense or sacred herbs, allowing the fragrant smoke to cleanse and purify the area.

Place the photograph or representation of the deceased in the center of the space. If possible, place the photograph or representation of the beloved pet or animal companion next to it.

Light the candles and place them around the photographs, creating a circle of gentle light. As you light each candle, focus on the love and connection between the deceased and their beloved pet.

Take a moment to center yourself and connect with your intentions. Feel the love and compassion in your heart as you prepare to invoke the reunion of the departed soul and their animal companion.

Begin to recite the following spell, speaking with sincerity and love:

"By the power of love, light, and divine decree,
I call upon the spirits to hear my plea.
In this sacred space, I ask for a sacred bond,
Between [name of the deceased] and [name of the beloved pet], so fond.

May the soul of [name of the deceased] find peace and rest,
And be reunited with their beloved companion, blessed.
In the realms beyond, where love knows no bounds,
Let [name of the beloved pet] be found.

O spirits of love, hear my sincere plea,
Bring [name of the deceased] and [name of the beloved pet] together, so free.
Across the veils of time and space,
Unite their souls in a loving embrace.

Let their spirits intertwine, forever entwined,
With love and companionship that is kind.
In the realm of eternal joy and delight,
Let [name of the deceased] and [name of the beloved pet] reunite.

With every breath, with every beat of the heart,
May their love and bond never depart.
Grant them eternal companionship and bliss,
In the realms of the afterlife, where all is amiss.

I offer this [name the offering] as a symbol of devotion,
To honor the love and connection, like an ocean.
May [name of the deceased] and [name of the beloved pet] be forever blessed,
In the sacred union, their souls caressed.

So mote it be."

Take a moment to sit or stand in silence, envisioning the reunion of the deceased and their beloved pet in the realms of the afterlife. Send your love, gratitude, and well wishes to both souls, knowing that they are united in love and eternal companionship.

When you are ready, extinguish the candles and leave the space in a state of reverence. You may choose to keep the photographs or representations of the deceased and the beloved pet in a special place or return them to their original locations, knowing that the spell has set the intention for their reunion.

Remember, this spell is a way to honor the bond between the deceased and their beloved pet or animal companion and to facilitate their reunion in the afterlife. It is a gesture of love, compassion, and eternal companionship. Trust in the power of love and the spiritual realm to bring about the reunion and find solace in knowing that their love transcends the physical plane.

170. Invocation of the goddess Taweret for fertility and abundance in the afterlife

Oh mighty Taweret, goddess of fertility and abundance,
I call upon you in this sacred space and time.
With reverence and respect, I seek your guidance and blessings,
For the soul of [deceased's name] as they embark on their journey beyond.

Taweret, protector of women and motherhood,
Embrace the soul of [deceased's name] with your loving presence.
Surround them with your nurturing energy and compassionate embrace,
And guide them towards the realm of eternal fertility and abundance.

In the afterlife, may [deceased's name] experience a bountiful harvest,
May their spirit be fertile with wisdom, love, and creativity.
May they be blessed with the abundance of joy, prosperity, and fulfillment,
And may their soul blossom like the lotus in the waters of eternity.

Taweret, ancient goddess of the cosmic river,
Flow through [deceased's name]'s journey, nurturing their soul.
Grant them the strength and resilience to overcome any obstacles,
And bless them with the fruitful blessings of your divine presence.

In the realm of the afterlife, may [deceased's name] find comfort and solace,
May they experience the fullness of life and the blessings of abundance.
May their soul be forever nourished and sustained by your loving energy,
As they embody the essence of fertility and abundance in its purest form.

Oh Taweret, goddess of fertility and abundance,
I offer my gratitude for your presence and blessings.
May your divine essence guide [deceased's name] in the afterlife,
And may their soul flourish with eternal fertility and abundance.

So be it, and so it is.

171. Invocation of the goddess Neith for wisdom and skill in the afterlife

Goddess Neith, renowned for your wisdom and skill,
I call upon your divine presence, my heart does thrill.
In the realm beyond, where souls find their rest,
I seek your guidance, Goddess Neith, I request.

Bearer of knowledge, master of the cosmic thread,
Your wisdom and insight, upon me, please shed.
Guide me through the realms of the afterlife,
With your divine wisdom, dispel all strife.

Goddess Neith, with your skillful hands,
Teach me the arts, the crafts, the sacred bands.
Grant me the knowledge and expertise,
To navigate the afterlife with grace and ease.

In this sacred space, I honor your name,
Neith, the weaver of destinies, beyond worldly fame.
Open the gates of wisdom, ancient and profound,
Let your teachings and skills in my spirit resound.

Grant me the ability to learn and to grow,
To acquire wisdom that only the afterlife can bestow.
With your guidance, let my spirit be uplifted,
In the realms beyond, may my skills be gifted.

Goddess Neith, I offer my reverence and devotion,
To you, the guardian of wisdom, an eternal ocean.
Bless me with your presence, in the afterlife's domain,
So that I may embody your wisdom, never in vain.

I thank you, Goddess Neith, for hearing my call,
May your wisdom and skill forever enthrall.
In the realms beyond, guide me on my way,
With your blessings, I shall thrive each day.

So mote it be.

Take a moment to feel the presence of Goddess Neith and express your gratitude for her wisdom and guidance. Trust in her power to bestow upon you the knowledge and skills needed to navigate the afterlife with grace and purpose.

172. Ritual of purification through the sacred chants of the eternal hymns

Prepare yourself for the ritual by finding a quiet and sacred space where you can focus without any disturbances. Light a candle or incense to create a sacred atmosphere. Sit or stand comfortably, with your back straight and your feet firmly grounded.

Take a few deep breaths, inhaling deeply through your nose and exhaling slowly through your mouth. Allow your body and mind to relax, letting go of any tension or distractions.

Close your eyes and imagine yourself surrounded by a soft, golden light. Feel the warmth and purity of this light enveloping your entire being, cleansing and purifying you from within.

Now, begin to chant softly, allowing the sacred sounds to flow from your lips. Let the vibrations of the sound reverberate through your body, resonating with your energy centers and purifying them.

As you chant, envision the sacred hymns reaching out to the heavens, carrying your intentions for purification and transformation. Feel the divine presence surrounding you, supporting you on this spiritual journey.

Continue chanting for as long as it feels right, allowing the energy to build and intensify. Let the sacred vibrations cleanse away any negativity or impurities, leaving you feeling light, clear, and renewed.

After some time, gradually slow down the chanting and come to a stillness. Take a moment to bask in the residual energy and absorb the purifying effects of the sacred hymns.

Express your gratitude to the divine forces that have guided and blessed you throughout this ritual. Offer a prayer or a simple gesture of thanks for the purification and transformation you have experienced.

Slowly open your eyes and take a few more deep breaths, feeling grounded and present in the moment. Carry the sense of purification and renewal with you as you go about your day, knowing that you have connected with the eternal hymns and received their cleansing power.

Remember, the ritual of purification through sacred chants can be performed regularly to maintain and deepen your spiritual cleansing.

173.   Spell for the liberation of the deceased's soul from the cycle of suffering

Note: This spell is intended to be performed by a knowledgeable practitioner with respect and reverence for the deceased. It is recommended to seek the guidance of an experienced spiritual practitioner or priest in conducting this ritual.

Ingredients:

A sacred space or altar
An image or representation of the deceased
Incense (such as sandalwood or frankincense)
A white candle
A small bowl of salt
A bowl of water
Procedure:

Prepare your sacred space or altar. Cleanse and purify the space by lighting the incense and allowing its fragrant smoke to waft through the area. Set up the image or representation of the deceased in a central position.

Light the white candle as a symbol of purity and divine light. Place it next to the image of the deceased.

Take a moment to center yourself and focus your intention on the liberation of the deceased's soul from the cycle of suffering. Visualize the deceased surrounded by a radiant light, free from any pain, anguish, or attachments.

Sprinkle a small amount of salt into the bowl of water, symbolizing purification and cleansing. Stir the water gently with your fingers, infusing it with your intention for liberation and release.

Hold your hands over the bowl of water and say the following incantation, or create your own heartfelt words:

"By the power of love and compassion,
I call upon the divine forces to intervene.
May the soul of [name of the deceased] be freed,
From the cycle of suffering and find eternal peace."

With reverence and respect, pour a few drops of the blessed water over the image or representation of the deceased. Visualize the water washing away any remnants of suffering or karmic burdens, leaving only purity and liberation.

Take a moment to express your heartfelt intentions and prayers for the soul of the deceased. Speak words of love, forgiveness, and well wishes. Feel free to share any personal messages or memories.

Sit in silence for a few moments, holding a space of peace and tranquility. Allow the energy of the ritual to settle and permeate the surroundings.

Express your gratitude to the divine and to the soul of the deceased for their presence and participation in this ritual. Extinguish the candle and give thanks for the guidance and blessings received.

Close the ritual by safely disposing of the blessed water and salt, returning the space to its normal state, and offering a final prayer or affirmation for the liberation and peace of the deceased.

Remember to approach this ritual with reverence and sincerity. It is a sacred act of compassion and love for the soul of the deceased, seeking their ultimate liberation from suffering and their journey toward eternal peace.

174.   Incantation to awaken the dormant spiritual senses within the deceased's spirit

Note: This incantation is intended to be spoken with reverence and respect for the deceased. It is recommended to perform this incantation in a quiet and sacred space, focusing your intention on awakening the dormant spiritual senses within the departed soul.

Begin by centering yourself and creating a calm and peaceful atmosphere. Take a few deep breaths, allowing yourself to relax and enter a meditative state. Visualize the presence of the deceased and imagine their spirit being receptive and open to the incantation.

Speak the following incantation with conviction and clarity:

"Spirit of [name of the deceased], hear my call,
Awaken from slumber, senses rise and stand tall.
Eyes to see the truth beyond the veil,
Ears to hear whispers of guidance, never to fail.

Nose to sense the subtle scents of spirit,
Tongue to taste the wisdom, no limit.
Skin to feel the energy that surrounds,
Heart to know love's presence, unbound.

Mind to comprehend the depths of divine,
Spiritual senses awakened, let them shine.
From this moment forth, in the realm unseen,
May the deceased's senses be keen.

I call upon the forces of light and love,
To bless and guide the spirit from above.
Awakened senses, bring clarity and insight,
To navigate the realms, day and night.

As I speak, so mote it be,
May the dormant senses awaken and be free.
With reverence and love, I set them aglow,
For the spirit's journey, to flourish and grow."

Take a few moments of silence after reciting the incantation, allowing the energy to settle and permeate the space. Express gratitude to the spirit of the deceased for their presence and willingness to awaken their dormant spiritual senses.

Close the ritual by offering a prayer or affirmation for the continued growth and enlightenment of the departed soul. Thank the divine and the spirit of the deceased for their participation and bid them farewell with love and light.

Remember to approach this incantation with sincerity and respect, understanding that it is a sacred act to awaken and honor the dormant spiritual senses of the departed.

175.   Ritual for the communion with the spirits of the celestial mountains and peaks

This ritual is designed to establish a connection with the spirits of the celestial mountains and peaks. It is recommended to perform this ritual outdoors, preferably in a mountainous or elevated area, where you can feel closer to the energy of the mountains. Here is a step-by-step guide:

Preparation:

Choose a day and time when you can be undisturbed and have ample time for the ritual.
Gather any items you may need, such as crystals, herbs, or offerings.
Dress comfortably and appropriately for the weather and the outdoor environment.

Grounding and Centering:

Find a quiet spot and take a few moments to ground yourself. Stand barefoot on the earth and take deep breaths to connect with the energy of the land.
Close your eyes and envision roots growing from your feet, grounding you deep into the earth. Feel the stability and strength of the earth beneath you.

Invocation:

Stand with your arms raised, palms facing the sky, and speak the following invocation:
"Spirits of the celestial mountains and peaks,
I call upon your ancient wisdom and mystique.
From high above, where heavens meet the land,
I seek your guidance, please extend your helping hand."

Offerings:

Prepare offerings that symbolize your respect and gratitude for the spirits of the mountains. These can include flowers, crystals, water, or other items of significance.
Place the offerings at the base of a tree or on a rock, creating a small altar dedicated to the spirits of the mountains.

Communion:

Sit or stand in a comfortable position, facing the mountains or peaks.

Close your eyes and imagine yourself surrounded by a vibrant and shimmering light. Open your senses to the energy of the mountains. Feel the strength, serenity, and grandeur of the peaks.
Meditate on the wisdom and teachings that the spirits of the mountains may offer you. Listen for any messages or insights that may come to you during this communion.

Gratitude and Farewell:

Express your gratitude to the spirits of the mountains for their presence and guidance. Offer a heartfelt thank you for any messages or insights received.
Slowly bring your awareness back to the present moment, feeling grounded and connected to the earth.

Closing:

Close the ritual by offering a final prayer or affirmation, expressing your intention to carry the wisdom and energy of the mountains with you.
Leave the offerings at the altar as a sign of respect and appreciation.
Take a moment to reflect on the experience and integrate any insights or feelings that arose during the ritual.

Remember, when communing with the spirits of the mountains, it is essential to approach them with respect, humility, and gratitude. Always be mindful of your surroundings and follow any local regulations or guidelines when practicing rituals in natural environments.

176.   Spell for the transmigration of the deceased's soul into the realm of eternal light and truth

This spell is intended to assist in the transmigration of the deceased's soul into the realm of eternal light and truth. It is a sacred invocation that calls upon divine forces to guide the soul to its ultimate destination. Here is a spell you can use:

Preparation:

Find a quiet and sacred space where you can perform the spell without interruption.
Gather a white candle, a piece of paper, and a pen or pencil.
Clear your mind and set your intention to facilitate the transmigration of the deceased's soul to the realm of eternal light and truth.

Candle Dedication:

Take the white candle and hold it in your hands, focusing your intention on its flame.
Say the following words or adapt them to fit your personal beliefs:
"I dedicate this candle to the divine light and truth,
May it guide the soul of [name of the deceased] in its journey.
May it illuminate the path and lead them to eternal peace and enlightenment."

Invocation:

Light the candle and place it in a safe holder on your altar or sacred space.
Close your eyes and take a few deep breaths to center yourself.
Visualize the presence of the deceased, surrounded by divine light and love.
Speak the following invocation or create your own heartfelt words:
"Divine forces of light and truth, I call upon you now.
Guide the soul of [name of the deceased] to its rightful place.
Illuminate their path with your radiant light,
And reveal the eternal truth that lies beyond."

Personal Message:

Take the piece of paper and write a personal message to the deceased.
Express your love, well wishes, and any final thoughts or blessings.
Fold the paper and hold it close to your heart, infusing it with your intentions.

Burning Ceremony:

Hold the folded paper over the flame of the candle, allowing it to catch fire.
Safely place the burning paper in a fireproof container or cauldron.
As you watch the paper burn, visualize the message being released to the divine
realms, reaching the deceased's soul and guiding them towards eternal light and truth.

Closing:

Express your gratitude to the divine forces for their guidance and assistance.
Extinguish the candle, either by snuffing it or blowing it out gently.
Take a moment to reflect on the spell and the connection you have made with the
deceased's soul.

Remember, this spell is a symbolic gesture to support the transition of the deceased's
soul. It is essential to perform it with reverence, love, and respect. Adapt the spell as
needed to align with your personal beliefs and practices.

177.   Invocation of the god Sobek for strength and protection in the afterlife

The following invocation is intended to invoke the presence and blessings of the god Sobek, known for his strength and protective qualities. Use this invocation to seek Sobek's guidance and support for the deceased in their journey through the afterlife:

Preparation:

Find a quiet and sacred space where you can focus without distractions.
Set up an altar or sacred area with an image or representation of Sobek.
Gather offerings such as fresh water, incense, and any items associated with Sobek, such as images of crocodiles or green stones.

Cleansing and Centering:

Take a moment to ground yourself and center your energy.
Light the incense and allow the smoke to purify the space and create a sacred atmosphere.
Take a few deep breaths, letting go of any distractions or concerns, and focusing your mind on the intention of invoking Sobek.

Invocation:

Stand before the altar or sacred area and extend your hands towards the representation of Sobek.
Speak the following invocation or adapt it to your personal words and beliefs:
"Mighty Sobek, powerful guardian and protector,
I call upon your presence in this sacred space.
In the realm of the afterlife, guide and watch over [name of the deceased].
Bestow upon them your strength and protection.
Keep them safe from harm and guide them through the challenges they may face.
Oh Sobek, Lord of the Nile, lend your aid and wisdom to [name of the deceased]
As they journey through the afterlife and seek eternal peace."

Offerings:

Present the offerings of fresh water and any other items you have gathered to the image or representation of Sobek.

Express your gratitude and respect for Sobek's presence and assistance in the afterlife journey of the deceased.

Connection and Meditation:

Close your eyes and visualize the presence of Sobek surrounding you and the altar. Imagine the strength and protection of Sobek enveloping the deceased, guiding them through the challenges of the afterlife and ensuring their safety.
Take a few moments to meditate on the energy of Sobek, feeling his presence and the support he provides.

Closing:

Express your gratitude to Sobek for his presence and assistance.
Leave the offerings on the altar for a period of time as a symbol of your connection and respect.
When you are ready, extinguish the incense and close the sacred space.

Remember, this invocation is a way to connect with the energy and essence of the god Sobek and seek his protection and strength for the deceased. Adapt the invocation and ritual to suit your personal beliefs and practices, and always approach the gods with reverence and respect.

178. Ritual of anointing with sacred crystals for spiritual clarity and insight

This ritual is designed to harness the energy and properties of sacred crystals to enhance spiritual clarity and insight. Follow these steps to perform the ritual:

Preparation:

Choose crystals that are known for their ability to promote clarity and insight, such as clear quartz, amethyst, selenite, or labradorite.
Find a quiet and sacred space where you can perform the ritual without interruptions.
Create a peaceful ambiance by lighting candles, burning incense, or playing soft music if desired.

Cleansing and Grounding:

Begin by cleansing yourself and the crystals. You can do this by holding the crystals under running water or smudging them with sage or palo santo.
Take a few moments to ground yourself by taking deep breaths and focusing your attention on the present moment.

Invocation:

Hold the crystals in your hands and close your eyes.
State your intention for the ritual, such as seeking spiritual clarity and insight.
Speak an invocation or prayer that resonates with you, calling upon the divine or higher powers to bless and empower the crystals for this purpose. You can use your own words or a pre-existing invocation that speaks to you.

Anointing:

Take one crystal at a time and hold it gently in your hand.
With a separate dropper or small brush, apply a few drops of anointing oil onto the crystal's surface. Choose an oil that corresponds to clarity and insight, such as frankincense, lavender, or sandalwood. Alternatively, you can use a diluted essential oil spray to mist the crystals.
As you anoint each crystal, visualize and intend that the oil infuses the crystal with its properties of clarity, insight, and spiritual wisdom.

Affirmation:

Hold the anointed crystal in your hands and speak an affirmation that aligns with your intention. For example, you can say, "I am open to receiving divine clarity and deep spiritual insight. These crystals guide me on my path of wisdom and understanding."

Meditation and Connection:

Sit or lie down in a comfortable position, holding the anointed crystals in your hands or placing them on your body where you feel guided.
Close your eyes and focus on your breath. Allow yourself to relax and enter a meditative state.
Visualize the crystals emitting a radiant light that fills your being with clarity, insight, and spiritual wisdom.
Stay in this meditative state for as long as you feel comfortable, allowing the energy of the crystals to permeate your being and bring forth insights and guidance.

Gratitude and Closure:

When you are ready, gently return your awareness to the present moment.
Express gratitude for the guidance and clarity received during the ritual.
Thank the crystals for their assistance and the higher powers you invoked for their presence and support.
Place the anointed crystals in a safe and sacred space, or carry them with you as a reminder of the spiritual clarity and insight you seek.

Remember, the power of the ritual comes from your intention, focus, and connection with the crystals. Adapt the ritual as needed to align with your personal beliefs and practices. Regularly cleanse and recharge the crystals to maintain their energetic potency.

179.   Spell for the transformation of the deceased into a vessel of divine transformation

This spell is intended to facilitate the transformation of the deceased into a vessel of divine transformation. It invokes the powers of the divine and sets the intention for the soul's metamorphosis. Perform this spell with reverence and a sincere belief in the transformative power of the divine.

Here is the spell:

Preparation:

Find a quiet and sacred space where you can perform the spell undisturbed.
Gather any items that hold personal significance or symbolism to the deceased or the concept of transformation. This could include candles, crystals, feathers, or objects representing elements of nature.
Create an altar or sacred space where you can place these items during the spell.

Centering and Grounding:

Take a few moments to center yourself and connect with your inner calm.
Close your eyes and take deep breaths, focusing on the sensation of your breath entering and leaving your body.
Visualize roots extending from your feet into the earth, grounding you and connecting you to its energy.

Invocation:

Light a candle or candles on your altar as a representation of the divine presence.
Speak an invocation to invite the divine energies of transformation to be present.
You can use your own words or adapt the following:
"I call upon the divine forces of transformation,
In this sacred space, I seek your assistance.
I invoke the power of change and renewal,
To guide the deceased into a vessel of divine transformation.
May their soul be reborn and infused with divine light.
Grant them the power to transcend and evolve,
As they embark on their journey of eternal transformation."

Personal Connection:

Take a moment to connect with the deceased and visualize their spirit being present with you.
Speak their name out loud and express your intention for their transformation.
Share any personal messages or words of love and support that you feel guided to communicate.

Symbolic Ritual:

Use the items you have gathered to create a symbolic ritual that represents the transformative journey.
For example, you can place feathers to symbolize the shedding of old limitations, or crystals to represent the awakening of higher consciousness.
Arrange these items on your altar or hold them in your hands as you focus on the transformative energy they represent.

Affirmation and Release:

State a powerful affirmation that affirms the deceased's transformation and release from earthly limitations. You can use your own words or adapt the following:
"I affirm the transformation of [name of the deceased].
Their spirit is now a vessel of divine transformation.
They are free from earthly limitations,
Embracing their eternal journey of growth and evolution.
May the divine light guide and protect them always."

Closing and Gratitude:

Express gratitude to the divine energies, the deceased, and any other spiritual guides or beings you feel connected to.
Thank them for their presence and assistance in this transformative process.
Blow out the candles, signaling the end of the spell.

Remember, this spell is a sacred act of intention and connection with the divine. The true power lies within your sincere belief and the energy you bring to the spell.
Perform this ritual with love, respect, and reverence for the deceased and the transformative process they are undertaking.

180. Incantation to invoke the blessings of the celestial rivers and streams

This incantation is designed to invoke the blessings of the celestial rivers and streams, connecting you to the flow of divine energy, healing, and abundance. By reciting this incantation with intention and reverence, you can tap into the sacred power and guidance of these celestial waters.

Here is the incantation:

"O mighty rivers and flowing streams,
From celestial realms, your blessings gleam.
I call upon your sacred waters pure,
To cleanse and heal, to guide and secure.

With each gentle current and sparkling flow,
Your wisdom and grace, I seek to know.
Through me, let your essence pour and glide,
A source of healing and nourishment, worldwide.

Like a river's journey, winding and long,
Carry me to a place where I belong.
Wash away all that no longer serves,
Revive my spirit, as new life observes.

By the banks of your ethereal streams,
I find solace, as in heavenly dreams.
Grant me your guidance, your currents deep,
In your sacred waters, my soul shall keep.

Flow through me, celestial rivers grand,
Envelop me in your blessings, hand in hand.
With gratitude, I honor your sacred course,
As I align with your divine force.

As above, so below, our spirits entwine,
In the rhythm of waters, eternal and divine.
Celestial rivers and streams, I call you near,
Embracing your blessings, forever I hold dear."

Recite this incantation with focus and intention, envisioning the celestial rivers and streams surrounding and infusing you with their blessings. Feel the cleansing, healing, and guidance they bring, and embrace their energy as it flows through you.

After reciting the incantation, take a few moments to sit in stillness and gratitude, allowing the energy of the celestial waters to integrate within you. You can also visualize yourself surrounded by a gentle flow of water, symbolizing the ongoing connection with the celestial rivers and their blessings.

Remember, the power of this incantation lies in your intention and belief. Embrace the flow of the celestial waters with an open heart and a receptive spirit, and trust that their blessings will manifest in your life.

181.   Ritual for the transfiguration of the deceased into a divine guardian of sacred wisdom

This ritual is intended to facilitate the transfiguration of the deceased into a divine guardian of sacred wisdom. By performing this ritual with reverence and intention, you can honor the spiritual journey of the departed and empower their essence to serve as a guardian of sacred wisdom.

Here is a suggested ritual:

Preparation:

Find a quiet and sacred space where you can perform the ritual undisturbed.
Create an altar or sacred space with items that symbolize wisdom and spiritual guidance, such as a book or scroll, a feather, a candle, and any other objects that hold personal significance.
Light the candle as a representation of divine light and guidance.
Invocation:

Begin by centering yourself and focusing your intention on honoring the deceased and their spiritual journey.
Call upon the divine energies and any deities or spiritual beings associated with wisdom and guardianship, such as Thoth or Athena.
Speak the following invocation or create your own, expressing your intention to transfigure the deceased into a guardian of sacred wisdom:
"Divine spirits of wisdom and guidance,
I call upon you in this sacred rite.
With reverence and love, I seek your presence,
To honor and empower the departed's spiritual light.

By the sacred flame and the symbols of wisdom,
I invoke the transfiguration of their essence.
Let them become a guardian of sacred wisdom,
A beacon of light, forever in divine presence."

Communion:

Take a moment to meditate and connect with the energy of the departed. Visualize their spirit merging with the divine light, becoming illuminated and transformed into a guardian of sacred wisdom.
Share any thoughts, messages, or gratitude you may have for the departed. Feel their presence and the wisdom they carried during their physical life.

Offering:

Offer the objects on the altar or sacred space as a symbolic gesture of honoring the departed and their journey towards becoming a guardian of sacred wisdom.
Speak your intentions aloud, stating that the departed's essence is now dedicated to serving as a guardian and guide for those seeking wisdom and spiritual guidance.

Closing:

Express your gratitude to the divine energies, deities, and spiritual beings who have witnessed and supported the ritual.
Extinguish the candle, signaling the completion of the ritual.

Remember, this ritual is a symbolic and spiritual act of honoring the deceased and their connection to wisdom. The power lies in your intention, love, and reverence for the departed. Trust that their essence will continue to guide and inspire others in their spiritual journeys.

182.   Spell for the reunion of the deceased's soul with their spiritual lineage

This spell is designed to facilitate the reunion of the deceased's soul with their spiritual lineage. It aims to create a sacred connection between the departed and their ancestors, guides, and spiritual lineage, allowing for guidance, support, and continued growth beyond the physical realm.

Here is a suggested spell:

Preparation:

Find a quiet and sacred space where you can perform the spell without interruption. Gather items that symbolize the deceased and their spiritual lineage, such as photographs, mementos, or symbolic objects that represent their ancestors or spiritual connections.
Light a candle or incense to create a sacred atmosphere.

Invocation:

Begin by centering yourself and focusing your intention on creating a bridge between the deceased's soul and their spiritual lineage.
Call upon the energies of the ancestors, guides, and spiritual lineage, expressing your sincere desire for the reunion of the departed's soul.
Speak the following invocation or create your own, speaking from your heart:
"Ancestors and guides of (name of the deceased),
Hear my call and feel my intention.
I stand here as a humble intermediary,
Seeking the reunion of (name of the deceased)'s soul with their spiritual lineage.

By the sacred flame and the power of love,
I open a portal of connection and divine reunion.
Let (name of the deceased)'s soul be embraced
By the wisdom, love, and guidance of their ancestors and spiritual guides.

May this sacred union bring comfort and strength,
A continuation of their spiritual journey beyond the physical.
Let their soul be guided and supported by their lineage,
Forever connected, forever protected, forever embraced."

Connection:

Hold the items symbolizing the deceased and their spiritual lineage in your hands.
Visualize a warm and loving light surrounding the objects, representing the reunion
and connection of the departed's soul with their spiritual lineage.
Feel the presence of the ancestors and guides, welcoming and embracing the
departed's soul with love and guidance.

Offering:

Place the objects representing the deceased and their spiritual lineage on the altar or
sacred space.
Express your gratitude and love for the ancestors, guides, and spiritual lineage for
their support and presence in this reunion.

Closing:

Take a moment to sit in stillness and gratitude, allowing the energy of the spell to
settle and integrate.
Express your heartfelt gratitude to the ancestors, guides, and spiritual lineage for their
love and continued support.
Blow out the candle or let the incense burn out naturally, symbolizing the
completion of the spell.

Remember, this spell is a symbolic and energetic act to foster the reunion of the
deceased's soul with their spiritual lineage. Trust in the power of the intention and
the love you put into the spell. The connection between the departed and their
spiritual lineage may continue to grow and evolve over time, providing guidance and
support to the departed's soul on their ongoing spiritual journey.

183. Invocation of the goddess Taweret for fertility and abundance in the afterlife

Goddess Taweret is a powerful deity associated with fertility, childbirth, and protection. Her presence and blessings can be invoked to bring fertility and abundance to the deceased in the afterlife. Here is an invocation to call upon the energy and guidance of the Goddess Taweret:

Preparation:

Find a quiet and sacred space where you can perform the invocation without interruption.
Create an altar or sacred space with items representing fertility and abundance, such as symbols of pregnancy, seeds, fruits, and flowers.
Light a candle or incense to set a sacred atmosphere.

Opening:

Take a few deep breaths to center yourself and connect with the energy of the space.
Light the candle or incense as a symbolic offering to the Goddess Taweret.
Close your eyes and visualize a gentle, nurturing presence surrounding you.

Invocation:

Speak the following invocation or create your own, speaking from your heart:
"Mighty Goddess Taweret, protector of life and bringer of abundance,
I call upon your presence and blessings in this sacred space.
Hear my voice and feel my sincere reverence as I seek your guidance.

In the realm of the afterlife, where life is transformed and renewed,
I ask for your divine intervention to bestow fertility and abundance upon (name of the deceased).
May their spirit be nourished and blessed with bountiful blessings.

Goddess Taweret, motherly and wise,
I implore you to bring forth the energy of fertility and growth.
Let the deceased be embraced by your loving and protective presence,
Ensuring their eternal prosperity and abundance.

May their journey in the afterlife be filled with joy, growth, and the manifestation of their desires.
Guide them through the cycles of rebirth and renewal,
And let the fruits of their spirit flourish in your divine care.

I offer my gratitude and devotion to you, Goddess Taweret,
For your unwavering support and blessings.
May your energy continue to flow through (name of the deceased),
Granting them fertility and abundance in the afterlife."

Connection:

Take a moment to imagine the energy of Goddess Taweret enveloping the space and filling it with her nurturing presence.
Visualize the deceased being embraced by her loving energy, surrounded by fertility and abundance.

Closing:

Express your gratitude to Goddess Taweret for her presence and blessings.
Blow out the candle or let the incense burn out naturally, symbolizing the completion of the invocation.

Remember, this invocation is a symbolic and energetic act to invoke the energy and blessings of Goddess Taweret for fertility and abundance in the afterlife. Trust in the power of your intention and the connection you have made with the goddess. May the deceased be blessed with a bountiful and prosperous journey in the afterlife.

184.   Ritual of purification through the sacred dances of the eternal rhythm

Dance has long been used as a form of expression, celebration, and purification. In this ritual, we will utilize the power of sacred dance to cleanse and purify the spirit. Here is a ritual for purification through the sacred dances of the eternal rhythm:

Preparation:

Find a quiet and sacred space where you can perform the ritual without interruption. Clear the space of any clutter and create an open area for movement.
Play music that resonates with your intentions and creates a sacred atmosphere.

Centering:

Stand tall and take a few deep breaths, allowing yourself to become fully present in the moment.
Close your eyes and visualize a vibrant and radiant light surrounding your body, purifying and energizing you.

Setting Intentions:

Set your intention for the dance ritual. It can be a general intention for purification or specific areas of your life that you wish to cleanse and release.
State your intentions aloud or silently, expressing your desire for purification and renewal.

Dance of Release:

Begin moving your body to the rhythm of the music, allowing the energy to flow through you.
Focus on releasing any negative or stagnant energies that may be weighing you down.
Let your movements be free and expressive, allowing your body to release tension and emotions.

Dance of Renewal:

As the music continues, shift your focus to inviting in positive and transformative energies.

Let your movements become more fluid and uplifting, symbolizing the renewal and rejuvenation of your spirit.

Visualize the energy of purification surrounding you, cleansing away any impurities and leaving you refreshed and revitalized.

Dance of Gratitude:

Slow down your movements and bring your dance to a gentle conclusion.

Take a moment to express gratitude for the opportunity to cleanse and purify your spirit through dance.

Place your hands over your heart and offer thanks for the renewal and transformation you have experienced.

Reflection and Integration:

Sit or stand in stillness and reflect on your dance experience.

Notice any shifts in your energy or emotions and acknowledge the cleansing and purifying effects of the ritual.

Take a few more deep breaths to ground yourself and integrate the energies of the ritual into your being.

Remember, this ritual is a personal and symbolic practice to purify and cleanse your spirit through the power of dance. Allow yourself to be fully present and let the movements flow naturally from within. Embrace the sacredness of the moment and the transformative potential of the eternal rhythm.

185.   Spell for the liberation of the deceased's soul from the illusions of the material world

This spell is designed to assist in the liberation of the deceased's soul from the illusions and attachments of the material world, allowing them to transcend to higher realms of consciousness and spiritual freedom. Here is a spell for the liberation of the deceased's soul:

You will need:

A quiet and sacred space
A white candle
Frankincense or sage incense
A small piece of paper
A pen or pencil
Steps:

Preparation:

Find a peaceful space where you can perform the spell without distractions.
Light the white candle and the frankincense or sage incense to create a sacred atmosphere.

Centering:

Close your eyes and take a few deep breaths to center yourself.
Visualize a protective white light surrounding you and the space, creating a safe and sacred environment.

Setting Intentions:

Take the small piece of paper and write down the intention for the deceased's soul liberation.
Be clear and specific in stating the desire for the soul to be freed from the illusions and attachments of the material world.

Incantation:

Hold the paper with both hands and repeat the following incantation three times:

"By the power of light and truth, I call upon the divine,
Release the soul from earthly binds, let illusions unwind.
Let the spirit soar, free and unbound,
Transcending the limitations, liberation is found."

Burning the Paper:

Light the paper with the flame of the candle and carefully place it in a fire-safe container.
As the paper burns, visualize the release of the deceased's soul from all illusions, attachments, and limitations.

Closing:

Take a moment to offer gratitude for the opportunity to assist in the liberation of the deceased's soul.

Allow the candle and incense to burn out naturally, or safely extinguish them. Remember, this spell is a symbolic and spiritual practice aimed at aiding the liberation of the deceased's soul. It is important to approach it with respect, sincerity, and a genuine desire for the soul's freedom. Allow the energy of the spell to flow and trust in the divine guidance and assistance that will support the liberation process.

186. Incantation to invoke the blessings of the celestial rivers and streams

Repeat the following incantation while visualizing the flowing waters and connecting with the energy of the celestial rivers and streams:

"By the rivers of the heavens, ancient and grand,
I invoke your blessings, a sacred command.
From celestial realms, your waters descend,
Pure and divine, on this journey I send.

Flowing with grace, your currents embrace,
Nourishing life, in every time and space.
Mighty rivers, your power I seek,
Your wisdom and blessings, within me, speak.

Gentle streams, with melodies sweet,
Carrying harmony, where waters meet.
Flow through my spirit, cleanse and renew,
Grant me your blessings, pure and true.

As above, so below, in perfect harmony,
Celestial rivers, flow through me.
I am one with your eternal streams,
Blessed by your currents, fulfilling my dreams.

By the rivers of the heavens, I now abide,
Guided by your wisdom, my spirit's guide.
With gratitude and reverence, my heart aligns,
To the celestial rivers, forever entwined."

Allow the words of the incantation to resonate within you as you imagine the celestial rivers and streams flowing through your being, purifying and rejuvenating your spirit. Embrace the connection with the ancient and powerful energies of these celestial waters, feeling their blessings and guidance surround you. Offer gratitude for their presence and envision the positive transformation and abundance they bring to your life.

Note: Remember to approach this incantation with reverence and focus, and adapt it to your personal beliefs and practices.

187. Invocation of the god Sobek for strength and protection in the afterlife

To invoke the divine presence of the God Sobek and seek his strength and protection in the afterlife, you can use the following invocation:

"Great Sobek, Mighty God of Strength and Protection,
I call upon you with reverence and devotion.
In this sacred space, I seek your divine presence,
To grant me your power and watchful essence.

O Ferocious Crocodile, with scales of might,
Grant me strength in my soul's eternal flight.
Protect me from dangers, both seen and unseen,
Guide me through the realms with your watchful keen.

With your jaws of power, devour my fears,
Infuse me with courage that perseveres.
Let your presence surround me like a shield,
As I navigate the afterlife's unknown field.

Sobek, I honor your ancient wisdom and grace,
In this life and beyond, you hold a sacred place.
Grant me your strength and unwavering protection,
As I embrace the eternal journey's direction.

I offer my devotion and respect to you, Sobek,
May your presence be with me, a divine connect.
In this invocation, I seek your blessing and aid,
In the afterlife's realm, let your strength pervade.

So be it."

Take a moment after the invocation to sit in stillness, connecting with the energy of Sobek and feeling his strength and protection surrounding you. Express gratitude for his presence and the blessings he bestows upon you.

Remember, this invocation should be performed with sincerity, respect, and an understanding of the divine power of Sobek.

188. Incantation to awaken the dormant spiritual gifts within the deceased's spirit

"By the light of the divine,
I call upon the gifts enshrined.
Awaken now, oh spirit dear,
Let your dormant powers appear.

From the depths of your sacred soul,
Let your gifts now be made whole.
Rise from slumber, oh hidden might,
Unveil your power, shining bright.

Open the gates, release the flame,
Let your gifts become your name.
From the realms beyond the sight,
Awaken now, embrace your light.

With love and reverence, I invoke,
The gifts that lie beneath the cloak.
Arise, awaken, come forth now,
Unleash the gifts that time did allow.

By the power of the divine,
I call upon your gifts to shine.
May they serve your higher quest,
And bring forth blessings and bequest.

As it is spoken, so shall it be,
Awakened gifts, set your spirit free.
Embrace your purpose, let it unfold,
As the divine plan now takes hold."

Recite this incantation with focus, intention, and belief in the awakening of the deceased's dormant spiritual gifts. Visualize their gifts stirring within their spirit, awakening and manifesting in all their glory. Offer your love and support to the deceased as they embrace their newfound gifts and align with their highest purpose.

189. Incantation to invoke the blessings of the celestial rain and dew

"From celestial realms, where raindrops fall,
And dewdrops glisten upon leaves so small,
I call upon the blessings of water divine,
To shower upon me, a sacred sign.

With each raindrop that kisses the ground,
May blessings and abundance always be found.
Like dew on petals in the early morn,
May blessings upon blessings be reborn.

Celestial rain, your touch so pure,
Cleanse and nourish, of this I'm sure.
With every droplet that graces the earth,
Bring healing, growth, and joyous rebirth.

Celestial dew, in the quiet of night,
Glistening like stars, a shimmering light.
Blessings of clarity, peace, and grace,
Fill my being in this sacred space.

As rain and dew bless the land and sea,
May celestial blessings now flow to me.
I embrace the gifts from skies above,
With gratitude, I receive their love.

Rain and dew, celestial and true,
I invoke your blessings, ever anew.
Guide me with your gentle touch,
As I walk this path, I love so much.

So mote it be."

Recite this incantation with focused intention and a sincere connection to the celestial energies of rain and dew. Visualize the blessings descending upon you, bringing abundance, purification, and renewal. Embrace the gratitude for the gifts of nature and the celestial realm. Remember to adapt the incantation to your personal beliefs and practices and speak with clarity and conviction.

190. Invocation of the goddess Ma'at for balance and justice in the afterlife

"Mighty Ma'at, goddess of truth,
In this sacred space, I seek your divine presence.
With a heart open and pure, I call upon thee,
To bring forth balance and justice in the afterlife's decree.

Your feather of truth, an emblem so fair,
Guides the departed on their journey beyond compare.
As they enter the realm of eternal rest,
Let your scales of justice weigh their deeds at their best.

Ma'at, embodiment of cosmic order and harmony,
I invoke your name with reverence and humility.
May your wisdom guide the scales of judgment,
Ensuring fairness and righteousness in every element.

Grant the departed soul a just and balanced fate,
Where their actions and intentions are truly weighed.
May their deeds align with your sacred principles,
As they navigate the afterlife's mystical intervals.

In your divine presence, I find solace and peace,
Knowing that justice and balance shall never cease.
Ma'at, goddess of truth and cosmic equilibrium,
I honor you and seek your guidance in this invocation.

By the power of Ma'at, let balance prevail,
In the afterlife's realm, where justice shall never fail."

As you recite this invocation, envision the presence of Ma'at, surrounded by a golden aura of justice and balance. Feel her divine energy infuse the space and bring forth a sense of harmony and righteousness.

Remember, approaching this invocation with sincerity, respect, and a genuine desire for balance and justice is crucial. The invocation of Ma'at can bring clarity and a sense of cosmic order to the afterlife journey.

191. Ritual of purification through the sacred chants of the eternal mantras

Prepare a serene and quiet space for your ritual. Create an altar adorned with meaningful symbols and objects that represent purity and spirituality. Light candles and burn incense to set a sacred atmosphere.

Sit in a comfortable position, with your spine straight and your palms resting gently on your lap. Take a few deep breaths to center yourself and quiet your mind.

Begin the ritual by chanting a mantra that resonates with purification and cleansing. You can choose a traditional mantra from a spiritual tradition or create one that holds personal significance to you. Examples of such mantras include:

Om Shuddham Namah (I bow to the pure essence within me)
Purify and cleanse my body, mind, and soul
Shanti, shanti, shanti (Peace, peace, peace)
Chant the mantra repeatedly, allowing its vibrations to permeate your entire being. Focus on the sound and meaning of the words, surrendering to the rhythm and melody of the chant.

As you chant, visualize a purifying light washing over you, dissolving any impurities or negativity. See this light entering your body, mind, and soul, cleansing and purifying every aspect of your being.

Continue chanting and visualizing for as long as feels right to you. Allow the energy of the mantra and the visualizations to deeply cleanse and purify you, releasing any stagnant or negative energies.

After some time, gradually bring the chanting to a close. Sit in silence for a few moments, allowing the purifying energy to settle within you. Express gratitude for the purification you have received.

Conclude the ritual by offering a prayer or affirmation for continued purification and spiritual growth. Blow out the candles, symbolizing the completion of the ritual.

May this ritual of purification through the sacred chants of the eternal mantras cleanse and purify your body, mind, and soul, bringing you closer to your divine essence and highest potential.

192. Spell for the transmigration of the deceased's soul into the realm of eternal love and unity

✧ Find a serene and quiet space where you can focus your energy and intention. Light a white or pink candle to symbolize love and purity.

✧ Take a few moments to ground yourself and enter a state of deep relaxation. Close your eyes and take slow, deep breaths, allowing any tension to melt away.

✧ Visualize the deceased's soul as a radiant light, shimmering with love and compassion. See this light expanding and encompassing their entire being.

✧ As you visualize the radiant light, recite the following incantation:

"By the power of love, by the power of light,
I call upon the realm of eternal delight.
Let the soul of [name of the deceased] transcend,
Into the realm of love that knows no end.
May their essence merge with the divine,
United in love, eternally entwined."

✧ Imagine the deceased's soul gently releasing any attachments to the physical realm and embracing the pure essence of love. Visualize them being surrounded by a warm and loving energy, guiding them towards the realm of eternal love and unity.

✧ Hold the image of the deceased's soul in your mind, radiating love and joy. Feel a deep sense of gratitude for their presence in your life and the love they shared.

✧ Allow the candle to burn for a few more moments, symbolizing the continued presence of love and light in the journey of the deceased's soul.

✧ When you feel ready, slowly open your eyes and extinguish the candle. Take a moment to reflect on the spell and the intentions you set.

Remember, this spell is a heartfelt offering to support the transition of the deceased's soul into a realm of eternal love and unity. Trust in the power of your intentions and the love that flows through you as you perform this spell.

193. Incantation to awaken the dormant spiritual potential within the deceased's spirit

"By the ancient powers that dwell within,
I call upon the divine to awaken and begin.
From depths unknown, I summon thee,
Awaken now, set the spirit free.

Rise, O dormant spirit, from slumber deep,
Unleash your essence, no longer asleep.
Ignite the fire within, let it burn bright,
Unveil the treasures hidden, bring forth the light.

Awaken the gifts, the power untold,
Within this soul, a story to unfold.
Release the wisdom, the ancient lore,
Open the gates, forevermore.

Spirit of the deceased, embrace this call,
Rise and soar, standing tall.
Unlock the potential, the boundless might,
Awaken, awaken, with this sacred rite.

By the forces of the cosmos, I declare,
The dormant spirit now awakens, aware.
Ignite the flame, let it blaze and grow,
Unleash the spiritual potential, let it flow.

So mote it be, the awakening is done,
The dormant spirit now has begun.
Embrace the journey, the path ahead,
With awakened spirit, may you be led."

Recite this incantation with focus, clarity, and intent, envisioning the dormant spiritual potential within the deceased's spirit awakening and coming to life. Feel the energy building and the spiritual essence unfolding. Trust in the power of the divine and the ancient forces to support the awakening process.

194. Incantation to invoke the blessings of the celestial mountains and valleys

"By the powers of Earth and Sky,
I invoke the blessings from mountains high.
From peaks that touch the heavens above,
To valleys deep, filled with life and love.

O majestic mountains, strong and grand,
Hold wisdom ancient, in your rocky land.
With towering heights and majestic grace,
Bestow your blessings upon this sacred space.

In valleys wide, where life finds its way,
Nurture and protect, by night and day.
From flowing rivers to fertile ground,
Your blessings in abundance, may they be found.

As above, so below, in harmony and peace,
May the blessings of mountains and valleys never cease.
Guide us in strength, in growth, and in grace,
Embrace us with your wisdom in this sacred space.

With gratitude and reverence, I call upon thee,
Celestial mountains and valleys, hear my plea.
Bless us with your energy, with peace and serenity,
As we journey through life, in harmony and unity.

So mote it be."

Note: As with any incantation, it is important to speak the words with intention, focus, and respect. Adjust the incantation as necessary to align with your personal beliefs and intentions.

195.   Invocation of the god Thoth for wisdom and knowledge in the afterlife

"Great Thoth, god of wisdom and knowledge,
I call upon you in this sacred hour.
With reverence and respect, I seek your presence,
To guide me on the path of enlightenment and understanding.

In the realm beyond, where mysteries unfold,
Grant me your divine wisdom to behold.
As I journey through the afterlife's domain,
May your guidance illuminate my way.

O Thoth, the scribe of the gods,
Bearer of the mighty knowledge and truth,
Bestow upon me your sacred teachings,
That I may gain insight and wisdom in the afterlife.

Grant me the understanding of ancient texts,
The deciphering of symbols and hieroglyphs.
Unveil the secrets hidden in the scrolls,
And awaken the dormant knowledge within my soul.

I seek your guidance, O wise Thoth,
To navigate the realms of the unknown.
With your wings of wisdom, I shall soar,
Through the vast expanse of eternal lore.

By the power of your sacred name,
I invoke your presence, Thoth, I acclaim.
Grant me the gift of divine wisdom,
That I may forever dwell in the light of your kingdom.

Hail, Thoth, the god of wisdom and knowledge,
I honor and invoke your divine presence.
Guide me in the afterlife's sacred quest,
And bless me with eternal enlightenment and rest."

196. Spell for the guidance of the deceased's soul through the celestial realms

"By the power of the sacred stars above,
I call upon the celestial realms with love.
As the soul of the departed embarks on its flight,
Guide it safely through the realms of light.

O celestial beings, guardians of the night,
I seek your guidance with all my might.
Wrap the departed in your celestial embrace,
Lead them through the heavens with divine grace.

Grant them wings to soar through the skies,
Navigating the celestial realms with wise eyes.
Guide them past the astral currents and streams,
To the realms where their highest purpose gleams.

Angels, spirits, and celestial guides,
Illuminate their path as the soul abides.
Protect them from darkness, fear, and strife,
Guide them towards the eternal source of life.

May the celestial realms open wide,
Revealing mysteries where truth resides.
Lead the departed to their rightful place,
Where their soul's journey finds solace and grace.

By the power of the celestial realms so grand,
I entrust the departed to your loving hand.
Guide them through the realms unknown,
To their destined place, let them be shown.

So mote it be."

197. Invocation of the goddess Hathor for beauty and rejuvenation in the afterlife

"Oh, radiant goddess Hathor, divine and fair,
I call upon your presence with utmost care.
Goddess of beauty, joy, and love divine,
In this sacred invocation, your light shall shine.

Hathor, graceful and enchanting in every way,
I beseech you now, hear my words, I pray.
In the realms beyond, where souls find rest,
Grant your blessings to the departed, blessed.

Wrap them in your loving, nurturing embrace,
As they journey through the eternal space.
Bathe them in your sacred rivers of rejuvenation,
Reviving their spirit with divine elation.

Goddess of the sun, moon, and stars above,
Bestow upon them your eternal love.
Restore their essence with your healing touch,
Envelop them in beauty that means so much.

Let their true essence shine like golden light,
Radiating from within, pure and bright.
Grant them the gift of eternal youth and grace,
As they dwell in the afterlife's celestial embrace.

Hathor, goddess of beauty and rejuvenation,
Guide the departed on their sacred transformation.
In your presence, may they find solace and peace,
Where beauty and joy forever increase.

I offer this invocation with reverence and love,
To you, Hathor, divine goddess above.
May your blessings of beauty and rejuvenation,
Bring eternal joy in the afterlife's glorious formation.

So mote it be."

198.   Incantation to awaken the dormant spiritual potential within the deceased's spirit

"By the power of the divine light,
I call upon the ancient forces of might.
Awaken now, oh dormant spirit,
Unveil your wisdom, let it freely emit.

From the depths of eternity, rise,
Unfold your gifts, let them materialize.
Break free from the slumber's hold,
Embrace your purpose, mighty and bold.

The divine spark within, ignite,
Illuminate the path, shining bright.
Tap into your infinite well of knowing,
Unleash your spiritual essence, ever-growing.

Spirit of the departed, now awakened,
Embark on a journey, unrestricted and unshaken.
Embrace your truth, your divine nature,
Reclaim your power, ascend to a higher stature.

With open heart and mind, let it be,
As I speak this incantation, so mote it be!"

Recite this incantation with focused intention and visualize the deceased's spirit awakening and embracing their dormant spiritual potential. Allow the energy of the words and your intention to resonate deeply within you and reach the spirit of the departed. Repeat the incantation as many times as you feel necessary, and trust that the awakening process is initiated.

Remember, the power lies within your intent and connection to the divine. Adapt the incantation as needed to align with your personal beliefs and practices.

199. Invocation of the god Anubis for guidance and guardianship in the afterlife

"Great Anubis, Lord of the Underworld,
Bearer of the scales of justice and guide of souls,
I invoke your presence and seek your guidance.

With your jackal-headed form and unwavering wisdom,
You lead the departed through the realm of the dead,
Guarding their souls and guiding them to their rightful place.

I call upon you, Anubis, in this sacred moment,
To watch over the deceased [name] as they journey in the afterlife.
Guide them through the trials and tribulations they may face,
Protect them from any malevolent forces that seek to harm.

O Anubis, the Opener of the Way,
Grant them safe passage and reveal to them the path of enlightenment.
Illuminate their soul with your divine light,
And guide them to their rightful destination.

In your presence, dear Anubis,
May [name] find solace and assurance,
Knowing that you are their faithful protector and guide,
In this life and the next.

I offer my gratitude and respect to you, Anubis,
For your unwavering guardianship and guidance.
May your presence bring comfort and peace,
As the departed soul embarks on their eternal journey.

So be it."

Note: This invocation should be performed with sincerity and respect for the deity. It is important to have the consent and intention of the deceased's loved ones before invoking any deities on their behalf.

1. Incantation to guide the deceased through the perilous realm of the Duat — Pg. 1

2. Ritual for the purification of the deceased's spirit through sacred herbs and oils — Pg. 2

3. Spell for the restoration of the deceased's physical body in the afterlife — Pg.4

4. Invocation of the god Anubis for guidance and protection in the journey of the soul — Pg. 6

5. Ritual of anointing with sacred waters for spiritual rejuvenation — Pg.7

6. Spell for the transformation of the deceased into a vessel of divine love and compassion — Pg. 8

7. Incantation to invoke the blessings of the celestial rivers and lakes — Pg.9

8. Ritual for the transfiguration of the deceased into a divine conduit of divine energy — Pg 11

9. Spell for the reunion of the deceased's soul with their ancestral lineage — Pg. 13

10. Ritual of purification through the sacred breath of the eternal winds — Pg. 15

11. Spell for the liberation of the deceased's soul from karmic bonds — Pg. 17

12. Incantation to awaken the dormant wisdom within the deceased's spirit — Pg. 19

13. Ritual for the communion with the spirits of the celestial constellations — Pg. 21

14. Spell for the transmigration of the deceased's soul into the realm of eternal knowledge — Pg. 23

15. Invocation of the god Ptah for creativity and manifestation in the afterlife — Pg. 25

16. Ritual of anointing with sacred crystals for spiritual clarity and protection — Pg. 27

17. Spell for the transformation of the deceased into a vessel of divine healing — Pg. 29

18. Incantation to invoke the blessings of the celestial mountains and valleys — Pg. 31

19. Ritual for the transfiguration of the deceased into a divine messenger of the gods — Pg. 33

20. Spell for the reunion of the deceased's soul with their spiritual guides and mentors — Pg. 35

21. Invocation of the goddess Hathor for joy and abundance in the afterlife — Pg. 37

22. Ritual of purification through the sacred movements of the eternal dance — Pg. 39

23. Spell for the liberation of the deceased's soul from earthly attachments — Pg. 41

24. Incantation to awaken the dormant inner strength within the deceased's spirit — Pg. 43

25. Ritual for the communion with the spirits of the celestial rain and thunder — Pg. 45

26. Spell for the transmigration of the deceased's soul into the realm of eternal harmony — Pg. 47

27. Invocation of the god Thoth for wisdom and knowledge in the afterlife — Pg. 49

28. Ritual of anointing with sacred symbols for spiritual empowerment and protection — Pg. 51

29. Spell for the transformation of the deceased into a vessel of divine guidance and wisdom — Pg. 53

30. Incantation to invoke the blessings of the celestial sunrises and sunsets — Pg. 55

31. Ritual for the transfiguration of the deceased into a divine weaver of cosmic destinies — Pg. 57

32. Spell for the reunion of the deceased's soul with their soul family and spiritual community — Pg. 59

33. Invocation of the goddess Isis for nurturing and protection in the afterlife — Pg. 61

34. Ritual of purification through the sacred fire of the eternal flame — Pg. 63

35. Spell for the liberation of the deceased's soul from the chains of illusion and ignorance — Pg. 65

36. Incantation to awaken the dormant divine spark within the deceased's spirit — Pg. 67

37. Ritual for the communion with the spirits of the celestial forests and meadows — Pg. 69

38. Spell for the transmigration of the deceased's soul into the realm of eternal peace and serenity — Pg. 71

39. Invocation of the god Sobek for strength and transformation in the afterlife — Pg. 73

40. Ritual of anointing with sacred colors for spiritual transformation and manifestation — Pg. 75

41. Spell for the transformation of the deceased into a vessel of divine protection and healing — Pg. 77

42. Incantation to invoke the blessings of the celestial moon phases and lunar cycles — Pg. 79

43. Ritual for the transfiguration of the deceased into a divine guardian of cosmic gateways — Pg. 81

44. Spell for the reunion of the deceased's soul with their soulmates and divine counterparts — Pg. 83

45. Invocation of the goddess Nut for guidance and expansion in the afterlife — Pg. 85

46. Spell for the liberation of the deceased's soul from the illusions of the material world — Pg. 87

47. Incantation to awaken the dormant spiritual gifts within the deceased's spirit — Pg. 89

48. Ritual for the communion with the spirits of the celestial oceans and seas — Pg. 91

49. Invocation of the god Horus for protection and vision in the afterlife — Pg. 93

50. Ritual of anointing with sacred feathers for spiritual elevation and connection — Pg. 95

51. Spell for the transformation of the deceased into a vessel of divine strength and courage — Pg. 97

52. Incantation to invoke the blessings of the celestial stars and galaxies — Pg. 99

53. Ritual for the transfiguration of the deceased into a divine keeper of ancient wisdom — Pg. 101

54. Spell for the reunion of the deceased's soul with their soul contracts and divine purpose — Pg. 103

55. Invocation of the goddess Sekhmet for healing and empowerment in the afterlife — Pg. 105

56. Ritual of purification through the sacred vibrations of the eternal sound — Pg. 107

57. Spell for the liberation of the deceased's soul from the cycles of birth and death — Pg. 109

58. Incantation to awaken the dormant spiritual senses within the deceased's spirit — Pg. 111

59.	Ritual for the communion with the spirits of the celestial birds and winged creatures	Pg. 113
60.	Spell for the transmigration of the deceased's soul into the realm of eternal light and truth	Pg. 115
61.	Invocation of the god Set for transformation and rebirth in the afterlife	Pg. 117
62.	Ritual of anointing with sacred incense for spiritual elevation and purification	Pg. 119
63.	Spell for the transformation of the deceased into a vessel of divine wisdom and understanding	Pg. 121
64.	Incantation to invoke the blessings of the celestial planets and celestial bodies	Pg. 123
65.	Ritual for the transfiguration of the deceased into a divine guardian of sacred knowledge	Pg. 125
66.	Spell for the reunion of the deceased's soul with their spiritual teachers and mentors	Pg. 127
67.	Invocation of the goddess Bastet for protection and grace in the afterlife	Pg. 129
68.	Ritual of purification through the sacred symbols of the eternal hieroglyphs	Pg. 131
69.	Ritual of purification through the sacred symbols of the eternal hieroglyphs	Pg. 133
70.	Ritual for the communion with the spirits of the celestial gardens and blossoms	Pg. 135
71.	Spell for the transmigration of the deceased's soul into the realm of eternal growth and evolution	Pg. 137
72.	Invocation of the god Ra for divine illumination and enlightenment in the afterlife	Pg. 139
73.	Ritual of anointing with sacred essences for spiritual transformation and transcendence	Pg. 141
74.	Spell for the transformation of the deceased into a vessel of divine harmony and balance	Pg. 143
75.	Incantation to invoke the blessings of the celestial winds and breezes	Pg. 145
76.	Ritual for the transfiguration of the deceased into a divine weaver of cosmic tapestries	Pg. 147
77.	Spell for the reunion of the deceased's soul with their spiritual guides and guardians	Pg. 149
78.	Invocation of the goddess Nephthys for protection and guidance in the afterlife	Pg. 151
79.	Ritual of purification through the sacred movements of the eternal dance	Pg. 153
80.	Spell for the liberation of the deceased's soul from the limitations of the physical body	Pg. 155
81.	Incantation to awaken the dormant divine essence within the deceased's spirit	Pg. 157
82.	Ritual for the communion with the spirits of the celestial rivers and streams	Pg. 159
83.	Spell for the transmigration of the deceased's soul into the realm of eternal serenity and peace	Pg. 161
84.	Invocation of the god Osiris for resurrection and rebirth in the afterlife	Pg. 163
85.	Ritual of anointing with sacred oils for spiritual healing and rejuvenation	Pg. 165
86.	Spell for the transformation of the deceased into a vessel of divine love and compassion	Pg. 167
87.	Ritual for the transfiguration of the deceased into a divine guardian of sacred rituals	Pg. 169
88.	Spell for the reunion of the deceased's soul with their spiritual allies and helpers	Pg. 171
89.	Invocation of the goddess Ma'at for balance and harmony in the afterlife	Pg. 173
90.	Ritual of purification through the sacred breath of the eternal winds	Pg. 175
91.	Spell for the liberation of the deceased's soul from the chains of karma	Pg. 177

92. Incantation to awaken the dormant inner wisdom within the deceased's spirit — Pg. 179
93. Ritual for the communion with the spirits of the celestial rainbows and colors — Pg. 181
94. Spell for the transmigration of the deceased's soul into the realm of eternal joy and bliss — Pg. 183
95. Ritual of purification through the sacred waters of the eternal Nile — Pg. 185
96. Spell for the protection of the deceased's soul from malevolent forces — Pg. 187
97. Ritual for the communion with the spirits of the sacred animals and totems — Pg. 189
98. Spell for the transmigration of the deceased's soul into the realm of eternal knowledge — Pg. 191
99. Ritual of anointing with sacred herbs for spiritual healing and transformation — Pg. 193
100. Spell for the transformation of the deceased into a vessel of divine power and authority — Pg. 195
101. Ritual for the transfiguration of the deceased into a divine messenger of the gods — Pg. 197
102. Spell for the reunion of the deceased's soul with their ancestral lineage — Pg. 199
103. Invocation of the goddess Isis for protection and nurturing in the afterlife — Pg. 201
104. Ritual of purification through the sacred fire of the eternal flame — Pg. 203
105. Spell for the liberation of the deceased's soul from earthly attachments — Pg. 205
106. Ritual for the communion with the spirits of the celestial trees and plants — Pg. 207
107. Spell for the transmigration of the deceased's soul into the realm of eternal peace — Pg. 209
108 .Invocation of the god Ptah for creation and manifestation in the afterlife — Pg. 211

109 .Ritual of anointing with sacred resins for spiritual elevation and enlightenment — Pg. 213

110. Spell for the transformation of the deceased into a vessel of divine grace and mercy — Pg. 215
111. Incantation to invoke the blessings of the celestial music and melodies — Pg. 217
112. Ritual for the transfiguration of the deceased into a divine protector of sacred spaces — Pg. 219
113. Spell for the reunion of the deceased's soul with their beloved pets and animal companions — Pg. 221
114. Invocation of the goddess Neith for wisdom and skill in the afterlife — Pg. 223
115. Ritual of purification through the sacred chants of the eternal hymns — Pg. 225
116. Spell for the liberation of the deceased's soul from the cycle of suffering — Pg. 227
117. Incantation to awaken the dormant spiritual senses within the deceased's spirit — Pg. 229
118. Ritual for the communion with the spirits of the celestial mountains and peaks — Pg. 231
119. Spell for the transmigration of the deceased's soul into the realm of eternal light and truth — Pg. 233
120. Ritual of anointing with sacred crystals for spiritual clarity and insight — Pg. 235
121. Spell for the transformation of the deceased into a vessel of divine transformation — Pg. 237
122. Ritual for the transfiguration of the deceased into a divine guardian of sacred wisdom — Pg. 239
123. Spell for the reunion of the deceased's soul with their spiritual lineage — Pg. 241
124. Ritual of purification through the sacred dances of the eternal rhythm — Pg. 243
125. Spell for the liberation of the deceased's soul from the illusions of the material world — Pg. 244
126. Incantation to awaken the dormant spiritual powers within the deceased's spirit — Pg. 245
127. Ritual for the communion with the spirits of the celestial stars and constellations — Pg. 249

128. Spell for the transmigration of the deceased's soul into the realm of eternal love and unity — Pg. 251

129. Invocation of the god Amun-Ra for divine protection and guidance in the afterlife — Pg. 253

130. Ritual of anointing with sacred incense for spiritual elevation and connection — Pg. 255

131. Incantation to invoke the blessings of the celestial birds and their songs — Pg. 257

132. Ritual for the transfiguration of the deceased into a divine guide of sacred paths — Pg. 259

133. Spell for the reunion of the deceased's soul with their spiritual teachers and mentors — Pg. 261

134. Invocation of the goddess Bastet for joy and protection in the afterlife — Pg. 263

135. Ritual of purification through the sacred symbols of the eternal hieroglyphs — Pg. 265

136. Spell for the liberation of the deceased's soul from the limitations of the physical body — Pg. 267

137. Incantation to awaken the dormant spiritual insights within the deceased's spirit — Pg. 269

138. Ritual for the communion with the spirits of the celestial clouds and rainbows — Pg. 271

139. Spell for the transmigration of the deceased's soul into the realm of eternal harmony — Pg. 273

140. Invocation of the god Horus for divine vision and guidance in the afterlife — Pg. 275

141. Ritual of anointing with sacred oils for spiritual empowerment and transformation — Pg. 277

142. Spell for the transformation of the deceased into a vessel of divine knowledge and understanding — Pg. 279

143. Incantation to invoke the blessings of the celestial sun and its radiant energy — Pg. 281

144. Ritual for the transfiguration of the deceased into a divine guardian of sacred secrets — Pg. 283

145. Spell for the reunion of the deceased's soul with their spiritual companions and allies — Pg. 285

146. Invocation of the goddess Nephthys for protection and healing in the afterlife — Pg. 287

147. Ritual of purification through the sacred breath of the eternal winds — Pg. 289

148. Spell for the liberation of the deceased's soul from the burdens of the past — Pg. 291

149. Incantation to awaken the dormant spiritual potentials within the deceased's spirit — Pg. 293

150. Ritual for the communion with the spirits of the celestial rain and dew — Pg. 294

151. Spell for the transmigration of the deceased's soul into the realm of eternal joy and bliss — Pg. 297

152. Invocation of the god Thoth for wisdom and knowledge in the afterlife — Pg. 299

153. Ritual of anointing with sacred herbs for spiritual healing and rejuvenation — Pg. 301

154. Spell for the transformation of the deceased into a vessel of divine power and authority — Pg. 303

155. Incantation to invoke the blessings of the celestial rainbows and colors — Pg. 305

156. Ritual for the transfiguration of the deceased into a divine messenger of the gods — Pg. 307

157. Invocation of the goddess Isis for protection and nurturing in the afterlife — Pg. 309

158. Ritual of purification through the sacred fire of the eternal flame — Pg. 311

159. Spell for the liberation of the deceased's soul from earthly attachments — Pg. 313

160. Incantation to awaken the dormant spiritual gifts within the deceased's spirit — Pg. 315

161. Ritual for the communion with the spirits of the celestial trees and plants — Pg. 317

162. Spell for the transmigration of the deceased's soul into the realm of eternal peace — Pg. 319

163. Invocation of the god Ptah for creation and manifestation in the afterlife — Pg. 321

164. Ritual of anointing with sacred resins for spiritual elevation and enlightenment — Pg. 323

165. Spell for the transformation of the deceased into a vessel of divine grace and — Pg. 325

mercy

166. Incantation to invoke the blessings of the celestial music and melodies   Pg. 327

167. Ritual for the transfiguration of the deceased into a divine protector of sacred spaces   Pg. 329

168. Spell for the transformation of the deceased into a vessel of divine light and wisdom   Pg. 332

169. Spell for the reunion of the deceased's soul with their beloved pets and animal companions   Pg. 333

170. Invocation of the goddess Taweret for fertility and abundance in the afterlife   Pg. 336

171. Invocation of the goddess Neith for wisdom and skill in the afterlife   Pg. 337

172. Ritual of purification through the sacred chants of the eternal hymns   Pg. 339

173. Spell for the liberation of the deceased's soul from the cycle of suffering   Pg. 341

174. Incantation to awaken the dormant spiritual senses within the deceased's spirit   Pg. 343

175. Ritual for the communion with the spirits of the celestial mountains and peaks   Pg. 345

176. Spell for the transmigration of the deceased's soul into the realm of eternal light and truth   Pg. 347

177. Invocation of the god Sobek for strength and protection in the afterlife   Pg. 349

178. Ritual of anointing with sacred crystals for spiritual clarity and insight   Pg. 351

179. Spell for the transformation of the deceased into a vessel of divine transformation   Pg. 353

180. Incantation to invoke the blessings of the celestial rivers and streams   Pg. 355

181. Ritual for the transfiguration of the deceased into a divine guardian of sacred wisdom   Pg. 357

182. Spell for the reunion of the deceased's soul with their spiritual lineage   Pg. 359

183. Invocation of the goddess Taweret for fertility and abundance in the afterlife   Pg. 361

184. Ritual of purification through the sacred dances of the eternal rhythm   Pg. 363

185. Spell for the liberation of the deceased's soul from the illusions of the material world   Pg. 365

186. Incantation to invoke the blessings of the celestial rivers and streams   Pg. 367

187. Invocation of the god Sobek for strength and protection in the afterlife   Pg. 368

188. Incantation to awaken the dormant spiritual gifts within the deceased's spirit   Pg. 369

189. Incantation to invoke the blessings of the celestial rain and dew   Pg. 370

190. Invocation of the goddess Ma'at for balance and justice in the afterlife   Pg. 371

191. Ritual of purification through the sacred chants of the eternal mantras   Pg. 372

192. Spell for the transmigration of the deceased's soul into the realm of eternal love and unity   Pg.373

193. Incantation to awaken the dormant spiritual potential within the deceased's spirit   Pg. 374

194. Incantation to invoke the blessings of the celestial mountains and valleys   Pg. 375

195. Invocation of the god Thoth for wisdom and knowledge in the afterlife   Pg. 376

196. Spell for the guidance of the deceased's soul through the celestial realms   Pg. 377

197. Invocation of the goddess Hathor for beauty and rejuvenation in the afterlife   Pg. 378

198. Incantation to awaken the dormant spiritual potential within the deceased's spirit   Pg. 379

199. Invocation of the god Anubis for guidance and guardianship in the afterlife   Pg. 380